D0689858

CARDENIO

OR

THE SECOND MAIDEN'S TRAGEDY

William Shakespeare

WILLIAM SHAKESPEARE

AND

JOHN FLETCHER

CARDENIO

OR

THE SECOND MAIDEN'S TRAGEDY

Charles Hamilton

Glenbridge Publishing Ltd.

Jacket engraving of William Shakespeare from the collection of Charles Hamilton

 For further information contact Glenbridge Publishing Ltd., 6010 W. Jewell Ave., Lakewood, Colorado.

Library of Congress Catalog Card Number: 93-73354

International Standard Book Number: 0-944435-24-6

To my sister, Elinor Hamilton Mattes,

with thanks for the many ways she

helped me when I was a boy

Other Books by Charles Hamilton

The Hitler Diaries

The Illustrated Letter

In Search of Shakespeare

American Autographs

Leaders of the Third Reich

Auction Madness

Great Forgers and Famous Fakes

The Signature of America

The Book of Autographs

Big Name Hunting (with Diane Hamilton)

Scribblers and Scoundrels

The Robot that Helped to Make a President

Lincoln in Photographs (with Lloyd Ostendorf)

Collecting Autographs and Manuscripts

Braddock's Defeat

Men of the Underworld

Cry of the Thunderbird

CONTENTS

INTRODUCTION

For three centuries lovers of Shakespeare have searched vainly for the Golden Fleece of literature—a lost play called *Cardenio*, allegedly by William Shakespeare and John Fletcher. There are references to performances of *Cardenio* at the court of King James I in 1613; and, forty years later, in 1653, a manuscript of *Cardenio* was officially entered in the *Stationers' Register* as a drama by Shakespeare and Fletcher. The lure of this missing play about Cardenio, a bizarre character in Cervantes's *Don Quixote*, has led lovers of Shakespeare on a chase through libraries and archives, into attics and ancient barns, and even abandoned privies.

In searching for the lost play, scholars have had to bear in mind that *Cardenio*, in order to be accepted as authentic, must meet all, or nearly all, of the following stringent requirements:

1. The play should reveal the recognizable creative touches of the joint authorship of Shakespeare and Fletcher, to whom it was attributed in 1653.

2. The play should bear one of its contemporary titles—Cardenio, Cardenno or Cardenna—or else be untitled.

3. If the play is in manuscript, it should exhibit clear indications that it was written for, or produced by, the King's Men, the performing company in which Shakespeare was a shareholder, actor, and playwright.

4. The play, if in manuscript, should be beyond cavil an original seventeenth-century document, preferably in the handwriting of, or partly in the handwriting of, Shakespeare or Fletcher.

5. The date of the play, if it bears a date, should fall some time between 1611 and 1613, roughly coinciding with its two recorded performances at the palatine wedding festivities in the court of James I at Whitehall in 1613. Cardenio may have been written or revamped especially for performance on this occasion.

6. The play should have as one of its sources the famous tale about Cardenio in Cervantes's *Don Quixote*.

There exists in the British Museum Library an anonymous manuscript that meets every one of these requirements. It is commonly known as *The Second Maiden's Tragedy*, the title put on it by the censor. In my opinion, it is the original manuscript of *Cardenio*.

Admittedly, *Cardenio* or *The Second Maiden's Tragedy* is one of Shakespeare's baffling Last Plays, like *Pericles* and *Cymbeline*, in the twilight of his genius. Scholars and lovers of Shakespeare offer all sorts of reasons to explain why these final plays are not quite up to Shakespeare's lofty standards. Homer is allowed to nod, but not Shakespeare. The man from Stratford must always be flawless, and if he falls short in any way we blame it on a collaborator or a compositor who didn't know his trade. If a play is badly structured, like *Pericles*, an uninspired or less-experienced dramatist monkeyed with it. If a play is confusing in plot and characterization and lacks the masterful touch, like *Cymbeline*, it is an erratic experiment. I am going to lay aside all such apologies for *Cardenio* and tell you what I believe may be the truth. Shakespeare was tired out. Possibly he was ill. Only five years away from death, he had labored hard all his life, had survived an awesome tragedy in the death of his eleven-year-old son, and was homesick for Stratford, the town he knew and loved as a boy.

As the manuscript of *Cardenio* is entirely in Shakespeare's own hand—the handwriting is identical down to the very dots on the *i's* with the script in Shakespeare's holograph will—and in every other way the play seems to fulfill the requirements of the lost *Cardenio*, it is a reasonable presumption that Shakespeare authored part of it, probably half or more of it. Certainly, *Cardenio* is a rough tumbling from the high peak of *The Tempest*, only a year or so earlier and one of Shakespeare's sublimest plays. Perhaps *The Tempest* was the brilliant flare of the candle just before it gutted.

To be sure, there are many touches of the Master in *Cardenio*: the cleverly crafted, swift-paced plot, the fierce confrontations, the frightening suspense, the obligatory scenes, the powerful phrase, the deft neologisms, the sweet-flowing lines, the triumph of good over evil. All here, all present and accounted for. It is in every way a splendid Shakespearean drama..

The laws of King James I of England required that all plays be censored. *Cardenio*, or *The Second Maiden's Tragedy* was submitted to the censor in October, 1611. It was still untitled, a newborn from the quill of Shakespeare. Two of the most important characters in the main plot, including the protagonist, had no name. The censor tacked a working title on the play—the "Second Mayden's tragedy."

The inspiration for *Cardenio* or *The Second Maiden's Tragedy* was a tale called "The History of Cardenio," embedded in Cervantes's *Don Quixote*, the great Spanish classic soon to be published in English for the first time (licensed for publication on January 19, 1612).

In the original manuscript, printed here, the three leading characters in Shakespeare's main plot appear as The Lady, The Tyrant, and Govianus. While Shakespeare's play was apparently still in production, *Don Quixote* was published. It was an immediate, sensational hit, comparable to the success of *Gone with the Wind* in our century. Overnight the names "Don Quixote" and "Cardenio" were on the tip of every tongue.

Always alert to *le dernier cri*, Shakespeare seized the opportunity to exploit the fame of Cervantes's characters. He and his co-author, John Fletcher, named their new play

Cardenio, and Shakespeare changed the name of his hero from Govianus to Cardenio, a logical and appropriate change, since Shakespeare's character Govianus was originally based upon the character Cardenio in *Don Quixote*. At the same time, Shakespeare may also have given his two unnamed characters the same names they had in the novel by changing The Lady to Luscinda and The Tyrant to Fernando, also alluded to as "Ferdinando" by Cervantes, who had difficulty remembering the names of his characters. Fletcher had already used the names of some of Cervantes's characters in his subplot, based upon a separate tale in "The History of Cardenio." Anselmo became Fletcher's Anselmus. Leonella remained Leonella. Lotario was modified to Votarius. Carmila became The Wife, and Leonella's lover, never given a name by Cervantes, was named Bellarius by Fletcher.

The original names used by Shakespeare and Fletcher still remain in this manuscript, just as they were before *Don Quixote* was published. You may well ask: If Shakespeare and Fletcher altered the names of their characters as I have indicated, why didn't they make these changes in the manuscript? They made no changes because no changes were necessary. Shakespeare's original manuscript served as the prompt copy, which, in Shakespeare's day, was known as "the book." The keeper of the book, or "book-keeper," was a managerial factotum who, among other duties, copied out from the book the parts for each actor to memorize and acted as the stage prompter. He had full charge of the single copy of the play that existed, usually the author's manuscript converted into the book. The book was the private property of the playhouse and was never intended for publication. Nor were outsiders permitted to read it. The book was always in the possession of the book-keeper during the day and was locked up at night to forestall theft by rival acting troupes. The book-keeper, of course, virtually knew the play by memory and was familiar with the roles of all the players. As stage prompter, he could easily change the names orally and no revisions were necessary in the manuscript.

I have here presented the play to you just as Shakespeare set it down in his own hand. I did not presume to alter the names of the characters. Thus I suggest that you follow the lead of the prompter and interpolate the correct names as you read: Cardenio for Govianus, Luscinda for The Lady, King Fernando for The Tyrant, and, in the subplot, Lotario for Votarius.

Written with John Fletcher in 1611 *Cardenio* was Shakespeare's penultimate romance play. *Henry VIII*, another Fletcher collaboration, was almost certainly his last drama and is, in my opinion, one of his poorest. As a play, it does not rise to the level of *Cardenio*. True, *Henry VIII* is replete with pageantry and lavish costumes and resounds with great speeches, but to me it suggests a string of newspaper headlines pasted together to form a stage presentation: Wolsey Gets Sack—His Emotional Farewell; Kate Aragon Jilted—Sobs Goodbye to King Hal; Beauty Weds the Beast!—Anne Boleyn Accepts Second-Hand Crown; Kudos for Infant Queen Liz—Seer Predicts She'll Be Number I.

The subplot of *Cardenio*, mostly written by Fletcher, is a tragicomedy based upon a tale in Cervantes's *Don Quixote*. Its swift-paced action ends with five dead characters on the stage.

The mood of the main plot of *Cardenio*, written by Shakespeare, is fierce and intense. Villainy is afoot and we sense it almost instantly. The unnamed protagonist, known as *The Tyrant* (King Fernando) is a usurper totally committed to the love of a beautiful woman who spurns his advances. He cares nothing for the power and wealth that come with his kingdom. The Tyrant impresses us at first by his kindness and generosity. He permits his enemy, the deposed king, Govianus (Cardenio), lover of The Lady (Luscinda), whose affection he covets, to remain in court. Further, The Tyrant apparently has the support and affection of most of his nobles. He is blunt and open about his fanatical love for The Lady and even admits to the deposed king that his only reason for seeking the throne was to win her affections.[1] The Tyrant's intentions are honest and noble. He wishes to marry The Lady and make her his queen. To this end he enlists the aid of her father, Helvetius, who becomes a willing panderer in the hope of winning the new monarch's favor. Even after an angry dispute with his reluctant daughter, Helvetius volunteers to compel his daughter to wed and bed the usurper.

Govianus deliberately provokes The Tyrant by subtle insults into putting him under arrest. The Tyrant later releases him. Meanwhile, Helvetius resolves an inner conflict of loyalty by an emotional apology to his daughter, who forgives him and returns his love. The Tyrant's gifts to The Lady continue to meet with rebuffs. After he has tried every possible means of winning her, he reveals the first symptom of the madness that will ultimately overtake and destroy him. He makes the error of sending soldiers to seize her. To preserve her honor, The Lady commits suicide by stabbing herself with Govianus's sword. So distraught is The Tyrant at the news of her death that he takes his second step into lunacy by ordering that the messenger who brought the bad news be slain. The Tyrant now transfers his consuming love for The Lady from the living woman to the bejeweled corpse. In a terrifying cathedral scene by dark of night, The Tyrant and three bumbling soldiers pry open The Lady's marble tomb. With the cowardly soldiers for comic relief, much like the gravediggers in *Hamlet* or the porters in *Macbeth*, The Tyrant exhumes The Lady's body and steals it from the cathedral. Soon afterward, Govianus comes with a page to kneel at her tomb and pray for her. As Govianus prays, a voice comes from the tomb: "I am not here." In a spectacular scene, the ghost of The Lady appears and explains that The Tyrant has stolen her body:

> I am now at court
> In his own private chamber. There he woos me
> And plies his suit to me with as serious pains
> As if the short flame of mortality
> Were lighted up again in my cold breast,
> Folds me within his arms and often sets
> A sinful kiss upon my senseless lip,
> Weeps when he sees the paleness of my cheek,
> And will send privately for a hand of art
> That may dissemble life upon my face
> To please his lustful eye. (IV, iv, 1775-84)

Govianus disguises himself as an embalmer and is hired by The Tyrant to "dissemble life" into the cheeks and body of the dead Lady. He completes the task and presents the usurper with her beautiful body, enticing and looking alive, but painted with poison. The Tyrant kisses the lips and dies. Despite his monstrous acts, The Tyrant gains our sympathy because he has sacrificed all for love. The Lady, too, wins our love and admiration because she repudiates riches and power and even gives up her life to preserve her honor and integrity. She is, in every sense, a creation of the Stratford Pygmalion who fashioned so many chaste and lovable women, totally different from dramatist Thomas Middleton's doxies and filching morts who would haul up their main buntlings for a grig.[2] Middleton is regarded by most scholars as the author of this play, but is it conceivable that Middleton, who specialized in vulgar and unappealing women, could have envisioned this pure and virgin Lady? Could he have portrayed The Tyrant who sacrificed his kingdom and his life for love? Professor David L. Frost describes Middleton as exhibiting a "constant equation in his plays of sexual desire with commercial acquisitiveness . . ."[3] Professor Frost further points out Middleton's "obsessive presumption that all human beings are dominated by egotism, pride and greed, that love is only lust under a fancy hat . . . ."[4]

Cardenio ends on a triumphant note. With Helvetius at his side, Govianus is restored to his throne. Reunited at last with the errant nobles of his court, whom he instantly forgives, and reconciled to the death of his beloved, King Govianus declares: "all the Kingdom's evils perish" (V, ii, 2212). The embalmed Lady, true instrument of his restoration, is honored for her *chastity* and *constancy* (Govianus's words), and at his orders is seated upon the throne and crowned queen before being carried reverently to her place of eternal rest.

The main plot of *Cardenio* fits the pattern of other tragicomic romances of Shakespeare perfectly. In his excellent guide, *The Shakespeare Handbook* (pp. 166, 167), Dr. Levi Fox writes:

> The last four complete plays [The collaborative *Cardenio* would make it five and *The Two Noble Kinsmen* six] that Shakespeare wrote, between 1608 and 1611, *Pericles, Cymbeline, The Winter's Tale*, and *The Tempest* . . . are all strikingly similar [and] are usually called the Romances. All four plays dwell richly on the . . . love between a father and a daughter, and the power of the princess [in *Cardenio*, The Lady] to restore to the king and his court, both truth and life . . . . In these Shakespearean romances, in each case, the ending is a triumph.

In *By Me, William Shakespeare* (N.Y.: 1980, p. 337), Robert Payne notes: "While the [romance] plays are very similar . . . in their intense preoccupation with innocence and the restoration of the kingdom to the rightful king, they are remarkably different in the characterization of the minor figures . . . ."

Including the collaborative dramas, the six romances of Shakespeare may be divided conveniently into two groups: plays involved with the perilous seas (*Pericles, The Winter's Tale*, and *The Tempest*), and those that take place in enchanted lands

(*Cymbeline, Cardenio,* and *The Two Noble Kinsmen*). In all of them, the harsher realities of life are often glossed over and the supernatural plays a vital role. Usually the capricious gods rile up the action, but in *Cardenio* it is The Lady's ghost that shapes the destiny of the characters.

The technical "defects" in *Cardenio* are, for the most part, shared by all of Shakespeare's other romance plays. Dr. Fox points out (*op. cit.*, p. 166): "The characters are preferably of royal or noble birth, and happily lack much psychological plausibility in their actions." An explanation for Shakespeare's fantasy-world plots and unreal characters was suggested by Hesketh Pearson in his *A Life of Shakespeare* (p. 168): "Shakespeare's later [romance] works are . . . attempts to make real all the perfect things in life that he had failed to find: purity, innocence, flawless love, charity, self-sacrifice, spirituality and ultimate happiness. These qualities [are] mostly figured in youthful heroines [whom] he surrounds with a crowd of . . . the most objectionable human beings he has met . . . ."

Many scholars aver that Shakespeare abandoned realism, such as we find in his great tragedies, and turned to romance drama because of the growing public demand for fantasy and spectacle, plus the fact that the Blackfriars theater, newly acquired by the King's Men (1608), was ideal for tragicomic plays. The rectangular theater, only about forty-five by sixty-five feet, could seat three hundred spectators. Its enclosed intimacy was adapted to the use of candles and lanterns, as in the nocturnal scenes in *Cardenio*. Further, the improved acoustics encouraged the inclusion in Shakespeare's dramas of *entr'acte* and occasional music and tender ballads, like the poetic eulogy sung by the page boy in *Cardenio*.

In a provocative study, *Shakespeare's Division of Experience* (N.Y.: 1982, pp. 290, 295, 296), Professor Marilyn French writes of Shakespeare's romance dramas: "Each play provides a different form, but all of them are experiments in achieving a vision in which 'feminine' values are triumphant . . . . The sexually opposed figures in these plays are fathers and daughters . . . . In all the romances, female chaste constancy is implicit . . . ."

The Lady in *Cardenio* is one of the most subtle creations of Shakespeare's wondrous imagination. To some she might appear static and no more fleshly than a marble Aphrodite by Praxiteles. In short, a character whom the dramatist looked upon as a mere foil for the protagonist. But I believe Shakespeare created The Lady as the embodiment of the perfect woman; beautiful and innocent, strong and brave, faithful to her lover and her ideals. She is inviolate and incorruptible; therefore, her character does not change to meet events and circumstances. In this respect, she forms a stark contrast to the beleaguered and indecisive Govianus and the psychopathic, love-tortured Tyrant, both of whom are constantly at war with their emotions and undergo drastic changes in character throughout the play.

The Lady defends her honor with dignity and nobility and dies without fanfare and with admirable courage. She leaves behind none of the rancor that clings to most suicides. She is undone by her own purity. Later, her ghost, incandescently beautiful and enticing, sustains the Olympian detachment that The Lady exhibited in life. Without specifically seeking vengeance, her ghost asks for protection of its mortal remains from The Tyrant's sexual molestation.

In his stage instructions, Shakespeare describes The Lady's ghost as it first appears to Govianus. Shakespeare's portrayal of The Lady is a beautiful vignette:

> On a sudden, in a kind of noise like a wind, the doors clattering, the tombstone flies open, and a great light appears in the midst of the tomb; his lady, as went out [died], standing just before him all in white, stuck with jewels, and a great crucifix on her breast. (IV, iv, 1746-51)

The second appearance of The Lady, lusciously served up to The Tyrant, is less terrifying but equally spectacular. Harold L. Stenger, Jr., writes of it: ". . . here is the entrance of the soldiers with the Lady's body with the elaborateness of a little masque."[5]

> They bring the body in a chair, dressed up in black velvet, which sets out the paleness of the hands and face, and a fair chain of pearl 'cross her breast, and the crucifix above it. He stands silent awhile, letting the music play, beckoning the Soldiers that bring her in to make obeisance to her, and he himself makes a low honour to the body and kisses the hand. (V, ii, 2022-25)

There are similar minuscule masques in *The Two Noble Kinsmen,* also by Shakespeare and Fletcher, that suggest a common authorship:

> Still music of recorders. Enter Emilia in white, her hair about her shoulders, with a wheaten wreath; one in white holding up her train, her hair stuck with flowers; one before her carrying a silver hind, in which being set upon the altar of Diana, her maids standing aloof, she sets fire to it. Then they curtsy and kneel. (*The Two Noble Kinsmen*, V, i, p. 151)

Later I shall discuss in detail exactly how Shakespeare and Fletcher utilized the story of Cardenio in Cervantes's *Don Quixote* for their main plot and "The Tale of the Curious Impertinent," also from the story of Cardenio, for their subplot.

In proclaiming *Cardenio* or *The Second Maiden's Tragedy* to be the work of a skilled dramatist, many critics have praised its adroit plotting, vivid scenes, and superlative stagecraft. But in my opinion, it is the beauty of the language and penetrating wisdom of *Cardenio* that clearly identify the play's authorship. Almost every page bears at least a fingertip touch of Shakespeare's genius. Here are a few excerpts:

> There's the kingdom
> Within yon valley fixed, while I stand here
> Kissing false hopes upon a frozen mountain. . . (I, i, 144-47)
>
> Down, villain, to thy everlasting weeping
> That canst rejoice so in the rape of virtue,

And sing light tunes in tempests. . . (III, 1115-17)

That when with ungoverned weapons they rush in,
Blinded with fury, they may take his death
Into the purple number of their deeds. . . (III, 1245-47)

When The Tyrant looks upon the corpse of The Lady, his moving tribute to her evokes the famed sonnet of Rupert Brooke that begins, "Oh! Death will find me, long before I tire/of watching you. . . ":

I never shall be weary to behold thee;
I could eternally stand thus and see thee. (IV, iii, 1624-25)

Many of the expressions and word usages in the main plot of *Cardenio* are redolent with the art of Shakespeare, startling and unusual, with frequent neologisms. The writer has a wondrous knack for using common words in uncommon ways and thus imparting to them a fresh and powerful meaning:

where she goes
Her eye *removes* the court (I, i, 149-50)

My knees shall *know* no other earthly lord (II, i, 744)

(On a tomb's cover): death's *marble lip* (III, 1315)

Have you *unlocked* your memory? (II, iii, 964)

The monument *woos* me! I must run and kiss it. (IV, iii, 1572)

(Giving orders to force open the tomb):
Pierce the *jaws*
Of this *cold, ponderous creature* (IV, iii, 1588-89)

O heav'n, *put armour on my spirit* (IV, iv, 1797)

My spirit *wrestles with my blood* (V, ii, 2009)

Reward my joys with *astonished silence* (V, ii, 2198)

'Tis as *unpossible* for living fire
To take hold there
As for dead ashes to burn back again (V, ii, 2116-2117)

Who for *the hate she owed* him, killed herself (IV, iii, 1681)

Shakespeare, of course, is celebrated for his apt remarks that become proverbs. The subplot is replete with them, a few adapted from the wit of Cervantes. But there are in the main plot many pithy sayings that seem to bear Shakespeare's touch:

> I need no spur, my lord. Honour pricks me. (I, i, 241)
>
> Look not after him that needs thee not (I, ii, 266)
>
> All the best arts
> Hath the most fools and drunkards to their
> masters (V, ii, 2086-87)
>
> That may thrive best
> Which the least hope looks after (II, iii, 1010)
>
> Search thy conscience for thy sins of youth;
> That's work enough for age (II, i, 729-30)

In Act I, Scene ii of the subplot, which I consider to be the joint work of Shakespeare and Fletcher, are many quotable lines. For example:

> What a wild seed
> Suspicion sows (I, ii, 402-403)
>
> All the world's a gamester (I, ii, 499)

Both the main plot and the subplot are rich in *double-entendres,* most of them of a bawdy turn. Shakespeare uses these *double-entendres* for comic relief. In the nocturnal cathedral scene, when The Tyrant orders the terrified soldiers to take up the body of the dead Lady, the first soldier says:

> I've took up many a woman in my days,
> But never with less pleasure (IV, iii, 1642-43)

Few Elizabethans were more adept at the oxymoron than Shakespeare. An interesting oxymoron occurs in *Cardenio* that seems to have the Master's touch:

> marry patience to my spirit!
> Give me a *sober fury*, I beseech thee,
> A rage that may not overcharge my blood (V, ii, 2067-69)

A play would not be Shakespeare's without a quorum of image clusters. Here is one of them—dawn [birth], liberty, health, and long life—from the final scene in *Cardenio*:

Welcome to mine eyes
As is the dayspring from the morning's womb
Unto that wretch whose nights are tedious,
As liberty to captives, health to labourers,
And life still to old people, never weary on't;
So welcome art thou to me. (V, ii, 2172-77)

In Act I, Scene ii of the subplot, which I have attributed to the combined genius of Shakespeare and Fletcher, are many beautiful passages. This one seems to bear the magic touch of the wizard of Stratford:

Dominions have their limits; the whole earth
Is but a prisoner. . .the sea her jailor,
That with a silver hoop locks in her body. . .
But the unbounded kingdom of the mind
Is as unlimitable as heaven. (I, ii, 257-263)

PART I

CARDENIO

or

THE SECOND MAIDEN'S TRAGEDY

PREFACE TO THE PLAY

Were most critics to rate the dramatists of the late Elizabethan and early Jacobean eras according to their position in the hierarchy of genius, they might list as the greatest, possibly in this order: Shakespeare, Jonson, Tourneur, Beaumont, and Fletcher. In the second group, a few rungs below: Middleton, Dekker, Webster, Chapman, Ford, Massinger, Marston, and Heywood. Still lower on the ladder: Nathaniel Field, Rowley, and Munday, followed by a host of lesser dramatists. All of these men were at work in 1611, when *Cardenio* was written.

It is surely a tribute to the anonymous play, here identified as *Cardenio*, that it is today ascribed by leading scholars to either Cyril Tourneur or Thomas Middleton, two of the outstanding dramatists of their era.

The beauty and dramatic impact of *Cardenio* has for almost two centuries been obscured by its great interest to scholars as a complete surviving manuscript play, handsomely penned with very few corrections, precisely as Heminges, Condell, and Ben Jonson described Shakespeare's manuscripts. Further, the play was fully readied for production, with stage directions for musicians and actors. *Cardenio* is also unique because it reveals exactly how Sir George Buc, the censor-general of Jacobean drama, went about his task. It survives in manuscript only because it was never published. Once a play was put into print, the manuscript or prompt copy was generally considered fit only to start fires or back pies.

Should you be hard pressed with other tasks and not have the leisure to peruse all of *Cardenio,* I urge you to read at least scenes two, three, and four of Act IV, in which the necrophilic Tyrant steals the body of The Lady and the theft is disclosed to her lover, Govianus. Judge for yourself whether the chilling beauty of these nocturnal scenes in the cathedral does not evoke the magic touch of the Wizard of Stratford.

NOTE ON THE TEXT

The text of this printing is based upon photocopies of the original manuscript (MS. Lansdowne 807) in the British Museum Library, W.W. Greg's 1909 Malone Society edition, Harold L. Stenger, Jr.'s modernized edition (1954), in typescript as a Ph.D. thesis, and Anne Lancashire's edition published by the Manchester University Press in 1978.

I have followed the scene divisions of Stenger and Lancashire and have modernized the spelling and introduced punctuation according to my own interpretation of the text. Finally, when necessary, I have added to or slightly altered Shakespeare's stage directions to clarify the action.

A glossary of obsolete words and obscure phrases will be found at the end of the play.

DRAMATIS PERSONAE

THE TYRANT a.k.a. KING FERNANDO, *a Usurper*

GOVIANUS a.k.a. CARDENIO, *the deposed King*

ANSELMUS a.k.a. ANSELMO, *his Brother*

VOTARIUS a.k.a. LOTARIO, *Friend to Anselmus*

HELVETIUS

MEMPHONIUS *Nobles*

SOPHONIRUS

BELLARIUS, *Lover of Leonella*

THE LADY a.k.a. LUSCINDA, *Daughter of Helvetius*

THE WIFE OF VOTARIUS a.k.a. CAMILLA

LEONELLA, *her Waiting-Woman*

NOBLES, SOLDIERS, and ATTENDANTS

CARDENIO
or
The Second Maiden's Tragedy

(ACT I, SCENE I)

The royal palace. Enter the new Usurping Tyrant, the nobles of his faction, Memphonius, Sophonirus, Helvetius, with others; the right heir Govianus, deposed.

A sennet

TYRANT: Thus high, my lords, your powers and constant loves
Hath fixed our glories like unmovèd stars
That know not what it is to fall or err.
We're the kingdom's love, and he that was
Flattered awhile, so stands before us now
Readier for doom than dignity.

GOVIANUS: So much
Can the adulterate friendship of mankind,
False Fortune's sister, bring to pass on kings,
And lay usurpers sunning in their glories
Like adders in warm beams.

TYRANT: There was but one
In whom my heart took pleasure (amongst women),
One in the whole creation, and in her
You dared to be my rival! Was't not bold?
Now we are king, she'll leave the lower path
And find the way to us. Helvetius!
It is thy daughter. Happier than a king
And far above him, for she kneels to thee
Whom we have kneeled to, richer in one smile
That came from her than she in all thy blessings!
If thou be'st proud, thou art to be forgiven;

It is no deadly sin in thee. While she lives,
High lust is not more natural to youth
Than that to thee. Be not afraid to die in't;
'Tis but the sign of joy. There is no gladness
But has a pride it lives by. That's the oil
That feeds it into flames. Let her be sent for
And honorably attended, as beseems
Her that we make our queen. My lords Memphonius
And Sophonirus, take into your care
The royal business of my heart. Conduct her
With a respect equal with that to us.
If more, it shall be pardoned; so still err,
You honour us, but ourself honours her.

MEMPHONIUS:

Aside

Strange fortune! Does he make his queen of her?

Exit Memphonius

SOPHONIRUS: I have a wife; would she were so preferred!
I could be but her subject; so I'm now:
I allow her her one friend to stop her mouth
And keep her quiet, gi' him his table free,
And the huge feeding of his great stone horse
On which he rides in pomp about the city
Only to speak to gallants in bay-windows.
Marry, his lodging he pays dearly for;
He gets me all my children; there I save by't.
Besides I draw my life out by the bargain
Some twelve years longer than the times appointed;
When my young prodigal gallant kicks up's heels
At one-and-thirty, and lies dead and rotten
Some five-and-forty years before I'm coffined.
'Tis the right way to keep a woman honest:
One friend is barricado to a hundred
And keeps 'em out. Nay more, a husband's sure
To have his children all of one man's getting,
And he that performs best can have no better.
I'm e'en as happy then that save a labour.

Exit Sophonirus

TYRANT: *To Helvetius*
Thy honours with thy daughter's love shall rise.
I shall read thy deservings in her eyes.

HELVETIUS: O may they be eternal books of pleasure
To show you all delight!

GOVIANUS: The loss of her sits closer to my heart
Than that of kingdom or the whorish pomp
Of this world's titles, that with flattery swells us
And makes us die like beasts fat for destruction.
O she's a woman, and her eye will stand
Upon advancement, never weary yonder;
But when she turns her head by chance and sees
The fortunes that are my companions,
She'll snatch her eyes off and repent the looking.

TYRANT: 'Tis well advised: we doom thee, Govianus,
To banishment for ever from our kingdom.

GOVIANUS: What could be worse to one whose heart is locked
Up in another's bosom! Banishment!
And why not death? Is that too easy for me?

TYRANT: But that the world would call our way to dignity
A path of blood, it should be the first act in all our reign.

GOVIANUS: She's lost for ever!
To Nobles
Farewell, virtuous men,
Too honest for your greatness. Now y'are mightier
Than when we knew the kingdom; your style's heavier.
Then, ponderous nobility, farewell!

FIRST NOBLEMAN: How's that, sir?

GOVIANUS: Weighty and serious!—O, sir, is it you?
I knew you one-and-twenty and a lord,
When your discretion sucked; is't come from nurse yet?
You seem to be a scholar; you were born better.

You have good lands; that's the best grounds of learning.
If you can conster but your doctor's bill,
Pierce your wife's waiting-women, and decline your tenants
Till they're all beggars with new fines and rackings,
Y'are scholar good enough for a lady's son
That's born to living. If you list to read,
Ride but to th' city and bestow your looks
On the court library, the mercers' books;
They'll quickly furnish you: do but entertain
A tailor for your tutor to expound
All the hard stuff to you, by what name and title
Soever they be called.

FIRST NOBLEMAN: I thank you, sir.

GOVIANUS: 'Tis happy you have learnt so much manners,
Since you have so little wit. Fare you well, sir!

TYRANT: Let him be stayed awhile.

SECOND NOBLEMAN: Stay!

FIRST NOBLEMAN: You must stay, sir.

GOVIANUS: He's not so honest, sure, to change his mind,
Revoke his doom. Hell has more hope on him.

TYRANT: We have not ended yet; the worst part's coming:
Thy banishment were gentle were that all.
But t'afflict thy soul, before thou goest
Thou shalt behold the heaven that thou must lose
In her that must be mine.
Then to be banished, then to be deprived,
Shows the full torment we provide for thee.

GOVIANUS: Here's a right tyrant now; he will not bate me
Th'affliction of my soul; he'll have all parts
Suffer together.

Enter the Nobles with the LADY clad in black

Now I see my loss;
I never shall recover't; my mind's beggared.

TYRANT: Black! Whence risse that cloud? Can such a thing be seen
In honour's glorious day, the sky so clear?
Why mourns the kingdom's mistress? Does she come
To meet advancement in a funeral garment?
Back! She forgot herself. 'Twas too much joy
That bred this error, and we heartily pardon't.
To the attending Nobles
Go, bring me her hither like an illustrious bride
With her best beams about her. Let her jewels
Be worth ten cities; that beseems our mistress,
And not a widow's case, a suit to weep in.

LADY: I am not to be altered.

TYRANT: How!

LADY: I have a mind
That must be shifted ere I cast off these,
Or else I shall wear strange colours. 'Tis not titles,
Nor all the bastard honours of this frame
That I am taken with. I come not hither
To please the eye of glory, but of goodness;
And that concerns not you, sir; you're for greatness
I dare not deal with you: I have found my match,
And I will never lose him.
Looks at Govianus

GOVIANUS:
If there be man
Above a king in fortunes, read my story
And you shall find him there. Farewell, poor kingdom!
To the Tyrant
Take it to help thee; thou hast need on't now.
I see thee in distress, more miserable
Than some thou lay'st taxations on, poor subjects!
Th'art all beset with storms, more overcast
Than ever any man that brightness flattered.
'Tis only wretchedness to be there with thee,
And happiness to be here.

TYRANT: Sure some dream crowned me.
If it were possible to be less than nothing,
I wake the man you seek for. There's the kingdom
Within yon valley fixed, while I stand here
Kissing false hopes upon a frozen mountain,
Without the confines. I am he that's banished.
The king walks yonder, chose by her affection,
Which is the surer side, for where she goes
Her eye removes the court. What is he here
Can spare a look? They're all employed on her.
Helvetius! Thou art not worth the waking neither;
I lose but time in thee. Go sleep again:
Like an old man, thou can'st do nothing;
Thou tak'st no pains at all to earn thine honours.
Which way shall we be able to pay thee
To thy content, when we receive not ours?
The master of the work must needs decay
When he wants means, and sees his servant play.

HELVETIUS: *To the Lady*
Have I bestowed so many blessings on thee,
And do they all return to me in curses?
Is that the use I ha' for 'em? Be not to me
A burden ten times heavier than my years!
Thou'd'st wont to be kind to me and observe
What I thought pleasing. Go, entreat the king!

LADY: I will do more for you, sir; y'are my father;
I'll kiss him, too.

She kisses Govianus

HELVETIUS: How am I dealt withal?

LADY: Why that's the usurper, sir; this is the king.
I happened righter than you thought I had.
And were all kingdoms of the earth his own,
As sure as this is not, and this dear gentleman
As poor as virtue and almost as friendless,
I would not change this misery for that sceptre
Wherein I had part with him. Sir, be cheerful.
'Tis not the reeling fortune of great state

Or low condition that I cast mine eye at.
It is the man I seek; the rest I lose
As things unworthy to be kept or noted.
Fortunes are but the outsides of true worth.
It is the mind that sets his master forth.

TYRANT: Has there so many bodies been hewn down
Like trees in progress, to cut out a way
That was ne'er known, for us and our affections,
And is our game so crossed? There stands the first
Of all her kind that ever refused greatness—
A woman to set light by sovereignty!
What age can bring her forth, and hide that book?
'Tis their desire most commonly to rule
More than their part comes to—sometimes their husbands.

HELVETIUS: 'Tis in your power, my lord, to force her to you
And pluck her from his arms.

TYRANT: Thou talk'st unkindly.
That had been done before thy thought begot it
If my affection could be so hard-hearted
To stand upon such payment. It must come
Gently and kindly, like a debt of love,
Or 'tis not worth receiving.

GOVIANUS: Now usurper,
I wish not happier freedom than the banishment
That thou hast laid upon me.

TYRANT: *Aside* O, he kills me
At mine own weapon! 'Tis I that live in exile.
Should she forsake the land, I'll feign some cause
Far from the grief itself to call it back.
To Govianus
That doom of banishment was but lent to thee
To make a trial of thy factious spirit,
Which flames in thy desire. Thou wouldst be gone.
There is some combination betwixt thee
And foreign plots; thou hast some powers to raise,
Which, to prevent, thy banishment we revoke,

Confine thee to thy house nearest our court,
And place a guard about thee. Lord Memphonius,
See it effected.

MEMPHONIUS: With best care, my lord.

GOVIANUS: Confine me? Here's my liberty in mine arms;
I wish no better to bring me content.
Love's best freedom is close prisonment!
Exeunt Lady and Govianus

TYRANT: Methinks the day e'en darkens at her absence.
I stand as in a shade, when a great cloud
Muffles the sun, whose beams shine afar off
On tow'rs and mountains; But I keep the valleys,
The place that is last served.

HELVETIUS: My lord!

TYRANT: Your reason, sir?

HELVETIUS: Your grace is mild to all but your own bosom.
They should have both been sent to several prisons,
And not committed to each other's arms.
There's a hot durance! He'll ne'er wish more freedom!

TYRANT: 'Tis true; let 'em be both forced back.
Stay, we command you!
Thou talk'st not like a statesman. Had my wrath
Took hold of such extremity at first,
They'd lived suspectful still, warned by their fears;
Where, now that liberty makes 'em more secure,
I'll take 'em at my pleasure. It gives thee
Freer access to play the father for us,
And ply her to our will.

HELVETIUS: Mass, so it does.
Let a man think on't twice, your grace hath happened
Upon a strange way, yet it proves the nearest.

TYRANT: Nay, more to vex his soul, give command straight

They be divided into several rooms,
Where he may only have a sight of her
To his mind's torment, but his arms and lips
Locked up like felons from her.

HELVETIUS: Now you win me.
I like that cruelty passing well, my lord.

TYRANT: Give order with all speed.

HELVETIUS: Though I be old,
I need no spur, my lord; honour pricks me.
I do beseech your grace look cheerfully.
You shall not want content if it be locked
In any blood of mine. The key's your own.
You shall command the words.

TYRANT: Say'st thou so, sir?
I were ingrateful then, should I see thee
Want honour, that provides content for me.
Exeunt. A Flourish

(ACT I, SCENE II)

The home of Anselmus. Enter Lord Anselmus, the deposed king's brother, with his friend, Votarius

VOTARIUS: Pray, sir, confine your thoughts and excuse me.
Methinks the deposed king your brother's sorrow
Should find you business enough.

ANSELMUS: How, Votarius!
Sorrow for him? Weak ignorance talks not like thee.
Why, he was never happier.

VOTARIUS: Pray prove that, sir.

ANSELMUS: H'as lost the kingdom, but his mind's restored.
Which is the larger empire, prithee tell me.
Dominions have their limits; the whole earth
Is but a prisoner, nor the sea her jailor,
That with a silver hoop locks in her body.
They're fellow prisoners, though the sea looks bigger
Because he is in office and pride swells him.
But the unbounded kingdom of the mind
Is as unlimitable as heaven, that glorious court of spirits,
All honest courtiers!
Sir, if thou lov'st me, turn thine eye to me,
And look not after him that needs thee not.
My brother's well attended; peace and pleasure
Are never from his sight. He has his mistress.
She brought those servants and bestowed them on him.
But who brings mine?

VOTARIUS: Had you not both long since
By a kind, worthy lady, your chaste wife?

ANSELMUS: That's it that I take pains with thee to be sure of.
What true report can I send to my soul
Of that I know not? We must only think
Our ladies are good people, and so live with 'em:
A fine security for them! Our own thoughts
Make the best fools of us; next to them, our wives.

But say she's all chaste, yet is that her goodness?
What labour is't for a woman to keep constant
That's never tried or tempted? Where's her fight?
The war's within her breast, her honest anger
Against the impudence of flesh and hell:
So let me know the lady of my rest,
Or I shall never sleep well. Give not me
The thing that is thought good, but what's approved so:
So wise men choose. O, what a lazy virtue
Is chastity in a woman if no sin
Should lay temptation to't! Prithee, set to her
And bring my peace along with thee.

VOTARIUS: You put to me
A business that will do my words more shame
Than ever they got honour among women.
Lascivious courtings among sinful mistresses
Come ever seasonably, please best.
But let the boldest ruffian touch the ear
Of modest ladies with adulterous sounds,
Their very looks confound him and force grace
Into that cheek where impudence sets her seal.
That work is never undertook with courage
That makes his master blush. However, sir,
What profit can return to you by knowing
That which you do already, with more toil?
That a man needs, in having a rich diamond,
Put it between a hammer and an anvil,
And not believing the true worth and value,
Break it in pieces to find out the goodness,
And in the finding lose it? Good sir, think on't!
Nor does it taste of wit to try their strengths
That are created sickly, nor of manhood.
We ought not to put blocks in women's ways,
For some too often fall upon plain ground.
Let me dissuade you, sir!

ANSELMUS: Have I a friend?
And has my love so little interest in him
That I must trust some stranger with my heart,
And go to seek him out?

VOTARIUS: Nay, hark you, sir!
I am so jealous of your weaknesses,
That rather than you should lie prostituted
Before a stranger's triumph, I would venture
A whole hour's shaming for you.

ANSELMUS: Be worth thy word, then!
Enter Wife
Aside. Yonder she comes. I'll have an ear to you both;
I love to have such things at the first hand.
He hides within hearing

VOTARIUS: I'll put him off with somewhat; guile in this
Falls in with honest dealing. O, who could move
Adultery to yon face! So rude a sin
May not come near the meekness of her eye.
My client's cause looks so dishonestly
I'll ne'er be seen to plead in't.

WIFE: What, Votarius!

VOTARIUS: Good morrow, virtuous madam.

WIFE: Was my lord
Seen lately here?

VOTARIUS: He's newly walked forth, lady.

WIFE: How was he attended?

VOTARIUS: Faith, I think with none, madam.

WIFE: That sorrow for the king his brother's fortune
Prevails too much with him, and leads him strangely
From company and delight.

VOTARIUS: *Aside*. How she's beguiled in him!
There's no such natural touch, search all his bosom.
Aloud
That grief's too bold with him indeed, sweet madam.
And draws him from the pleasure of his time,

But 'tis a business of affection
That must be done. We owe a pity, madam,
To all men's misery, but especially
To those afflictions that claim kindred of us.
We're forced to feel 'em: all compassion else
Is but a work of charity, this, of nature,
And ties our pity in a bond of blood.

WIFE: Yet, sir, there is a date set to all sorrows.
Nothing is everlasting in this world.
Your counsel will prevail: persuade him, good sir,
To fall into life's happiness again,
And leave the desolate path. I want his company:
He walks at midnight in thick shady [dark] woods
Where scarce the moon is starlight. I have watched him
In silver nights when all the earth was dressed
Up like a virgin in white innocent beams;
Stood in my window cold and thinly clad
T'observe him through the bounty of the moon
That liberally bestowed her graces on me.
And when the morning dew began to fall,
Then was my time to weep. H'as lost his kindness,
Forgot the way of wedlock, and become
A stranger to the joys and rites of love.
He's not so good as a lord ought to be.
Pray tell him so from me, sir.
Exit Wife

VOTARIUS: That will I, madam.
How must I dress a strange dish for his humour.
Enter Anselmus from his hiding place

ANSELMUS: *Aside*. Call you this courting? Life, not one word near it!
There was no syllable but was twelve score off.
My faith, hot temptation! Woman's chastity
In such a conflict had great need of one
To keep the bridge. 'Twas dangerous for the time.
Why, what fantastic faiths are in these days
Made without substance! Whom should a man trust
In matters about love?
Anselmus comes forward

VOTARIUS: Mass, here he comes, too!

ANSELMUS: How now, Votarius! What's the news for us?

VOTARIUS: You set me to a task, sir, that will find
Ten ages work enough, and then unfinished.
Bring sin before her! Why, it stands more quaking
Than if a judge should frown on't. Three such fits
Would shake it into goodness, and quite beggar
The under-kingdom. Not the art of man,
Woman or devil—

ANSELMUS: O, peace, man! Prithee, peace!

VOTARIUS: Can make her fit for lust.

ANSELMUS: Yet again, sir?
Where lives that mistress of thine, Votarius,
That taught thee to dissemble? I'd fain learn;
She makes good scholars.

VOTARIUS: How, my lord!

ANSELMUS: Thou art the son of falsehood. Prithee, leave me.
How truly constant, charitable, and helpful
Is woman unto woman in affairs
That touch affection and the peace of spirit;
But man to man, how crooked and unkind;
I thank my jealousy I heard thee all,
For I heard nothing; now thou'rt sure I did.

VOTARIUS: Now by this light, then, wipe but off this score,
Since y'are so bent, and if I ever run
In debt again to falsehood and dissemblance,
For want of better means, tear the remembrance of me
From your best thoughts.

ANSELMUS: For thy vow's sake, I pardon thee
Thy oath is now sufficient watch itself
Over thy actions. I discharge my jealousy:
I ha' no more use for't now. To give thee way

I'll have an absence made purposely for thee,
And presently take horse. I'll leave behind me
An opportunity that shall fear no starting.
Let thy pains deserve it.

VOTARIUS: I am bound to't.

ANSELMUS: For a small time, farewell then. Hark thee!
Anselmus whispers in his ear

VOTARIUS: O good sir!
It will do wondrous well.
Exit Anselmus
What a wild seed
Suspicion sows in him, and takes small ground for't!
But happy were this lord if he would leave
To tempt his fate and be resolved he were so!
He would be but too rich.
Man has some enemy still that keeps him back
In all his fortunes, and his mind is his,
And that's a mighty adversary. I had rather
Have twenty kings my enemies than that part;
For let me be at war with earth and hell
So that be friends with me! I ha' sworn to make
A trial of her faith. I must put on
A courtier's face and do't; mine own will shame me.

Enter Wife

WIFE: This is most strange of all! How one distraction
Seconds another!

VOTARIUS: What's the news, sweet madam?

WIFE: H'as took his horse, but left his leave untaken.
What should I think on't, sir? Did ever lord
Depart so rudely from his lady's presence?

VOTARIUS: Did he forget your lip?

WIFE: He forgot all
That nobleness remembers.

VOTARIUS: I'm ashamed on him.
Let me help, madam, to repair his manners,
And mend that unkind fault.

WIFE: Sir! Pray, forbear!
You forget worse than he.

VOTARIUS: *Aside.* So virtue save me,
I have enough already.

WIFE: 'Tis himself
Must make amends, good sir, for his own faults.

VOTARIUS: *Aside.* I would he'd do't then, and ne'er trouble mein't.
Aloud
But, madam, you perceive he takes the course
To be far off from that. He's rode from home,
But his unkindness stays, and keeps with you.
Let whose will please his wife; he rides his horse;
That's all the care he takes. I pity you, madam;
Y'ave an unpleasing lord. Would 'twere not so.
I should rejoice with you.
You're young, the very spring's upon you now.
The roses on your cheeks are but new blown.
Take you together, y'are a pleasant garden
Where all the sweetness of man's comfort breathes.
But what is it to be a work of beauty
And want the heart that should delight in you?
You still retain your goodness in yourself,
But then you lose your glory, which is all.
The grace of every benefit is the use,
And is't not pity you should want your grace?
Look you like one whose lord should walk in groves
About the peace of midnight? Alas, madam,
'Tis to me wondrous how you should spare the day
From amorous clips, much less the general season
When all the world's a gamester!
That face deserves a friend of heart and spirit,
Discourse, and motion, indeed such a one
That should observe you, madam, without ceasing,
And not a weary lord.

WIFE: Sure I was married, sir,
In a dear year of love, when scarcity
And famine of affection vexed poor ladies,
Which makes my heart so needy. It ne'er knew
Plenty of comfort yet.

VOTARIUS: Why, that's your folly,
To keep your mind so miserably, madam.
Change into better times; I'll lead you to 'em.
What bounty shall your friend expect for his?
O you that can be hard to your own heart,
But would you use your friend's? If I thought kindly,
I'd be the man myself to serve your pleasure.

WIFE: Now, sir!

VOTARIUS: Nay, and ne'er miss you, too. I'd not come sneaking
Like a retainer once a week or so
To show myself before you for my livery;
I'd follow business like a household servant,
Carry my work before me, and dispatch
Before my lord be up, and make no words on't—
The sign of a good servant.

WIFE: 'Tis not friendly done, sir,
To take a lady at advantage thus:
Set all her wrongs before her, and then tempt her.

VOTARIUS: *Aside*. Heart! I grow fond myself! 'Twas well
she waked me
Before the dead sleep of adultery took me;
'Twas stealing on me. Up, you honest thoughts,
And keep watch for your master! I must hence.
I do not like my health; 't'as a strange relish.
Pray heaven I plucked mine eyes back time enough!
I'll never see her more. I praised the garden
But little thought a bed of snakes lay hid in't.
He prepares to leave

WIFE: *Aside*. I know not how I am! I'll call my woman—
Stay, for I fear thou'rt too far gone already.

VOTARIUS: *Aside*. I'll see her but once more. Do thy worst, love!
Thou art too young, fond boy, to master me.
He returns to the Wife
I come to tell you, madam, and that plainly
I'll see your face no more. Take't how you please.

WIFE: You will not offer violence to me, sir,
In my lord's absence! What does that touch you
If I want comfort?

VOTARIUS: Will you take your answer?

WIFE: It is not honest in you to tempt woman:
When her distresses takes away her strength,
How is she able to withstand her enemy?

VOTARIUS: I would fain leave your sight and I could possible.

WIFE: What is't to you, good sir, if I be pleased
To weep myself away, and run thus violently
Into the arms of death, and kiss destruction?
Does this concern you now?

VOTARIUS: Ay, marry, does it!
What serve these arms for but to pluck you back,
These lips but to prevent all other tasters,
And keep that cup of nectar for themselves?
Aside
Heart, I'm beguiled again! Forgive me, heav'n,
My lips have been naught with her! Sin's mere witchcraft.
Break all the engines of life's frame in pieces,
I will be master once, and whip the boy
Home to his mother's lap. Face, fare thee well!
Exit Votarius

WIFE: Votarius! Sir! My friend! Thank heav'n, he's gone.
And he shall never come so near again;
I'll have my frailty watched over. Henceforward
I'll no more trust it single. It betrays me
Into the hands of folly. Where's my woman?

Enter Leonella

My trusty Leonella!

LEONELLA: Call you, madam?

WIFE: Call I? I want attendance! Where are you?

LEONELLA: Never far from you, madam.

WIFE: Pray be nearer,
Or there is some that will, and thank you, too,
May perhaps bribe you to be absent from me.

LEONELLA: How madam?

WIFE: Is that strange to a lady's woman?
There are such things i'th world, many such buyers
And sellers of a woman's name and honour,
Though you be young in bribes, and never came
To the flesh-market yet. Beshrew your heart
For keeping so long from me!

LEONELLA: What ail you, madam?

WIFE: Somewhat commands me, and takes all the power
Of myself from me.

LEONELLA: What should that be, lady?

WIFE: When did you see Votarius?

LEONELLA: *Aside.* Is that next?
Nay, then I have your ladyship in the wind.
Aloud
I saw him lately, madam.

WIFE: Whom didst see?

LEONELLA: Votarius!

WIFE: What have I to do with him
More than another man? Say he be fair,

And has parts proper both of mind and body,
You praise him but in vain in telling me so.

LEONELLA: *Aside*. Yea, madam, are you prattling in your sleep?
'Tis well my lord and you lie in two beds.

WIFE: I was ne'er so ill. I thank you, Leonella,
My negligent woman! Here you showed your service.

LEONELLA: *Aside*. Life! Have I a power or means to stop a sluice
At a high water? What would sh'ave me do in't?

WIFE: I charge thee, while thou liv'st with me, henceforward
Use not an hour's absence from my sight.

Exit Wife

LEONELLA: By my faith, madam, you shall pardon me.
I have a love of mine own to look to,
And he must have his breakfast. Pist! Bellarius!

Enter Bellarius, muffled in his cloak

BELLARIUS: Leonella!

LEONELLA: Come forth, and show yourself a gentleman,
Although most commonly they hide their heads,
As you do there, methinks! And why a taffety muffler?
Show your face, man! I'm not ashamed on you.

BELLARIUS: I fear the servants.

LEONELLA: And they fear their mistresses, and ne'er think on you;
Their thoughts are upon dinner and great dishes.
If one thing hap, impossible to fail to
(I can see so far in't), you shall walk boldly, sir,
And openly in view through every room
About the house, and let the proudest meet thee;
I charge you give no way to 'em.

BELLARIUS: How thou talk'st!

LEONELLA: I can avoid the fool, and give you reason for't.

BELLARIUS: 'Tis more than I should do, if I asked more on thee.
I prithee tell me how.

LEONELLA: With ease, i'faith, sir.
My lady's heart is wondrous busy, sir,
About the entertainment of a friend too;
And she and I must bear with one another,
Or we shall make but a madhouse betwixt us.

BELLARIUS: I'm bold to throw my cloak off at this news,
Which I ne'er durst before, and kiss thee freelier.
What is he, sirrah?

LEONELLA: Faith, an indifferent fellow
With good long legs—a near friend of my lord's.

BELLARIUS: A near friend of my lady's, you would say!
His name, I prithee?

LEONELLA: One Votarius, sir.

BELLARIUS: What sayest thou?

LEONELLA: He walks under the same title.

BELLARIUS: The only enemy that my life can show me!

LEONELLA: Your enemy! Let my spleen then alone with him.
Stay you your anger; I'll confound him for you.

BELLARIUS: As how, I prithee?

LEONELLA: I'll prevent his venery.
He shall ne'er lie with my lady.

BELLARIUS: Troth, I thank you.
Life, that's the way to save him! Art thou mad?
Whereas the other way he confounds himself,
And lies more naked to revenge and mischief.

LEONELLA: Then let him lie with her, and the devil go with him!

He shall have all my furtherance.

BELLARIUS: Why, now you pray heartily, and speak to purpose.

Exeunt.

(ACT II, SCENE I)

The house of Govianus's imprisonment. Enter The Lady of Govianus, with a Servant

LADY: Who is't would speak with us?

SERVANT: My lord your father.

LADY: My father! Pray make haste; he waits too long.
Entreat him hither.
Exit Servant
In spite of all
The tyrant's cruelties, we have got that friendship
E'en of the guard that he has placed about us.
My lord and I have free access together,
As much as I would ask of liberty.
They'll trust us largely now, and keep sometimes
Three hours from us, a rare courtesy
In jailors' children. Some mild news, I hope,
Comes with my father.
Enter Helvetius
No, his looks are sad;
There is some further tyranny. Let it fall!
Our constant suff'rings shall amaze it.
She kneels before her father

HELVETIUS: Rise.
I will not bless thee. Thy obedience
Is after custom, as most rich men pray,
Whose saint is only fashion and vainglory.
So 'tis with thee in thy dissembled duty;
There is no religion in't, no reverent love;
Only for fashion and the praise of men.

LADY: Why should you think so, sir.

HELVETIUS: Think? You come too late
If you seek there for me. I know't and see't.
I'll sooner give my blessing to a drunkard,
Whom the ridiculous power of wine makes humble,
As foolish use makes thee. Base-spirited girl,
That can'st not think above disgrace and beggary,
When glory is set for thee and thy seed,
Advancement for thy father, beside joy
Able to make a latter spring in me
In this my fourscore summer, and renew me
With a reversion yet of heat and youth!
But the dejection of thy mind and spirit
Makes me, thy father, guilty of a fault
That draws thy birth in question, and e'en wrongs
Thy mother in her ashes, being at peace
With heaven and man. Had not her life and virtues
Been seals unto her faith, I should think thee now
The work of some hired servant, some house-tailor,
And no one part of my endeavor in thee.
Had I neglected greatness, or not rather
Pursued almost to my eternal hazard,
Thou'dst ne'er been a lord's daughter.

LADY: Had I been
A shepherd's, I'd been happier and more peaceful.

HELVETIUS: Thy very seed will curse thee in thy age
When they shall hear the story of thy weakness:
How in thy youth thy fortunes tendered thee
A kingdom for thy servant, which thou left'st
Basely to serve thyself. What does thou in this
But merely cozen thy posterity
Of royalty and succession, and thyself
Of dignity present?

LADY: Sir, your king did well
'Mongst all his nobles to pick out yourself
And send you with these words. His politic grace
Knew what he did, for well he might imagine
None else should have been heard:
They'd had their answer

Before the question had been half-way through.
But, dearest sir, I owe to you a reverence,
A debt which both begins and ends with life,
Never till then discharged; 'tis so long-lasting
Yet could you be more precious than a father,
Which, next a husband, is the richest treasure
Mortality can show us, you should pardon me
(And yet confess too that you found me kind)
To hear your words, though I withstood your mind.

HELVETIUS: Say you so, daughter? Troth, I thank you kindly,
I am in hope to rise well by your means,
Or you to rise yourself. We're both beholding to you.
Well, since I cannot win you, I commend you;
I praise your constancy and pardon you.
Take Govianus to you, make the most of him;
Pick out your husband there, so you'll but grant me
One light request that follows.

LADY: Heaven forbid else, sir!

HELVETIUS: Give me the choosing of your friend, that's all.

LADY: How, sir, my friend! A light request indeed!
Somewhat too light, sir, either for my wearing
Or your own gravity, and you look on't well!

HELVETIUS: Pish! Talk like a courtier, girl, not like a fool!
Thou know'st the end of greatness, and hast wit
Above the flight of twenty feathered mistresses
That glister in the sun of princes' favours.
Thou hast discourse in thee fit for a king's fellowship,
A princely carriage and astonishing presence.
What should a husband do with all this goodness?
Alas, one end on't is too much for him,
Nor is it fit a subject should be master
Of such a jewel. 'Tis in the king's power
To take it for the forfeit; but I come
To bear thee gently to his bed of honours,
All force forgotten. The king commends him to thee
With more than the humility of a servant,

That since thou wilt not yield to be his queen,
Be yet his mistress. He shall be content
With that or nothing; he shall ask no more
And with what easiness that is performed
Most of your women know. Having a husband,
That kindness costs thee nothing: y'ave that in
All over and above to your first bargain,
And that's a brave advantage for a woman
If she be wise, as I suspect not thee.
And having youth, and beauty, and a husband,
Thou'st all the wish of woman. Take thy time, then;
Make thy best market.

LADY: Can you assure me, sir,
Whether my father spake this? Or some spirit
Of evil-wishing that has for a time
Hired his voice of him to beguile me that way,
Presuming on his power and my obedience?
I'd gladly know, that I might frame my answer
According to the speaker.

HELVETIUS: How now, baggage!
Am I in question with thee? Does thy scorn cast
So thick an ignorance before thine eyes
That I am forgotten too? Who is't speaks to thee
But thy father?

Enter Govianus, discharging a pistol

GOVIANUS: The more monstrous he!

Helvetius falls

Art down but with the bare voice of my fury?
Up, ancient sinner! Thou'rt but mocked with death.
I missed thee purposely; thank this dear creature.
O, hadst thou been anything beside her father
I'd made a fearful separation on thee.
I would have sent thy soul to a darker prison
Than any made of clay, and thy dead body
As a token to the lustful king thy master.
Art thou struck down so soon with the short sound
Of this small earthen instrument, and dost thou
So little fear th' eternal noise of hell?

What's she? Does she not bear thy daughter's name?
How stirs thy blood, sir? Is there a dead feeling
Of all things fatherly and honest in thee?
Say thou couldst be content, for greatness' sake,
To end the last act of thy life in panderism
(As you perhaps will say your betters do),
Must it needs follow that unmanly sin
Can work upon the weakness of no woman
But her whose name and honour natural love
Bids thee preserve more charily than eyesight,
Health, or thy senses? Can promotion's thirst
Make such a father? Turn a grave old lord
To a white-headed squire? Make him so base
To buy his honours with his daughter's soul
And the perpetual shaming of his blood?
Hast thou the leisure, thou forgetful man,
To think upon advancement at these years?
What wouldst thou do with greatness? Dost thou hope
To fray death with't? Or hast thou that conceit
That honour will restore thy youth again?
Thou art but mocked, old fellow! 'Tis not so;
Thy hopes abuse thee. Follow thine own business
And list not to the sirens of the world.
Alas, thou hadst more need kneel at an altar
Than to a chair of state,
And search thy conscience for thy sins of youth;
That's work enough for age; it needs no greater.
Thou'rt called within. Thy very eyes look inward
To teach thy thoughts the way, and thy affections.
But miserable notes that conscience sings
That cannot truly pray, for flattering kings.

HELVETIUS: This was well searched indeed, and without favouring.
Blessing reward thee! Such a wound as mine
Did need a pitiless surgeon. Smart on, soul!
Thou'lt feel the less hereafter. Sir, I thank you.
I ever saw my life in a false glass
Until this friendly hour. With what fair faces
My sins would look on me! But now truth shows 'em,
How loathsome and how monstrous are their forms!

Be you my king and master still! Henceforward
My knee shall know no other earthly lord,
Well may I spend this life to do you service,
That sets my soul in her eternal way.
He kneels

GOVIANUS: Rise! Rise, Helvetius!

HELVETIUS: I'll see both your hands
Set to my pardon first.

GOVIANUS: Mine shall bring hers.

LADY: Now, sir, I honour you for your goodness chiefly,
Y'are my most worthy father; you speak like him.
The first voice was not his. My joy and reverence
Strive which should be most seen. Let our hands, sir,
Raise you from earth thus high, and may it prove
The Lady and Govianus raise him up
The first ascent of your immortal rising
Never to fall again!

HELVETIUS: A spring of blessings
Keep ever with thee, and the fruit thy lord's.

GOVIANUS: I ha' lost an enemy and have found a father.
Exeunt

(ACT II, SCENE II)

The home of Anselmus. Enter Votarius, sadly

VOTARIUS: All's gone; there's nothing but the prodigal left
I have played away my soul at one short game
Where e'en the winner loses.
Pursuing sin, how often did I shun thee!
How swift art thou afoot, beyond man's goodness,
Which has a lazy pace! So was I catched.
A curse upon the cause! Man in these days
Is not content to have his lady honest
And so rest pleased with her without more toil,
But he must have her tried, forsooth, and tempted.
And when she proves a queen then he lies quiet:
Like one that has a watch of curious making,
Thinking to be more cunning than the workman,
Never gives over tampering with the wheels
Till either spring be weakened, balance bowed,
Or some wrong pin put in, and so spoils all.
How could I curse myself! Most business else
Delight in the dispatch, that's the best grace to't;
Only this work of blind, repented lust
Hangs shame and sadness on his master's cheek,
Yet wise men take no warning.

Enter Wife

Nor can I now;
Her very sight strikes my repentance backward;
It cannot stand against her. Chamber thoughts
And words that have sport in 'em, they're for ladies.

WIFE: My best and dearest servant!

VOTARIUS: Worthiest mistress!

Enter Leonella

LEONELLA: Madam!

WIFE: Who's that? My woman! She's myself.
Proceed, sir.

LEONELLA: Not if you love your honour, madam.
I came to give you warning my lord's come.

VOTARIUS: How!

WIFE: My lord?

VOTARIUS: *Aside*. Alas, poor vessels, how this tempest
tosses 'em!
They're driven both asunder in a twinkling.
Down goes the sails here, and the main mast yonder.
Here rides a bark with better fortune yet;
I fear no tossing, come what weather will,
I have a trick to hold out water still.

VOTARIUS: *Aside*. His very name shoots like a fever through me.
Now hot, now cold. Which cheek shall I turn toward him,
For fear he should read guiltiness in my looks?
I would he would keep from home like a wise man;
'Tis no place for him now. I would not see him
Of any friend alive! It is not fit
We two should come together; we have abused
Each other mightily: he used me ill
To employ me thus, and I ha' used him worse!
I'm too much even with him.
Enter Anselmus
Yonder's a sight on him.

WIFE: My loved and honoured lord! Most welcome, sir.
They kiss

LEONELLA: *Aside*. O, there's a kiss! Methinks my lord
might taste
Dissimulation rank in't, if he had wit.
He takes but of the breath of his friend's lip.
A second kiss is hers, but that she keeps
For her first friend. We women have no cunning.

WIFE: You parted strangely from me.

ANSELMUS: That's forgotten!

Votarius! I make speed to be in thine arms.

VOTARIUS: You never come too soon, sir.
Anselmus and Votarius converse apart

ANSELMUS: How goes business?

VOTARIUS: Pray think upon some other subject, sir.
What news at court?

ANSELMUS: Pish, answer me!

VOTARIUS: Alas, sir, would you have me work by wonders,
To strike fire out of ice? Y'are a strange lord, sir.
Put me to possible things and find 'em finished
At your return to me; I can say no more.

ANSELMUS: I see by this thou didst not try her thoroughly.

VOTARIUS: How, sir, not thoroughly! By this light he lives not
That could make trial of a woman better.

ANSELMUS: I fear thou wast too slack.

VOTARIUS: Good faith, you wrong me, sir.
She never found it so.

ANSELMUS: Then I've a jewel;
And nothing shall be thought too precious for her.
I may advance my forehead and boast purely.
Methinks I see her worth with clear eyes now.
O, when a man's opinion is at peace
'Tis a fine life to marry! No state's like it.
To his Wife
My worthy lady, freely I confess
To thy wronged heart. My passion had alate
Put rudeness on me, which I now put off.
I will no more seem so unfashionable
For pleasure and the chamber of the lady.

WIFE: I'm glad you're changed so well, sir.

VOTARIUS: Thank himself for't.
Exeunt Wife and Anselmus

LEONELLA: *Aside*. This comes like physic when the party's dead.
Flows kindness now, when 'tis so ill-deserved?
This is the fortune still. Well, for this trick
I'll save my husband and his friend a labour;
I'll never marry as long as I'm honest,
For commonly queens have the kindest husbands.
Exit Leonella; manet Votarius

VOTARIUS: I do not like his company now; 'tis irksome;
His eye offends me. Methinks 'tis not kindly
We two should live together in one house.
And 'tis impossible to remove me hence.
I must not give way first. She's my mistress,
And that's a degree kinder than a wife.
Women are always better to their friends
Than to their husbands, and more true to them.
Then let the worst give place, whom she'as least need on
He that can best be spared, and that's her husband.
I do not like his overboldness with her;
He's too familiar with the face I love.
I fear the sickness of affection.
I feel a grudging on't; I shall grow jealous
E'en of that pleasure which she has by law,
I shall go near with her.
Enter Bellarius, passing over the stage
Life, 'tis Bellarius, my rank enemy!
Mine eye snatched so much sight of him. What's his business?
His face half-darkened, stealing through the house
With a whoremaster's pace. I like it not!
This lady will be served like a great woman,
With more attendants, I perceive, than one.
She has her shift of friends. Mine enemy one!
Do we both shun each other's company
In all assemblies public, at all meetings,
And drink to one another in one mistress?
My very thought's my poison. 'Tis high time
To seek for help. Where is our head physician,

A doctor of my making and that lecher's?
O, woman! when thou once leav'st to be good,
Thou car'st not who stands next thee. Every sin
Is a companion for thee, for thy once-cracked honesty
Is like the breaking of whole money;
It never comes to good, but wastes away.
Enter Anselmus

ANSELMUS: Votarius!

VOTARIUS: Ha!

ANSELMUS: We miss you, sir, within.

VOTARIUS: I missed you more without. Would you had come sooner, sir!

ANSELMUS: Why, what's the business?

VOTARIUS: You should ha' seen a fellow,
A common bawdy-house ferret, one Bellarius,
Steal through this room, his whorish, barren face
Three-quarters muffled. He is somewhere hid
About the house, sir.

ANSELMUS: Which way took the villain,
That marriage felon, one that robs the mind
Twenty times worse than any highway-striker?
Speak! Which way took he?

VOTARIUS: Marry, my lord, I think—
Let me see, which way was't, now? Up yon stairs.

ANSELMUS: The way to chambering! Did not I say still
All thy temptations were too faint and lazy?
Thou dids't not play 'em home.

VOTARIUS: To tell you true, sir,
I found her yielding ere I left her last,
And wavering in her faith.

ANSELMUS: Did I not think so!

VOTARIUS: That makes me suspect him.

ANSELMUS: Why, partial man,
Coulds't thou hide this from me, so dearly sought for,
And rather waste thy pity upon her?
Thou'rt not so kind as my heart praised thee to me.
Hark!

Sound of footsteps, above

VOTARIUS: 'Tis his footing, certain.

ANSELMUS: Are you chambered?
I'll fetch you from aloft!

Exit Anselmus

VOTARIUS: He takes my work,
And toils to bring me ease. This use I'll make on him:
His care shall watch to keep all strange thieves out,
Whiles I familiarly go in and rob him,
Like one that knows the house.
But how has rashness and my jealousy used me:
Out of my vengeance to mine enemy
Confessed her yielding! I have locked myself
From mine own liberty with that key. Revenge
Does no man good but to his greater harm.
Suspect and malice, like a mingled cup,
Made me soon drunk. I knew not what I spoke,
And that may get me pardon.

Enter Anselmus, a dagger in his hand,
with Leonella

LEONELLA: Why, my lord!

ANSELMUS: Confess, thou mystical panderess! Run, Votarius,
To the back gate; the guilty slave leaped out
And scaped me so.

Exit Votarius

This strumpet locked him up
In her own chamber.

LEONELLA: Hold, my lord! I might.
He is my husband, sir.

ANSELMUS: O, soul of cunning,
Came that arch-subtlety from thy lady's counsel
Or thine own sudden craft? Confess to me
How oft thou hast been a bawd to their close actions,
Or all thy light goes out!

LEONELLA: My lord, believe me.
In troth I love a man too well myself
To bring him to my mistress.

ANSELMUS: Leave thy sporting!
Or my next offer makes thy heart weep blood.

LEONELLA: O, spare that strength, my lord, and I'll reveal
A secret that concerns you, for this does not.

ANSELMUS: Back, back my fury, then!
It shall not touch thy breast. Speak freely,
what is't?

LEONELLA: Votarius and my lady are false gamesters;
They use foul play, my lord.

ANSELMUS: Thou liest!

LEONELLA: Reward me then
For all together: if it prove not so,
I'll never bestow time to ask your pity.

ANSELMUS: Votarius and thy lady! 'Twill ask days
Ere it be settled in belief. So rise!
Go get thee to thy chamber.

Exit Anselmus

LEONELLA: A pox on you!
You hindered me of better business, thank you.
H'as frayed a secret from me. Would he were whipped!
Faith, from a woman a thing's quickly slipped.

Exit

(ACT II, SCENE III)

The royal court. Enter The Tyrant with Sophonirus, Memphonius and other Nobles. A flourish

TYRANT: My joys have all false hearts! There's nothing true to me
That's either kind or pleasant. I'm hardly dealt withal.
I must not miss her. I want her sight too long.
Where's this old fellow?

SOPHONIRUS: Here's one, my lord, of threescore and seventeen.

TYRANT: Push! That old limber ass puts in his head still.
Helvetius! Where is he?

MEMPHONIUS: Not yet returned, my lord.

Enter Helvetius

TYRANT: Your lordship lies!
Here comes the kingdom's father. Who amongst you
Dares say this worthy man has not made speed?
I would fain hear that fellow!

SOPHONIRUS: *Aside.* I'll not be he.
I like the standing of my head too well
To have it mended.

TYRANT: *To Helvetius.* Thy sight quickens me.
I find a better health when thou art present
Than all times else can bring me. Is the answer
As pleasing as thyself?

HELVETIUS: Of what, my lord?

TYRANT: Of what? Fie, no! He did not say so, did he?

SOPHONIRUS: O no, my lord, not he spoke no such word.
Aside. I'll say as he would ha't, for I'd be loath
To have my body used like butcher's meat.

TYRANT: When comes she to our bed?

HELVETIUS: Who, my lord?

TYRANT: Hark! You heard that plain amongst you?

SOPHONIRUS: O my lord, as plain as my wife's tongue,
That drowns a saunce bell.
Aside. Let me alone to lay about for honour:
I'll shift for one.

TYRANT: When comes the lady, sir,
That Govianus keeps?

HELVETIUS: Why, that's my daughter!

TYRANT: O, is it so? Have you unlocked your memory?
What says she to us?

HELVETIUS: Nothing.

TYRANT: How thou tempt'st us!
What didst thou say to her, being sent from us?

HELVETIUS: More than was honest, yet it was but little.

TYRANT: How cruelly thou work'st upon our patience,
Having advantage 'cause thou art her father!
But be not bold too far: if duty leave thee,
Respect will fall from us.

HELVETIUS: Have I kept life
So long till it looks white upon my head,
Been threescore years a courtier, and a flatterer
Not above threescore hours, which time's repented
Amongst my greatest follies, and am I at these days
Fit for no place but bawd to mine own flesh?
You'll prefer all your old courtiers to good services.
If your lust keep but hot some twenty winters,
We are like to have a virtuous world of wives,
Daughters and sisters, besides kinswomen

And cousin-germans removed up and down,
Where'er you please to have 'em! Are white hairs
A colour fit for pandars and flesh-brokers,
Which are the honoured ornaments of age,
To which e'en kings owe reverence as they're men
And greater in their goodness than their greatness?
And must I take my pay all in base money?
I was a lord born, set by all court grace,
And am I thrust now to a squire's place?

TYRANT: *Aside*. How comes the moon to change so in this man,
That was at full but now in all performance,
And swifter than my wishes? I beshrew that virtue
That busied herself with him: she might have found
Some other work. The man was fit for me
Before she spoiled him. She has wronged my heart in't
And marred me a good workman. Now his art fails him,
What makes the man at court? This is no place
For fellows of no parts. He lives not here
That puts himself from action when we need him.
To Helvetius
I take off all thy honours and bestow 'em
On any of this rank that will deserve 'em.

SOPHONIRUS: My lord, that's I. Trouble your grace no further.
I'll undertake to bring her to your bed
With some ten words. Marry, they're special charms;
No lady can withstand 'em. A witch taught me 'em
If you doubt me, I'll leave my wife in pawn
For my true loyalty, and your majesty
May pass away the time till I return.
I have a care in all things.

TYRANT: That may thrive best
Which the least hope looks after; but, however,
Force shall help nature: I'll be too sure now.
Thy willingness may be fortunate; we employ thee.

SOPHONIRUS: Then I'll go fetch my wife, and take my journey.

TYRANT: Stay! We require no pledge; we think thee honest.

SOPHONIRUS: *Aside*. Troth, the worse luck for me! We
had both been made by't:
It was the way to make my wife great, too.

TYRANT: *To Helvetius*. I'll teach you to be wide and
strange to me!
Thou'lt feel thyself light shortly. I'll not leave thee
A title to put on but the bare name
That men must call thee by, and know thee miserable.

HELVETIUS: 'Tis miserable, king, to be of thy making
And leave a better workman. If thy honours
Only keep life in baseness, take 'em to thee
And give 'em to the hungry; there's one gapes.

SOPHONIRUS: One that will swallow you, sir, for that jest.
And all your titles after.

HELVETIUS: The devil follow 'em!
There's room enough for him too. Leave me, thou king,
As poor as truth—the gentlewoman I now serve
And never will forsake her for her plainness—
That shall not alter me.

TYRANT: No? Our guard within there!
Enter Guard

GUARD: My lord!

TYRANT: Bear that old fellow to our castle prisoner.
Give charge he be kept close.

HELVETIUS: Close prisoner,
Why, my heart thanks thee. I shall have more time
And liberty to virtue in one hour
Than all these threescore years I was a courtier.
So by imprisonment I sustain great loss;
Heaven opens to that man the world keeps close.
Exit Helvetius, with Guard

SOPHONIRUS: But I'll not go to prison to try that.

Give me the open world; there's a good air.

TYRANT: I would fain send death after him, but I dare not.
He knows I dare not; that would give just cause
Of her unkindness everlasting to me.
His life may thank his daughter. Sophonirus,
Here, take this jewel, bear it as a token
To our heart's saint. 'Twill do thy words no harm;
Speech may do much, but wealth's a greater charm
Than any made of words. And, to be sure,
If one or both should fail, I provide farther.
Call forth those resolute fellows whom our clemency
Saved from a death of shame in time of war
For field offences; give 'em charge from us
They arm themselves with speed, beset the house
Of Govianus round, that if thou fail'st,
Or stay'st beyond the time thou leav'st with them,
They may with violence break in themselves
And seize her for our use.

Exeunt Tyrant and his court. Manet Sophonirus

SOPHONIRUS: They're not so saucy
To seize her for their own, I hope,
As there are many knaves will begin first
And bring their lords the bottom. I have been served so
A hundred times myself by a scurvy page
That I kept once but my wife loved him,
And I could not help it

A flourish. Exit Sophonirus

(ACT III)

The house of Govianus's imprisonment. Enter Govianus with his Lady and a Servant

GOVIANUS: What is he?

SERVANT: An old lord come from the court.

GOVIANUS: He should be wise, by's years. He will not dare
To come about such business; 'tis not man's work.
Art sure he desired conference with thy lady?

SERVANT: Sure, sir!

GOVIANUS: Faith, thou'rt mistook; 'tis with me, certain.
Let's do the man no wrong. Go, know it truly, sir.

SERVANT: *Aside*. This' a strange humour; we must know
things twice.
Exit Servant

GOVIANUS: There's no man is so dull but he will weigh
The work he undertakes, and set about it
E'en in the best sobriety of his judgment,
With all his senses watchful. Then his guilt
Does equal his for whom 'tis undertaken.
Enter Servant
What says he now?

SERVANT: E'en as he said at first, sir!
'Has business to my lady from the king.

GOVIANUS: Still from the king! He will not come near, will he?

SERVANT: Yes, when he knows he shall, sir.

GOVIANUS: I cannot think it:
Let him be tried!

SERVANT: Small trial will serve him, I warrant you, sir.

GOVIANUS: Sure honesty has left man; has fear forsook him?
Yes, faith, there is no fear where there's no grace.

LADY: What way shall I devise to gi'm his answer?
Denial is not strong enough to serve, sir.

GOVIANUS: No, 't must have other helps.
Enter Sophonirus
I see he dares!
O Patience! I shall lose a friend of thee!

SOPHONIRUS: I bring thee, precious lady, this dear stone,
And commendations from the king my master.
Govianus unsheathes his sword

GOVIANUS: I set before thee, panderous lord, this steel,
And much good do't thy heart! Fall to, and spare not!
He stabs Sophonirus

LADY: 'Las, what have you done, my lord!

GOVIANUS: Why, sent a bawd
Home to his lodging; nothing else, sweetheart.

SOPHONIRUS: Well, you have killed me, sir, and there's an end.
But you'll get nothing by the hand, my lord,
When all your cards are counted. There be gamesters
Not far off, will set upon the winner
And make a poor lord on you ere th'ave left you.
I'm fetched in like a fool to pay the reckoning,
Yet you'll save nothing by't.

GOVIANUS: What riddle's this?

SOPHONIRUS: There she stands by thee now, who yet ere midnight
Must lie by the king's side.

GOVIANUS: Who speaks that lie?

SOPHONIRUS: One hour will make it true! She cannot 'scape
No more than I from death. Y'ave a great game on't,
And you look well about you, that's my comfort.
The house is round beset with armed men
That know their time, when to break in and seize on her.

LADY: My lord!

GOVIANUS: 'Tis boldly done to trouble me
When I've such business to despatch. Within, there!
Enter Servant

SERVANT: My lord!

GOVIANUS: Look out, and tell me what thou see'st.
Exit Servant

SOPHONIRUS: How quickly now my death will be revenged,
Before the king's first sleep! I depart laughing
To think upon the deed.
Sophonirus dies

GOVIANUS: 'Tis thy banquet.
Down, villain, to thy everlasting weeping,
That canst rejoice so in the rape of virtue,
And sing light tunes in tempests, when near shipwrecked,
And have no plank to save us!
Enter Servant
Now, sir, quickly!

SERVANT: Which way soe'er I cast mine eye, my lord,
Out of all parts o' th' house, I may see fellows
Gathered in companies, and all whispering,
Like men for treachery busy.

GOVIANUS: 'Tis confirmed.

SERVANT: Their eyes still fixed upon the doors and windows.

GOVIANUS: I think thou'st never done; thou lov'st to talk on't.
'Tis fine discourse; prithee, find other business.

SERVANT: Nay, I'm gone. I'm a man quickly sneaped.
Exit Servant

GOVIANUS: H'as flattered me with safety for this hour.

LADY: Have you leisure to stand idle? Why, my lord,
It is for me they come.

GOVIANUS: For thee, my glory,
The riches of my youth. It is for thee!

LADY: Then is your care so cold? Will you be robbed,
And have such warning of the thieves? Come on, sir,
Fall to your business! Lay your hands about you!
Do not think scorn to work. A resolute captain
Will rather fling the treasure of his bark
Into whales' throats than pirates should be gorged
with't.
Be not less man than he. Thou art master yet,
And all's at thy disposing. Take thy time;
Prevent mine enemy! Away with me!
Let me no more be seen! I'm like that treasure,
Dangerous to him that keeps it. Rid thy hands on't.

GOVIANUS: I cannot lose thee so.

LADY: Shall I be taken,
And lost the cruel'st way? Then wouldst thou curse
That love that sent forth pity to my life.
Too late thou wouldst!

GOVIANUS: O, this extremity!
Hast thou no way to 'scape 'em but in soul?
Must I meet peace in thy destruction,
Or will it ne'er come at me?
'Tis a most miserable way to get it.
I had rather be content to live without it
Than pay so dear for't and yet lose it too.

LADY: Sir, you do nothing; there's no valour in you;
Y'are the worst friend to a lady in affliction
That ever love made his companion.
For honour's sake despatch me! Thy own thoughts
Should stir thee to this act more than my weakness.
The sufferer should not do't. I speak thy part,
Dull and forgetful man, and all to help thee.
Is it thy mind to have me seized upon
And borne with violence to the tyrant's bed,
There forced unto the lust of all his days?

GOVIANUS: O, no! Thou liv'st no longer, now I think on't;
I take thee at all hazard.

LADY: O, stay! Hold, sir!

GOVIANUS: Lady, what had you made me done now!
You never cease till you prepare me cruel 'gainst my heart,
And then you turn't upon my hand and mock me.

LADY: Cowardly flesh!
Thou show'st thy faintness still. I felt thee shake,
E'en when the storm came near thee. Thou'rt the same.
But 'twas not for thy fear I put death by.
I had forgot a chief and worthy business,
Whose strange neglect would have made me forgotten
Where I desire to be remembered most.
I will be ready straight, sir.
She kneels in prayer

GOVIANUS: O, poor lady!
Why might not she expire now in that prayer,
Since she must die, and never try worse ways?
'Tis not so happy, for we often see
Condemned men sick to death, yet 'tis their fortune
To recover to their execution
And rise again in health to set in shame.
What if I steal a death unseen of her now,
And close up all my miseries with mine eyes? O, fie!
And leave her here alone! That were unmanly.

LADY: My lord, be now as sudden as you please, sir;
I am ready to your hand.

GOVIANUS: But that's not ready.
'Tis the hardest work that ever man was put to;
I know not which way to begin to come to't.
Believe me, I shall never kill thee well.
I shall but shame myself. It were but folly,
Dear soul, to boast of more than I can perform.
I shall not have the power to do thee right in't.
Thou deserv'st death with speed, a quick despatch,
The pain but of a twinkling, and so sleep.
If I do't, I shall make thee live too long,
And so spoil all that way. I prithee excuse me!

LADY: I should not be disturbed, and you did well, sir.
I have prepared myself for rest and silence,
And took leave of words. I am like one
Removing from her house, that locks up all,
And rather than she would displace her goods,
Makes shift with anything for the time she stays.
A knock
Then look not for more speech: th'extremity speaks
Enough to serve us both had we no tongues!
Knocking within
Hark!

WITHIN: Lord Sophonirus!

GOVIANUS: Which hand shall I take?

LADY: Art thou yet ignorant? There is no way
But through my bosom.

GOVIANUS: Must I lose thee then?

LADY: Th'are but thine enemies that tell thee so.
His lust may part me from thee, but death, never;
Thou canst not lose me there, for, dying thine,
Thou dost enjoy me still. Kings cannot rob thee.
Knocking within

WITHIN: Do you hear, my lord?

LADY: Is it yet time, or no?
Honour remember thee!

GOVIANUS: I must! Come, prepare thyself!

LADY: Never more dearly welcome!
Govianus runs at her, and falls by the way in a swound
Alas, sir!
My lord! My love! O, thou poor-spirited man!
He's gone before me. Did I trust to thee,
And has thou served me so? Left all the work
Upon my head, and stole away so smoothly?
There was not equal suffering shown in this;
And yet I cannot blame thee. Every man
Would seek his rest. Eternal peace sleep with thee!
She takes up the sword of Govianus
Thou art my servant now. Come, thou hast lost
A fearful master, but art now preferred
Unto the service of a resolute lady,
One that knows how to employ thee and scorns death
As much as great men fear it. Where's hell's ministers?
A great knocking
The tyrant's watch and guard? 'Tis of much worth
When with this key the prisoner can slip forth.
The Lady kills herself. A great knock again

GOVIANUS: *Awakening*. How now! What noise is this? I heard doors beaten.
Where are my servants? Let men knock so loud
Their master cannot sleep!

WITHIN: The time's expired,
And we'll break in, my lord!

GOVIANUS: Ha! Where's my sword?
I had forgot my business. O, 'tis done,
And never was beholding to my hand!
Was I so hard to thee? So respectless of thee

To put all this to thee, Why, it was more
Than I was able to perform myself
With all the courage that I could take to me.
It tired me. I was fain to fall and rest;
And hast thou, valiant woman, overcome
Thy honour's enemies with thine own white hand,
Where virgin-victory sits, all without help?
Eternal praise go with thee! Spare not now;
Make all the haste you can. I'll plant this bawd
Against the door, the fittest place for him,
That when with ungoverned weapons they rush in,
Blinded with fury, they may take his death
Into the purple number of their deeds,
And wipe it off from mine.

He places the corpse of Sophonirus against the door.
A knocking within

How now, forbear!
My lord's at hand!

WITHIN: My lord, and ten lords more!
I hope the king's officers are above 'em all.

Enter the Fellows, well-weaponed
They stab Sophonirus

GOVIANUS: Life, what do you do! Take heed! Bless the old man!

FIRST FELLOW: My Lord, All-Ass, my lord, he's gone!

SECOND FELLOW: Heart, farewell he, then.
We have no eyes to pierce through inch boards
'Twas his own folly; the king must be served,
And shall. The best is we shall ne'er be hanged for't,
There's such a number guilty.

GOVIANUS: Poor my lord!
He went some twice ambassador, and behaved himself
So wittily in all his actions.

SECOND FELLOW: *Seeing the Lady's body.* My lord! What's she?

GOVIANUS: Let me see!
What should she be? Now I remember her.

O, she was a worthy creature
Before destruction grew so inward with her.

FIRST FELLOW: Well, for her worthiness, that's no work of ours.
You have a lady, sir; the king commands her
To court with speed, and we must force her thither.

GOVIANUS: Alas, she'll never strive with you; she was born
E'en with the spirit of meekness. Is't for the king?

FIRST FELLOW: For his own royal and most gracious lust,
Or let me ne'er be trusted.

GOVIANUS: Take her, then.

SECOND FELLOW: Spoke like an honest subject, by my troth.
I'd do the like myself to serve my prince.
Where is she, sir?

GOVIANUS: Look but upon yon face,
Then do but tell me where you think she is.

SECOND FELLOW: Life, she's not here.

GOVIANUS: She's yonder.

FIRST FELLOW: Faith, she's gone
Where we shall ne'er come at her, I see that.

GOVIANUS: *Aside*. No, nor thy master neither. Now I praise
Her resolution. 'Tis a triumph to me
When I see those about her.

SECOND FELLOW: How came this, sir?
The king must know.

GOVIANUS: From yon old fellow's prattling.
All your intents he revealed largely to her,
And she was troubled with a foolish pride
To stand upon her honour, and so died.
'Twas a strange trick of her. Few of your ladies

In ordinary will believe it. They abhor it.
They'll sooner kill themselves with lust than for it.

FIRST FELLOW: We have done the king good service to kill him.
More than we were aware on; but this news
Will make a mad court. 'Twill be a hard office
To be a flatterer now. His grace will run
Into so many moods there'll be no finding on him:
As good seek a wild hare without a hound now.
Speaks to corpse of Sophonirus
A vengeance of your babbling! These old fellows
Will harken after secrets as their lives,
But keep 'em in e'en as they keep their wives.

ALL: We have watched fairly.
Exeunt Fellows. Manet Govianus

GOVIANUS: What a comfort 'tis
To see 'em gone without her! Faith, she told me
Her everlasting sleep would bring me joy,
Yet I was still unwilling to believe her,
Her life was so sweet to me: like some man
In time of sickness that would rather wish
(To please his fearful flesh) his former health
Restored to him than death; when, after trial,
If it were possible, ten thousand worlds
Could not entice him to return again
And walk upon the earth from whence he flew;
So stood my wish, joyed in her life and breath,
Now gone, there is no heav'n but after death.
Come, thou delicious treasure of mankind:
To him that knows what virtuous woman is,
And can discreetly love her. The whole world
Yields not a jewel like her, ransack rocks
And caves beneath the deep. O, thou fair spring
Of honest and religious desires,
Fountain of weeping honour, I will kiss thee
After death's marble lip! Thou'rt cold enough
To lie entombed now by my father's side
Without offense in kindred. There I'll place thee
With one I loved the dearest next to thee.
Help me to mourn, all that love chastity.
Exit

(ACT IV, SCENE I)

The home of Anselmus. Enter Votarius with Anselmus's Wife

VOTARIUS: Prithee forgive me, madam; come, thou shalt!

WIFE: I'faith, 'twas strangely done, sir.

VOTARIUS: I confess it.

WIFE: Is that enough to help it, sir? 'Tis easy
To draw a lady's honour in suspicion,
But not so soon recovered and confirmed
To the first faith again from whence you brought it.
Your wit was fetched out about other business,
Or such forgetfulness had never seized you.

VOTARIUS: 'Twas but an overflowing, a spring tide
In my affection, raised by too much love;
And that's the worst words you can give it, madam.

WIFE: Jealous of me!

VOTARIUS: Life, you'd a' sworn yourself, madam,
Had you been in my body, and changed cases,
To see a fellow with a guilty pace
Glide through the room, his face three-quarters nighted,
As if a deed of darkness had hung on him.

WIFE: I tell you twice, 'twas my bold woman's friend.
Hell take her impudence!

VOTARIUS: Why, I have done, madam.

WIFE: Y'ave done too late, sir. Who shall do the rest now?
Confessed me yielding! Was thy way too free?

Why, didst thou long to be restrained? Pray, speak, sir!

VOTARIUS: A man cannot cozen you of the sin of weakness,
Or borrow it of a woman for one hour,
But how he's wondered at. Where, search your lives,
We shall ne'er find it from you; we can suffer you
To play away our days in idleness,
And hide your imperfections with our loves,
Or the most part of you would appear strange creatures;
And now 'tis but our chance to make an offer,
And snatch at folly, running, yet to see
How earnest y'are against us, as if we had robbed you
Or the best gift your natural mother left you.

WIFE: 'Tis worth a kiss, i'faith, and thou shalt ha't,
Were there not one more left for my lord's supper.
And now, sir, I've bethought myself.

VOTARIUS: That's happy!

WIFE: You say we're weak; but the best wits on you all
Are glad of our advice, for aught I see,
And hardly thrive without us.

VOTARIUS: I'll say so too,
To give you encouragement and advance your virtues
'Tis not good always to keep down a woman.

WIFE: Well, sir, since y'ave begun to make my lord
A doubtful man of me, keep on that course,
And ply his faith still with that poor belief
That I'm inclining unto wantonness.
Take heed you pass no further now.

VOTARIUS: Why, dost think
I'll be twice mad together in one moon?
That were too much for any freeman's son
After his father's funeral.

WIFE: Well, then thus, sir,
Upholding still the same, as being emboldened

By some loose glance of mine, you shall attempt
(After y'ave placed my lord in some near closet)
To thrust yourself into my chamber rudely,
As if the game went forward to your thinking,
Then leave the rest to me. I'll so reward thee
With bitterness of words—but prithee pardon 'em—
My lord shall swear me into honesty
Enough to serve his mind all his life after.
Nay, for a need, I'll draw some rapier forth,
That shall come near my hand as 'twere by chance,
And set a lively face upon my rage,
But fear thou nothing. I too dearly love thee
To let harm touch thee.

VOTARIUS: O, it likes me rarely!
I'll choose a precious time for't.
Exit Votarius

WIFE: Go thy ways; I'm glad I had it for thee.
Enter Leonella

LEONELLA: Madam, my lord entreats your company.

WIFE: Pshaw, ye!

LEONELLA: Pshaw, ye! My lord entreats your company.

WIFE: What now?
Are ye so short-heeled?

LEONELLA: I am as my betters are, then.

WIFE: How come you by such impudence alate, minion?
Y'are not content to entertain your playfellow
In your own chamber closely, which I think
Is large allowance for a lady's woman.
There's many a good knight's daughter is in service
And cannot get such favour of her mistress
But what she has by stealth; she and the chambermaid
Are glad of one between 'em; and must you
Give such bold freedom to your long-nosed fellow
That every room must take a taste of him?

LEONELLA: Does that offend your ladyship?

WIFE: How think you, forsooth?

LEONELLA: Then he shall do't again.

WIFE: What!

LEONELLA: And again, madam!
So often till it please your ladyship;
And when you like it, he shall do't no more.

WIFE: What's this?

LEONELLA: I know no difference, virtuous madam,
But in love all have privilege alike.

WIFE: Y'are a bold queen.

LEONELLA: And are not you, my mistress?

WIFE: This' well, i'faith!

LEONELLA: You spare not your own flesh no more than I;
Hell take me and I spare you.

WIFE: *Aside.* O, the wrongs
That ladies do their honours when they make
Their slaves familiar with their weaknesses!
They're ever thus rewarded for that deed;
They stand in fear e'en of the groom they feed.
I must be forced to speak my woman fair now,
And be first friends with her. Nay, all too little.
She may undo me at her pleasure else;
She knows the way so well, myself not better,
My wanton folly made a key for her
To all the private treasure of my heart;
She may do what she list.

Aloud

Come, Leonella,
I am not angry with thee.

LEONELLA: Pish!

WIFE: Faith, I am not.

LEONELLA: Why, what care I and you be!

WIFE: Prithee, forgive me.

LEONELLA: I have nothing to say to you.

WIFE: Come, thou shalt wear this jewel for my sake.
A kiss and friends; we'll never quarrel more.

LEONELLA: Nay, choose you, faith; the best is, and you do.
You know who'll have the worst on't.

WIFE: *Aside.* True; myself.

LEONELLA: *Aside.* Little thinks she I have set her forth already.
I please my lord, yet keep her in awe too.

WIFE: One thing I had forgot; I prithee, wench,
Steal to Votarius closely, and remember him
To wear some privy armour then about him,
That I may feign a fury without fear.

LEONELLA: Armour! When, madam?

WIFE: See now, I chid thee
When I least thought upon thee: thou'rt my best hand.
I cannot be without thee. Thus then, sirrah:
To bear away suspicion from the thoughts
Of ruder-list'ning servants about house,
I have advised Votarius at fit time
Boldly to force his way into my chamber,
The admittance being denied him, and the passage
Kept strict by thee, my necessary woman.
(La! There I should ha' missed thy help again!)
At which attempt I'll take occasion
To dissemble such an anger that the world

Shall ever after swear us to their thoughts
As clear and free from any fleshly knowledge,
As nearest kindred are, or ought to be,
Or what can more express it, if that failed.

LEONELLA: You know I'm always at your service, madam,
But why some privy armour?

WIFE: Marry, sweetheart,
The best is yet forgotten; thou shalt hang
A weapon in some corner of the chamber,
Yonder, or there—

LEONELLA: Or anywhere. Why, i'faith, madam,
Do you think I'm to learn how to hang a weapon?
As much as I'm uncapable of what follows,
I've all your mind without books. Think it done, madam.

WIFE: Thanks, my good wench; I'll never call thee worse.
Exit Wife

LEONELLA: Faith, y'are like to ha't again, and you do, madam.
Enter Bellairius

BELLARIUS: What, art alone?

LEONELLA: Cuds me, what make you here, sir?
You're a bold long-nosed fellow.

BELLARIUS: How!

LEONELLA: So my lady says.
Faith, she and I have had a bout for you, sir,
But she got nothing by't.

BELLARIUS: Did I not say still
Thou wouldst be too adventurous!

LEONELLA: Ne'er a whit, sir.
I made her glad to seek my friendship first.

BELLARIUS: By my faith, that showed well. If you come off
So brave a conqueress, to't again and spare not,
I know not which way you should get more honour.

LEONELLA: She trusts me now to cast a mist, forsooth,
Before the servants' eyes. I must remember
Votarius to come once with privy armour
Into her chamber, when with feigned fury
And rapier drawn, which I must lay a purpose
Ready for her dissemblance, she will seem
T'act wonders for her juggling honesty.

BELLARIUS: I wish no riper vengeance! Canst conceive me?
Votarius is my enemy.

LEONELLA: That's stale news, sir.

BELLARIUS: Mark what I say to thee; forget of purpose
That privy armour; do not bless his soul
With so much warning, nor his hated body
With such sure safety. Here express thy love:
Lay some empoisoned weapon next her hand,
That in that play he may be lost for ever.
I'd have him kept no longer; away with him!
One touch will set him flying! Let him go!

LEONELLA: Bribe me but with a kiss, it shall be so.

Exeunt

(ACT IV, SCENE II)

The royal court. Enter Tyrant, wondrous discontentedly. Nobles afar off.

FIRST NOBLE: My lord!

TYRANT: Begone, or never see life more!
I'll send thee far enough from court.
Exit First Noble
Memphonius!
Where's he now?

MEMPHONIUS: Ever at your highness' service.

TYRANT: How ar'st thou be so near, when we have threatened
Death to thy fellow! Have we lost our power?
Or thou thy fear? Leave us in time of grace;
'Twill be too late anon.

MEMPHONIUS: *Aside, leaving*. I think 'tis so with thee already

TYRANT: Dead! And I so healthful!
There's no equality in this. Stay!

MEMPHONIUS: Sir?

TYRANT: Where is that fellow brought the first report to us?

MEMPHONIUS: He waits without.

TYRANT: I charge thee give command
That he be executed speedily,
As thou't stand firm thyself.

MEMPHONIUS: *Aside.* Now by my faith
His tongue has helped his neck to a sweet bargain.
Exit Memphonius

TYRANT: Her own fair hand so cruel! Did she choose
Destruction before me? Was I no better?

How much am I exalted to my face,
And where I would be graced, how little worthy!
There's few kings know how rich they are in goodness,
Or what estate they have in grace and virtue.
There is so much deceit in glozers' tongues
The truth is taken from us; we know nothing
But what is for their purpose. That's our stint;
We are allowed no more. O, wretched greatness!
I'll cause a sessions for my flatterers
And have 'em all hanged up. 'Tis done too late.
O she's destroyed, married to death and silence,
Which nothing can divorce, riches nor laws,
Nor all the violence that this fame can raise.
I've lost the comfort of her sight for ever.
I cannot call this life that flames within me,
But everlasting torment lighted up
To show my soul her beggary! A new joy
Is come to visit me in spite of death!
It takes me of that sudden, I'm ashamed
Of my provision, but a friend will bear. Within there!

Enter Soldiers

FIRST SOLDIER: Sir!

SECOND SOLDIER: My lord!

TYRANT: The men I wished for, for secrecy and employment.
Go, give order that Govianus be released.

FOURTH SOLDIER: Released, sir?

TYRANT: Set free. And then I trust he will fly the kingdom,
And never know my purpose. Run, sir!

Exit Fourth Soldier

To First Soldier. You!
Bring me the keys of the cathedral straight.

FIRST SOLDIER: *Aside.* Are you so holy now? Do you curse all day
And go to pray at midnight?

Exit First Soldier

TYRANT: Provide you, sirs, close lanthorns and a pickaxe.
Away, be speedy!

SECOND SOLDIER: *Aside*. Lanthorns and a pickaxe?
Life, does he mean to bury himself alive, too?
Exeunt Second and Third Soldiers

TYRANT: Death nor the marble prison my love sleeps in
Shall keep her body locked up from mine arms;
I must not be so cozened; though her life
Was like a widow's state, made o'er in policy
To defeat me and my too confident heart.
'Twas a most cruel wisdom to herself,
As much to me that loved her. What, returned?
Enter First Soldier

FIRST SOLDIER: Here be the keys, my lord.

TYRANT: I thank thy speed.
Here come the rest full-furnished.
Enter Second and Third Soldiers
Follow me
And wealth shall follow you.
Exit Tyrant

FIRST SOLDIER: Wealth! By this light,
We go to rob a church! I hold my life
The money will ne'er thrive; that's a sure saw:
"What's got from grace is ever spent in law."
Exeunt. Enter Mr. Goughe [as Memphonius]

MEMPHONIUS: What strange fits grow upon him! Here alate
His soul has got a very dreadful leader,
What should he make in the cathedral now,
The hour so deep in night? All his intents
Are contrary to men; in spirit or blood
He waxes heavy in his noble mind.
His moods are such they cannot bear the weight,
Nor will not long, if there be truth in whispers.
The honorable father of the state,
Noble Helvetius, all the lords agree
By some close policy shortly to set free.
Exit

(ACT IV, SCENE III)

Within the cathedral. Enter the Tyrant with Soldiers at a farther door, which opened, brings him to the tomb where the Lady lies buried. The tomb is here discovered, richly set forth.

TYRANT: Softly, softly!
Let's give this place the peace that it requires.
The vaults e'en chide our steps with murmuring sounds,
For making bold so late. It must be done.

FIRST SOLDIER: I fear nothing but the whorish ghost of a queen I kept once. She swore she would so haunt me I should never pray in quiet for her, and I have kept myself from church this fifteen year to prevent her.

TYRANT: The monument woos me! I must run and kiss it.
Now trust me if the tears do not e'en stand
Upon the marble. What slow springs have I!
'Twas weeping to itself before I came.
How pity strikes e'en through insensible things
And makes them shame our dullness!
Thou house of silence, and the calms of rest
After tempestuous life, I claim of thee
A mistress, one of the most beauteous sleepers
That ever lay so cold, not yet due to thee
By natural death, but cruelly forced hither
Many a year before the world could spare her.
We miss her 'mongst the glories of our court
When they be numbered up. All thy still strength,
Thou grey-eyed monument, shall not keep her from us.
To Second Soldier
Strike, villain! though the echo rail us all
Into ridiculous deafness! Pierce the jaws
Of this cold ponderous creature.

SECOND SOLDIER: Sir!

TYRANT: Why strik'st thou not?

SECOND SOLDIER: I shall not hold the axe fast, I'm afraid, sir.

TYRANT: O shame of men! A soldier and so fearful!

SECOND SOLDIER: 'Tis out of my element to be in a church, sir.
Give me the open field and turn me loose, sir.

TYRANT: True, there thou hast room enough to run away!
To First Soldier
Take thou the axe from him.

FIRST SOLDIER: I beseech your grace,
'Twill come to a worse hand. You'll find us all
Of one mind for the church, I can assure you, sir.

TYRANT: Nor thou?

THIRD SOLDIER: I love not to disquiet ghosts
Of any people living. That's my humour, sir.

TYRANT: O slaves of one opinion!
To Second Soldier
Give me't from thee,
Thou man made out of fear.

SECOND SOLDIER: By my faith,
I'm glad I'm rid on't. I that was ne'er before in a cathedral
And have the batt'ring of a lady's tomb
Lie hard upon my conscience at first coming!
I should get much by that! It shall be a warning to me;
I'll ne'er come here again.

TYRANT: *Striking at the tomb.* No? Wilt not yield?
Art thou so loath to part from her?

FIRST SOLDIER: Life, what means he?
Has he no feeling with him? By this light, if I be not
afraid to stay any longer. I'm a stone-cutter! Very few
will go nigh to turn me of some religion or other, and so
make me forfeit my lieutenantship.

TYRANT: O, have we got the mastery? Help, you vassals!
Freeze you in idleness and can see us sweat?

SECOND SOLDIER: We sweat with fear as much as work can make us.

TYRANT: Remove the stone, that I may see my mistress.
Set to your hands, you villains, and that nimbly,
Or the same axe shall make you all fly open!

ALL: O, good my lord!

TYRANT: I must not be delayed.

FIRST SOLDIER: This is ten thousand times worse than ent'ring upon a breech. 'Tis the first stone that ever I took off from any lady; marry, I have brought 'em many: fair diamonds, sapphires, rubies—

They lift off the stone

TYRANT: O blessed object!
I never shall be weary to behold thee;
I could eternally stand thus and see thee.
Why, 'tis not possible death should look so fair;
Life is not more illustrious when health smiles on't.
She's only pale, the colour of the court,
And most attractive; mistresses most strive for't,
And their lascivious servants best effect it.
Where be these lazy hands again?

ALL SOLDIERS: My lord!

TYRANT: Take up her body.

FIRST SOLDIER: How, my lord?

TYRANT: Her body!

FIRST SOLDIER: She's dead, my lord!

TYRANT: True; if she were alive
Such slaves as you should not come near to touch her.
Do't, and with all best reverence. Place her here.

Holds out his arms

FIRST SOLDIER: Not only, sir, with reverence, but with fear.
You shall have more than your own asking once.
I am afraid of nothing but she'll rise
At the first jog and save us all a labour.

SECOND SOLDIER: Then we were best take her up, and never touch her!

FIRST SOLDIER: Life, how can that be? Does fear make thee mad?
I've took up many a woman in my days,
But never with less pleasure; I protest.

TYRANT: O, the moon rises! What reflection
Is thrown about this sanctified building,
E'en in a twinkling! How the monuments glister
As if death's palaces were all massy silver
And scorned the name of marble! Art thou cold?
I have no faith in't yet; I believe none.
Madam! 'Tis I, sweet lady. Prithee speak!
'Tis thy love calls on thee—thy king, thy servant.
No? Not a word? All prisoners to pale silence?
I'll prove a kiss.

FIRST SOLDIER: *Aside*. Here's fine chill venery!
'Twould make a pander's heels ache; I'll be sworn
All my teeth chatter in my head to see't.

TYRANT: B'th' mass, thou'rt cold indeed! Beshrew thee for't!
Unkind to thine own blood? Hard-hearted lady!
What injury hast thou offered to the youth
And pleasure of thy days! Refuse the court
And steal to this hard lodging! Was that wisdom?
O, I could chide thee with mine eye brimfull,
And weep out my forgiveness when I ha' done.
Nothing hurt thee but want of woman's counsel.
Hads't thou but asked th'opinion of most ladies,
Thou'dst never come to this! They would have told thee
How dear a treasure life and youth had been.
'Tis *that* they fear to lose; the very name
Can make more gaudy tremblers in a minute
Than heaven or sin or hell. Those are last thought on.

And where got'st thou such boldness from the rest
Of all thy timorous sex to do a deed here
Upon thyself would plunge the world's best soldier
And make him twice bethink him and again,
And yet give over? Since thy life has left me,
I'll clasp the body for the spirit that dwelt in't,
And love the house still for the mistress' sake.
Thou art mine now, spite of destruction
And Govianus, and I will possess thee.
I once read of a Herod, whose affection
Pursued a virgin's love as I did thine,
Who, for the hate she owed him, killed herself,
As thou too rashly didst, without all pity.
Yet he preserved her body dead in honey
And kept her long after her funeral.
But I'll unlock the treasure-house of art
With keys of gold and bestow all on thee.
Here, slaves, receive her humbly from our arms.
Upon your knees, you villains! All's too little
If you should sweep the pavement with your lips.

FIRST SOLDIER: *Aside*. What strange brooms he invents!

TYRANT: So reverently
Bear her before us gently to our palace.
Place you the stone again where first we found it.
Exeunt with body. Manet First Soldier

FIRST SOLDIER: Life, must this on now to deceive all comers,
And cover emptiness? 'Tis for all the world
Like a great city-pie brought to a table
Where there be many hands that lay about;
The lid's shut close when all the meat's picked out,
Yet stands to make a show and cozen people.
Exit

(ACT IV, SCENE IV)

Within the cathedral, before the Lady's tomb. Enter Govianus in black, a book in his hand, his Page carrying a torch before him

GOVIANUS: Already mine eyes melts. The monument
No sooner stood before it but a tear
Ran swiftly from me to express her duty.
Temple of honour, I salute thee early,
The time that my griefs rise! Chamber of peace,
Where wounded virtue sleeps locked from the world,
I bring to be acquainted with thy silence
Sorrows that love no noise: they dwell all inward,
Where truth and love in every man should dwell.
Be ready, boy! Give me the strain again.
'Twill show well here, whilst in my grief's devotion
At every rest mine eye lets fall a bead
To keep the number perfect.

Govianus kneels at the tomb, wondrous passionately. His Page sings

The Song

If ever pity were well-placed
On true desert and virtuous honour,
It could ne'er be better graced.
Freely then, bestow't upon her.

Never lady earned her fame
In virtue's war with greater strife.
To preserve her constant name
She gave up beauty, youth and life.
There she sleeps
And here he weeps,
The lord unto so rare a wife.

Weep, weep and mourn! Lament,
You virgins that pass by her.
For if praise come by death again
I doubt few will lie nigh her.

GOVIANUS: Thou art an honest boy. 'Tis done like one
That has a feeling of his master's passions.
And the unmatched worth of his dead mistress.
Thy better years shall find me good to thee
When understanding ripens in thy soul,
Which truly makes the man, and not long time.
Prithee withdraw a little, and attend me
At cloister door.

PAGE: It shall be done, my lord.

The Page withdraws

GOVIANUS: Eternal maid of honour, whose chaste body
Lies here like virtue's close and hidden seed,
To spring forth glorious to eternity
At the everlasting harvest—

WITHIN: I am not here.

GOVIANUS: What's that? Who is not here? I'm forced to question it—
Some idle sounds the beaten vaults send forth.

On a sudden, in a kind of noise like a wind, the doors clattering, the tombstone flies open, and a great light appears in the midst of the tomb; his Lady as went out, standing just before him all in white, stuck with jewels, and a great crucifix on her breast.

Enter Lady, Rich Robinson

GOVIANUS: Mercy look to me! Faith, I fly to thee!
Keep a strong watch about me! (Now thy friendship!)
O never came astonishment and fear
So pleasing to mankind! I take delight
To have my breast shake and my hair stand stiff.
If this be horror, let it never die!
Come all the pains of hell in that shape to me,
I could endure 'em smiling. Keep me still
In terror, I beseech thee. I'd not change

This fever for felicity of man,
Or all the pleasures of ten thousand ages.

LADY: Dear lord, I come to tell you all my wrongs.

GOVIANUS: Welcome! Who wrongs the spirit of my love?
Thou art above the injuries of blood;
They cannot reach thee now. What dares offend thee?
No life that has the weight of flesh upon't
And treads as I do can now wrong my mistress.

LADY: The peace that death allows me is not mine.
The monument is robbed! Behold, I'm gone,
My body taken up!

Govianus lifts up the stone

'Tis gone indeed!
What villain dares so fearfully run in debt
To black eternity?

LADY: He that dares do more—
The Tyrant!

GOVIANUS: All the miseries below
Reward his boldness!

LADY: I am now at court
In his own private chamber. There he woos me
And plies his suit to me with as serious pains
As if the short flame of mortality
Were lighted up again in my cold breast,
Folds me within his arms and often sets
A sinful kiss upon my senseless lip,
Weeps when he sees the paleness of my cheek,
And will send privately for a hand of art
That may dissemble life upon my face
To please his lustful eye.

GOVIANUS: O piteous wrongs!
Inhuman injuries without grace or mercy!

LADY: I leave 'em to thy thought, dearest of men.

My rest is lost! Thou must restore't again.

GOVIANUS: O, fly me not so soon!

LADY: Farewell, true lord.

Exit Lady

GOVIANUS: I cannot spare thee yet. I'll make myself
Over to death too, and we'll walk together
Like loving spirits: I prithee let's do so.
She's snatched away by fate and I talk sickly;
I must dispatch this business upon earth
Before I take that journey.
I'll to my brother for his aid or counsel.
So wronged! O heav'n, put armour on my spirit!
Her body I will place in her first rest
Or in th'attempt lock death into my breast.

Exit

(ACT V, SCENE I)

The home of Anselmus. Enter Votarius with Anselmus, the husband

VOTARIUS: You shall stand here, my lord, unseen and hear all.
Do I deal now like a right friend with you?

ANSELMUS: Like a most faithful.

VOTARIUS: You shall have her mind e'en as it comes to me,
Though I undo her by't. Your friendship, sir,
Is the sweet mistress that I only serve.
I prize the roughness of a man's embrace
Before the soft lips of a hundred ladies.

ANSELMUS: And that's an honest mind of thee.

VOTARIUS: Lock yourself, sir,
Into that closet, and be sure none see you!
Trust not a creature. We'll have all run clear,
E'en as the heart affords it.

ANSELMUS: 'Tis a match, sir.

Exit Anselmus

VOTARIUS: Troth, he says true there. 'Tis a match indeed.
He does not know the strength of his own words,
For if he did there were no mast'ring on him.
H'as cleft the pin in two with a blind man's eyes.
Though I shoot wide, I'll cozen him of the game.

Exit Votarius. Enter Leonella above, in a gallery, with her love Bellarius

LEONELLA: Doest thou see thine enemy walk?

BELLARIUS: I would I did not.

LEONELLA: Prithee rest quiet, man; I have fee'd one for him—
A trusty catchpole, too, that will be sure on him.
Thou know'st this gallery well; 'tis at thy use now;
'T'as been at mine full often. Thou may'st sit
Like a most private gallant in yon corner,
See all the play, and ne'er be seen thyself.

BELLARIUS: Therefore I chose it.

LEONELLA: Thou shalt see my lady
Play her part naturally, more to the life
Than she's aware on.

BELLARIUS: There must I be pleased.
Thou'rt one of the actors; thou't be missed anon.

LEONELLA: Alas, a woman's action's always ready.
Yet I'll down, now I think on't.

BELLARIUS: Do: 'tis time, i'faith.
Descendet Leonella. Reenter Anselmus

ANSELMUS: I know not yet where I should plant belief,
I am so strangely tossed between two tales,
I'm told by my wife's woman the deed's done,
And in Votarius' tongue 'tis yet to come;
The castle is but upon yielding yet.
'Tis not delivered up. Well, we shall find
The mystery shortly. I will entertain
The patience of a prisoner i'th' meantime.
Anselmus locks himself in. Enter
Anselmus's Wife with Leonella

WIFE: Is all set ready, wench?

LEONELLA: Pish, madam, all!

WIFE: Tell me not so. She lives not for a lady
That has less peace than I.

LEONELLA: Nay, good sweet madam,
You would not think how much this passion alters you.
It drinks up all the beauty of your cheek;
I promise you, madam, you have lost much blood.

WIFE: Let it draw death upon me, for till then
I shall be mistress of no true content.
Who could endure hourly temptation
And bear it as I do?

LEONELLA: Nay, that's most certain—
Unless it were myself again: I can do't.
I suffer the like daily; you should complain, madam.

WIFE: Which way? Were that wisdom? Prithee, wench, to whom?

LEONELLA: To him that makes all whole again—my lord!
To one that, if he be a kind good husband,
Will let you bear no more than you are able.

WIFE: Thou know'st not what thou speak'st. Why, my lord's he
That gives him the house-freedom, all his boldness,
Keeps him a purpose here to war with me.

LEONELLA: Now I hold wiser of my lord than so.
He knows the world; he would not be so idle.

WIFE: I speak sad truth to thee. I am not private
In mine own chamber, such his impudence is.
Nay, my repenting-time is scarce blessed from him;
He will offend my prayers.

LEONELLA: Out upon him
I believe, madam, he's of no religion.

WIFE: He serves my lord, and that's enough for him,
And he preys upon poor ladies like myself.
There's all the gentleman's devotion!

LEONELLA: Marry, the devil of hell give him his blessing!

WIFE: Pray watch the door, and suffer none to trouble us,
Unless it be my lord.

LEONELLA: *Aside.* 'Twas finely spoke, that!
My lord indeed is the most trouble to her.
Now I must show a piece of service here.
How do I spend my days! Life, shall I never
Get higher than a lady's doorkeeper?
I must be married as my lady is, first,
And then my maid may do as much for me.

WIFE: O miserable time! Except my lord
Do wake in honourable pity to me,
And rid this vicious gamester from his house,
Whom I have checked so often, here I vow
I'll imitate my noble sister's fate,
Late mistress to the worthy Govianus,
And cast away my life as she did hers.
Enter Votarius to the door within

LEONELLA: Back! Y'are too forward, sir! There's no coming for you.

VOTARIUS: How, Mistress Len, my lady's smock-woman!
Am I no farther in your duty yet?

LEONELLA: Duty! Look for't of them you keep under, sir.

VOTARIUS: You'll let me in?

LEONELLA: Who would you speak withal?

VOTARIUS: With the best lady you make curtsy to.

LEONELLA: She will not speak with you.

VOTARIUS: Have you her mind?
I scorn to take her answer of her broker.

LEONELLA: Madam!

WIFE: What's there? How now, sir! What's your business?
We see your boldness plain.

VOTARIUS: I came to see you, madam.

WIFE: Farewell, then! Though 'twas impudence too much
When I was private.

VOTARIUS: Madam!

WIFE: Life, he was born
To beggar all my patience!

VOTARIUS: I'm bold
Still to prefer my love. Your woman hears me not.

WIFE: Where's modesty and honour? Have I not thrice
Answered thy lust?

LEONELLA: *Aside*. By'r lady, I think oftener.

WIFE: And ar'st thou yet look with temptation on us?
Since nothing will prevail, come death! Come vengeance!
I will forget the weakness of my kind
And force thee from my chamber.
She thrusts at Votarius with the sword

VOTARIUS: How now, lady!
'Uds life! You prick me, madam!

WIFE: *Aside*. Prithee, peace!
I will not hurt thee.
Aloud
Will you yet be gone, sir?

LEONELLA: He's upon going, I think

VOTARIUS: Madam! Heart, you deal false with me. O, I feel it!
Y'are a most treacherous lady! This thy glory?
My breast is all afire! O!—
Votarius dies

LEONELLA: Ha, ha, ha!

ANSELMUS: Ha! I believe her constancy too late,
Confirmed e'en in the blood of my best friend.
He seizes the sword from his Wife. Enter Bellarius
Take thou my vengeance, thou bold, perjurious strumpet,
That dust accuse thy virtuous lady falsely.
Kills Leonella

BELLARIUS: O deadly poison after a sweet banquet!
What make I here? I had forgot my part!
I am an actor too, and ne'er thought on't.
The blackness of this season cannot miss me.
To Anselmus. Sirrah! You, lord!
Bellarius draws a sword

WIFE: Is he there? Welcome, ruin!

BELLARIUS: There is a life due to me in that bosom
For this poor gentlewoman.

ANSELMUS: And art thou then receiver?
I'll pay thee largely, slave, for thy last 'scape.
They make a dangerous pass at one another. The wife purposely runs between, and is killed by them both

WIFE: I come, Votarius!
Dies

ANSELMUS: Hold, if manhood guide thee!
O what has fury done?

BELLARIUS: What has it done now?
Why, killed an honourable whore, that's all.

ANSELMUS: Villain! I'll seal that lie upon thy heart.
A constant lady!
He kneels at his Wife's side

BELLARIUS: Go to the devil, as could be!
Heart! Must I prick you forward? Either up,
Or, sir, I'll take my chance. Thou couldst kill her
Without repenting that deserved more pity!
And spend'st thy time and tears upon a queen—

ANSELMUS: Slave!

BELLARIUS: —That was deceived once in her own deceit,
They fight, and each is mortally stabbed
As I am now. The poison I prepared
Upon that weapon for mine enemy's bosom
Is bold to take acquaintance of my blood too,
And serves us both to make up death withal.

ANSELMUS: I ask no more of destiny but to fall
Close by the chaste side of my virtuous mistress.
If all the treasure of my weeping strength
Be left so wealthy but to purchase that,
I have the dear wish of a great man's spirit.
Yet favour me, O yet.
Touches Wife
I thank thee, fate;
I expire cheerfully, and give death a smile.
Anselmus swoons and appears to die

BELLARIUS: O rage! I pity now mine enemy's flesh.
Enter Govianus with Servants

GOVIANUS: Where should he be?

FIRST SERVANT: My lady, sir, will tell you.
She's in her chamber here.

SECOND SERVANT: *Seeing bodies*. O my lord!

GOVIANUS: Peace!—My honorable brother—madam—all!
So many dreadful deeds, and not one tongue
Left to proclaim 'em!

BELLARIUS: Yes, here! If a voice

Some minute long may satisfy your ear,
I've that time allowed it.

GOVIANUS: 'Tis enough.
Bestow it quickly, ere death snatch it from thee.

BELLARIUS: That lord your brother made his friend Votarius
To tempt his lady. She was won to lust,
The act revealed here by her serving-woman.
But that wise, close adulteress, stored with art
To prey upon the weakness of that lord,
Dissembled a great rage upon her love,
And indeed killed him, which so won her husband
He slew this right discoverer in his fury,
Who, being my mistress, I was moved in heart
To take some pains with him, and h'as paid me for't.
As for the cunning lady, I commend her;
She performed that which never woman tried:
She ran upon two weapons, and so died.
Now you have all, I hope I shall sleep quiet.
Dies

ANSELMUS: O, thunder that awakes me e'en from death,
And makes me curse my confidence with cold lips,
I feel his words in flames about my soul;
H'as more than killed me.

GOVIANUS: Brother!

ANSELMUS: I repent the smile
That I bestowed on destiny! A whore!
Speaks to Body of Wife
I fling thee thus from my believing breast
With all the strength I have. My rage is great,
Although my veins grow beggars. Now I sue
To die far from thee! May we never meet!
Were my soul bid to joy's eternal banquet,
And were assured to find thee there a guest,
I'd sup with torments, and refuse that feast.
O thou beguiler of man's easy trust!
'The serpent's wisdom is in women's lust.'
Dies

GOVIANUS: Is death so long a-coming to mankind
It must be met half ways? 'Las, the full time
Is to eternity but a minute.
Was that so long to stay? O cruel speed!
There's few men pay their debts before their day.
If they be ready at their time, 'tis well—
And but a few that are so. What strange haste
Was made among these people! My heart weeps for't.
To Servants
Go, bear these bodies to a place more comely.
Servants take out bodies
Brother, I came for thy advice, but I
Find thee so ill a counsellor to thyself
That I repent my pains, and depart sighing.
The body of my love is still at court;
I am not well to think on't. The poor spirit
Was with me once again about it, troth;
And I can put off no more for shame,
Though I desire to have it haunt me still
And never to give over, 'tis so pleasing.
I must to court: I've plighted my faith to't;
'T'as opened me the way to the revenge.
Tyrant, I'll run thee on a dangerous shelf,
Though I be forced to fly this land myself.

(ACT V, SCENE II)

The royal court. Enter the Tyrant with Attendants

TYRANT: In vain my spirit wrestles with my blood;
Affection will be mistress here on earth.
The house is hers, the soul is but a tenant.
I ha' tasked myself but with the abstinence
Of one poor hour, yet cannot conquer that.
I cannot keep from sight of her so long.
I starve mine eye too much. Go, bring her forth,
As we have caused her body to be decked
In all the glorious riches of our palace.
Our mind has felt a famine for the time;
All comfort has been dear and scarce with us.

The times are altered since.

Sounds of music within

Strike on, sweet harmony!

Enter Soldiers with the Lady

A braver world comes toward us.

They bring the body in a chair, dressed up in black velvet, which sets out the paleness of the hands and face, and a fair chain of pearl 'cross her breast, and the crucifix above it. He stands silent awhile, letting the music play, beckoning the soldiers that bring her in to make obeisance to her, and he himself makes a low honour to the body and kisses the hand.

A song within, in voices

Song

O, what is beauty, that's so much adored?
A flattering glass that cozens her beholders,
One night of death makes it look pale and horrid:
The dainty preserved flesh, how soon it moulders!
To love it living, it bewitcheth many,
But after life is seldom heard of any.

FIRST SOLDIER: By this hand, mere idolatry! I make curtsy
To my damnation. I have learnt so much,
Though I could never know the meaning yet
Of all my Latin prayers, nor ne'er sought for't.

TYRANT: How pleasing art thou to us even in death!
I love thee yet, above all women living,
And shall do sev'n year hence.
I can see nothing to be mended in thee
But the too constant paleness of thy cheek.
I'd give the kingdom but to purchase there
The breadth of a red rose in natural colour,
And think it the best bargain that ever king made yet.
But fate's my hindrance,
And I must only rest content with art;
And that I'll have in spite on't. Is he come, sir?

SECOND SOLDIER: Who, my lord?

TYRANT: Dull! The fellow that we sent
For a court schoomaster, a picture drawer,
A lady's forenoon tutor. Is he come, sir?

FIRST SOLDIER: Not yet returned, my lord.

TYRANT: The fool belike
Makes his choice carefully, for so we charged him,
To fit our close deeds with some private hand.
It is no shame for thee, most silent mistress,
To stand in need of art, when youth
And all thy warm friends has forsook thee.
Women alive are glad to seek her friendship
To make up the fair number of their graces,
Or else the reckoning would fall short sometimes,
And servants would look out for better wages.

Enter Third Soldier with Govianus, disguised

SECOND SOLDIER: He's come, my lord.

TYRANT: Depart then.

Exeunt Soldiers. Manet Third Soldier

Is that he?

THIRD SOLDIER: The privatest I could get, my lord.

GOVIANUS: *Aside*. O heaven, marry patience to my spirit!
Give me a sober fury, I beseech thee,
A rage that may not overcharge my blood
And do myself most hurt! 'Tis strange to me
To see thee here at court, and gone from hence.
Didst thou make haste to leave the world for this?
And kept in the worst corner?
O, who dares play with destiny but he
That wears security so thick upon him
The thought of death and hell cannot pierce through?

TYRANT: 'Twas circumspectly carried.

To Third Soldier

Leave us; go.

To Govianus

Be nearer, sir; thou'rt much commended to us.

GOVIANUS: It is the hand, my lord, commends the workman.

TYRANT: Thou speak'st both modesty and truth in that.
We need that art that thou art master of.

GOVIANUS: My king is master both of that and me.

TYRANT: Look on yon face and tell me what it wants.

GOVIANUS: Which, that, sir?

TYRANT: That! What wants it?

GOVIANUS: Troth, my lord
Some thousand years' sleep and a marble pillow.

TYRANT: What's that?

Aside

Observe it still! All the best arts
Hath the most fools and drunkards to their masters

Aloud

Thy apprehension has too gross a film
To be employed at court. What colour wants she?

GOVIANUS: By my troth, all, sir; I see none she has,
Nor none she cares for.

TYRANT: *Aside.* I am overmatched here.

GOVIANUS: A lower chamber with less noise were kindlier
For her, poor woman, whatsoe'er she was.

TYRANT: But how if we be pleased to have it thus,
And thou well hired to do what we command?
Is not your work for money?

GOVIANUS: Yes, my lord;

I would not trust at court and I could choose.

TYRANT: Let but thy art hide death upon her face,
That now looks fearfully on us, and but strive
To give our eye delight in that pale part
Which draws so many pities from these springs,
And thy reward for't shall outlast thy end,
And reach to thy friend's fortunes, and his friend.

GOVIANUS: Say you so, my lord? I'll work out my heart then
But I'll show art enough.

TYRANT: About it, then!
I never wished so seriously for health
After long sickness.

GOVIANUS: *Aside*. A religious trembling shakes me by the hand,
And bids me put by such unhallowed business,
But revenge calls for't, and it must go forward.
'Tis time the spirit of my love took rest;
Poor soul, 'tis weary, much abused and toiled.
Govianus paints the face of the body

TYRANT: Could I now send for one to renew heat
Within her bosom, that were a fine workman;
I should but too much love him. But alas,
'Tis as unpossible for living fire
To take hold there as for dead ashes to burn back again
Into those hard tough bodies whence they fell.
Life is removed from her now, as the warmth
Of the bright sun from us when it makes winter
And kills with unkind coldness. So is't yonder;
An everlasting frost hangs now upon her.
And in such a season men will force
A heat into their bloods with exercise
In spite of extreme weather, so shall we
By art force beauty on yon lady's face;
Though death sit frowning on't a storm of hail
To beat it off, our pleasure shall prevail.

GOVIANUS: My lord!

TYRANT: Hast done so soon?

GOVIANUS: That's as your grace
Gives approbation.

TYRANT: O, she lives again!
She'll presently speak to me. Keep her up;
I'll have her swoon no more; there's treachery in't.
Does she not feel warm to thee?

GOVIANUS: Very little, sir.

TYRANT: The heat wants cherishing then. Our arms and lips
Shall labour life into her. Wake, sweet mistress!
He kisses the lips of the body
'Tis I that call thee at the door of life. Ha!
I talk so long to death, I'm sick myself.
Methinks an evil scent still follows me.

GOVIANUS: Maybe 'tis nothing but the colour, sir,
That I laid on.

TYRANT: Is that so strong?

GOVIANUS: Yes, faith, sir,
'Twas the best poison I could get for money.
Govianus throws off his disguise

TYRANT: Govianus!

GOVIANUS: O, thou sacrilegious villain!
Thou thief of rest, robber of monuments!
Cannot the body after funeral
Sleep in the grave for thee? Must it be raised
Only to please the wickedness of thine eye?
Does all things end with death, and not thy lust?
Hast thou devised a new way to damnation,
More dreadful than the soul of any sin
Did ever pass yet between earth and hell?
Dost strive to be particularly plagued
Above all ghosts beside? Is thy pride such

Thou scorn'st a partner in thy torments too?

TYRANT: What fury gave thee boldness to attempt
This deed? For which I'll doom thee with a death
Beyond the Frenchmen's tortures.

GOVIANUS: I smile at thee.
Draw all the death that ever mankind suffered
Unto one head, to help thine own invention,
And make my end as rare as this thy sin,
And full as fearful to the eyes of women!
My spirit shall fly singing to his lodging
In midst of that rough weather. Doom me, Tyrant.
Had I feared death, I'd never appeared noble
To seal this act upon me, which e'en honours me
Unto my mistress' spirit. It loves me for't.
I told my heart 'twould prove destruction to't.
Who, hearing 'twas for her, charged me to do't.

TYRANT: Thy glories shall be shortened! Who's within there?
Enter the Ghost, in the same form as
the Lady is dressed in the chair.
I called not thee, thou enemy to firmness,
Mortality's earthquake!

GOVIANUS: Welcome to mine eyes
As is the day spring from the morning's womb
Unto that wretch whose nights are tedious!
As liberty to captives, health to labourers,
And life still to old people, never weary on't;
So welcome art thou to me. The deed's done,
Thou queen of spirits; he has his end upon him.
Thy body shall return to rise again,
For thy abuser falls, and has no power
To vex thee farther now.

LADY: My truest love!
Life ever honoured here, and blessed above.

TYRANT: O, if there be a hell for flesh and spirit,
'Tis built within this bosom.

Enter Nobles
My lords, treason!

GOVIANUS: Now death, I'm for thee. Welcome!

TYRANT: Your king's poisoned!

MEMPHONIUS: The King of heaven be praised for't!

TYRANT: Lay hold on him—
On Govianus!

MEMPHONIUS: E'en with the best loves
And truest hearts that ever subjects owed.

TYRANT: How's that? I charge you all, lay hands on him.

MEMPHONIUS: Look you, my lord, your will shall be obeyed:
Here comes another; we'll have his hand too.
Enter Helvetius

HELVETIUS: You shall have both mine, if that work go forward,
Beside my voice and knee.

TYRANT: Helvetius!
Then my destruction was confirmed amongst 'em;
Premeditation wrought it. O my torments!

ALL: Live Govianus long our virtuous king!
A flourish

TYRANT: That thunder strikes me dead.
The Tyrant dies

GOVIANUS: I cannot better
Reward my joys than with astonished silence,
For all the wealth of words is not of power
To make up thanks for you, my honoured lords!
I'm like a man plucked up from many waters,
That never looked for help, and am here placed
Upon this cheerful mountain, where prosperity

Shoots forth her richest beam.

MEMPHONIUS: Long-injured lord,
The tyranny of his actions grew so weighty,
His life so vicious—

HELVETIUS: To which this is witness—
Monster in sin!—this, the disquieted body
Of my too resolute child in honour's war.

MEMPHONIUS: —That he became as hateful to our minds—

HELVETIUS: As death's unwelcome to a house of riches,
Or what can more express it.

GOVIANUS: Well, he's gone;
And all the kingdom's evils perish with him!
And since the body of that virtuous lady
Is taken from her rest, in memory
Of her admired mistress, 'tis our will
It receive honour dead, as it took part
With us in all afflictions when it lived.
Here place her in this throne, crown her our queen,
The first and last that ever we make ours,
Her constancy strikes so much firmness in us.
That honour done, let her be solemnly borne
Unto the house of peace from whence she came,
As Queen of Silence.

The Spirit enters again and stays to go out with the body, as if it were attending it

O welcome, blessed spirit!
Thou need'st not mistrust me; I have a care
As jealous as thine own. We'll see it done,
And not believe report; our zeal is such
We cannot reverence chastity too much.
Lead on! I would those ladies that fill honour's rooms
Might all be borne so honest to their tombs.

Recorders or other solemn music plays them out

Finis

GLOSSARY OF OBSOLETE WORDS AND PHRASES

ACT I

Line

3. *Sennet*. trumpet call
43. *great stone horse*. stallion
53. *barricado*. barrier
88. *conster*. construe
89. *pierce your wife's waiting women*. an Elizabethan pun
90. *fines and sackings*. fees and improperly high rents
92. *living*. property
94. *mercers' books*. clothier's accounts
115. *risse*. rose
187. *hide that book*. an unclear phrase, possibly a slip of Shakespeare's pen
248. *A Flourish*. trumpet fanfare
315. *jealous*. protective
448. *clips*. embraces
449. *gamester*. gambler; lewd person
521. *Beshrew*. curses upon
539. *use*. spend

ACT II

605. *use*. custom
702. *earthen*. earthly
873. *cracking of whole money*. a cracked coin loses much of its value and generally continues to crack even more
883. *highway-striker*. footpad
900. *saunce bell*. sanctus bell, or church bell
1067. *saucy*. savage

ACT III

1084. *grace*. God's forgiveness for sin
1089. *dear*. valuable
1112. *sneaped*. reproved
1252. *All-Ass*. alas (a pun on the character of Sophonirus)
1290. *Finding on him*. pinning him down

ACT IV

1387. *short-heeled*. wanton
1454. *hang a weapon*. (*weapon* was a slang word for penis. This phrase is one of the many *double-entendres* in the play)
1509. *glozers'*. flatterers'
1627. *illustrious*. bright
1653. *prove*. try
1696. *city-pie*. possibly a large London pie
1703. *duty*. respect

ACT V

1821. *fee'd*. bribed
1822. *catchpole*. a petty official
1831. *woman's action*. a *double-entendre*
1899. *prefer*. urge
2101. *pities from these springs*. tears from these eyes
2132. *treachery*. magic or witchcraft
2173. *dayspring*. daybreak

PART II

CHAPTER I

SHAKESPEARE'S "LOST" PLAY

In their *First Folio* preface "To the great Variety of Readers," the editors, John Heminges and Henry Condell, both friends and fellow actors of Shakespeare, are very explicit that in their folio edition Shakespeare's plays are "absolute in their numbers as he conceived them."[1] They allow for no new plays. They leave no room for any accusation of omission. And, since the admission of *Pericles* (1664) into the sacred canon, the iron door has been slammed on all comers, even on *The Two Noble Kinsmen*, which so clearly reveals the Master's touch. We are thus confronted with the inevitable question: If *The Second Maiden's Tragedy* is actually *Cardenio*, written by Shakespeare and Fletcher, why didn't Heminges and Condell include it in *The First Folio*? Here are some of the possible reasons:

1. *Cardenio* wasn't up to Shakespeare's standards. In his will, the writing of which I shall discuss in the next chapter, Shakespeare left a bequest of twenty-six shillings and eight pence in gold to each of his fellow actors—Richard Burbage, John Heminges, and Henry Condell—to buy a memorial ring. These three men, major stockholders in *The Globe* and *Blackfriars* theaters, amongst them owned the prompt copies of many of Shakespeare's plays not yet in print. Despite their lack of experience in authorship, they were in a unique position to edit and publish Shakespeare's plays. Ben Jonson had already startled the literary world by publishing his *Works* in 1616, the year of Shakespeare's death. Jonson's publication of his plays as "works" was an audacious act and fetched him a mighty lambasting from the critics, since plays were in those days considered "throwaways" and not literary works of permanent value. Did Shakespeare, then living in retirement and certainly aware of Jonson's project, contemplate a volume of his own collected plays? And, if so, did he, when apprised of his impending death, leave by oral bequest his pertinent papers and any printed quartos he may have possessed to Heminges and Condell, and possibly Burbage, instructing them on which plays to include in their complete edition of his dramas? Burbage, who had acted in all or most of Shakespeare's plays and knew many of the great lines from memory, abdicated his share of the task when he died in 1619.[2] In their preface, Heminges and Condell, the two survivors, wrote: "It had bene a thing, we confesse, worthie to have bene wished,

that the author himselfe had liv'd to have set forth and overseen his owne writings; but since it hath bin ordain'd otherwise, and he by death departed from that right, we pray you do not envie his friends the office of their care and paine to have collected and publish'd them."[3] The phrase "had liv'd to" rather than simply "had" suggests that Shakespeare had contemplated a complete edition of his plays, but died before he could prepare it. If so, the absence of *Cardenio*, or *The Second Maiden's Tragedy,* as well as *Pericles* and *The Two Noble Kinsmen,* from the *First Folio* may have been at Shakespeare's explicit request.

2. *Cardenio* was more a work by Fletcher than by Shakespeare and logically would belong in Fletcher's works rather than Shakespeare's. This possibility is also suggested by the fact that in the *Stationers' Register, Cardenio* is listed as by "Mr. Fletcher. & Shakespeare," with the name of the lesser dramatist first. However, Humphrey Moseley, the publisher who registered *Cardenio* in 1653, did not include it in his *Comedies and Tragedies* of Beaumont and Fletcher (1647), although it is quite possible Moseley did not own the manuscript or rights to *Cardenio* at that time.

3. Heminges and Condell were unable to locate the promptbook of *Cardenio*, and since the play had been performed early in June 1613, only three weeks before the great fire that burned down *The Globe* (June 29, 1613), they may have concluded that the manuscript play was in the theater and went up in flames with the rest of *The Globe's* properties and therefore never bothered to search for it.

4. It is remotely possible, too, that *Cardenio* may have been incorrectly filed among other dramas under its alternate title, *The Second Maiden's Tragedy* and thus escaped the attention of Heminges and Condell.

5. Heminges and Condell may have located the manuscript too late to include it in their oversized volume of Shakespeare's dramatic works.

6. The most obvious and compelling reason for Heminges and Condell to omit *Cardenio,* or *The Second Maiden's Tragedy* from *The First Folio* was because the mores of England were changing in 1623. In the twelve years since *Cardenio* was written, the carefree Jacobean era had begun to merge into the age of Puritanism. It is quite possible that Heminges and Condell felt that *Cardenio,* with its violent plot featuring murder and necrophilia, might have bestirred their readers against Shakespeare and even injured the sale of his collected plays. As matters turned out, they were right.

The great age of drama was drawing to a close. In 1642, only ten years after the publication of the second folio edition of Shakespeare's plays, the Houses of Parliament declared that all public performances of stage plays should cease; and six years later, a more severe edict ordered that all theaters be dismantled and all actors, even of private performances, be publicly whipped and each member of the audience be fined. The drama lay dead for fifteen years. When it was revived in 1656, Shakespeare was looked upon as an out-of-date playwright whose "crude" dramas reeked with murder and violence.

His beautiful plays were dismantled and rewritten by jingle men who staged them in bowdlerized versions, stripped of their poetry and violence, and with totally altered plots.

There is no disagreement on what the manuscript of *Cardenio,* or *The Second Maiden's Tragedy* looks like today. Labelled *Lansdowne 807* (folios 29-56 in a slender-bound volume), it rubs iambs with interlopers on either side—*The Queen of Corsica* by Francis Jaques (folios 2-28) and *The Bugbears* (folios 57-77), plus a ragtailed fragment (folios 78-88). Perhaps I should not allude to these other plays, long forgotten, as interlopers. They may, indeed, have been holy guardians for one of the most precious manuscripts in the world, protecting its flanks from mutilation. The manuscript comprises twenty-three folio leaves, numbered in pencil 29-56, plus five small slips of paper containing alterations or additions, affixed to the margins. The folio pages measure about 7 x 11 inches, and each page contains about fifty-six lines of handsomely penned text.[4]

The present mid-eighteenth century paper cover of the manuscript adds little to our knowledge:

The Second Maydens Tragedy
October 31st
1611
By Thomas Goffe George Chapman
By Will Shakespear
A Tragedy indeed

The names Thomas Goffe, George Chapman, and Will Shakespear were written by successive owners, and the third owner (possibly John Warburton, who will be discussed later in this chapter) crossed off the names of Thomas Goffe and George Chapman and identified the writer as Will Shakspear. Chapman is, perhaps, a viable prospect for authorship, but Goffe, who was born in 1592, does not seem a likely prospect by reason of his youth in 1611 and the nature of his surviving dramas.

Attributions to Shakespeare, alias W.S. and W. Sh., are so frequently met with on seventeenth century printed plays and poetry manuscripts in commonplace books that I am contemplating an article to be entitled, "Verses Shakespeare Never Wrote." I hope that no reader of this book will give any credence to the presumptuous cover attribution—I certainly do not—for the evidence I shall adduce for Shakespeare and Fletcher's authorship of *Cardenio* or *The Second Maiden's Tragedy* lies elsewhere.

By way of introduction to a detailed discussion of the links between *Cardenio* and *The Second Maiden's Tragedy*, here is a brief summary of my evidence:

1. As the play was still untitled when the censor approved it for performance (October, 1611), he christened it *The Second Maiden's Tragedy.* Shakespeare and Fletcher may later have added another title, thus: *The History of Cardenio* or *The Second Maiden's Tragedy.*

2. The name "Cardenio" is taken from one of the most exotic and popular characters in the runaway best seller, *Don Quixote* and would pique interest in the new play.

3. By a logical process of elimination, *The Second Maiden's Tragedy* appears to be the play that was twice performed in 1613 at Court under the title *Cardenno* or *Cardenna.* The spelling of the royal clerks was seldom consistent and at times was even grotesque.

4. When the publisher Humphrey Moseley bought a large collection of promptbooks from the King's Men (about 1647-1653), the forty-two-year-old title wrapper of *Cardenio* may have been falling apart. If lost, the play would be left nameless, except for the censor's title written on the last page. To protect his claim to the title *Cardenio,* in the event that the cover wrapper disintegrated or got lost and nobody (which was often the case) could recall the play's name, Moseley may have separately registered the subtitle, or he may have possessed a duplicate, variant, or revised manuscript of *Cardenio* entitled *The Second Maiden's Tragedy.*[5]

5. About a century later, a manuscript collector named John Warburton acquired Moseley's stock of promptbooks. *Cardenio* had vanished. Obviously it "disappeared" the very moment its title wrapper crumbled away. In its stead was nothing but a plain, old drama, *The Second Maiden's Tragedy*, an anonymous play that nobody had ever heard of.

Sometime early in October 1611, we may surmise, the completed manuscript, untitled and a bit rough around the edges, had been delivered by the authors to the censor, George Buc,[6] whose official job was to delete all passages or allusions that might be offensive to the crown. Harold L. Stenger, Jr. has commented on the severity of the censorship:[7] "The censor's ban was heavy-handed, absolute, and extensive over the widest possible area of dramatic depiction. The portrayal of a king in any unfavorable light whatsoever, whether touching upon his actions as a monarch or his failings as a man, was forbidden. Any action tinged in the slightest degree with sedition or disloyalty was forbidden. . ."[8] A few references to regicide, a subject that haunted the timorous James I, were rigorously expunged. For example, the remark of The Tyrant, *Your King's poisoned* (V, iii, 2185), was censored into *I am poisoned.*

Stenger has brilliantly encapsulated the disastrous effect of Buc's censorship:

> The censor's cuts were made without regard to literary worth. Esthetically several of the deleted passages rank among the finest in the play. . . With their removal nearly all the trenchancy would be bled out of the play; the spirit of irony and satire, so obviously indigenous to the mind of its author, removed, would take the spice out of the dish and leave a flat gruel indeed. Probably the greatest loss, however, would be the veiling of reality as this playwright understood it. The author's finest attribute is an ability to look at life clearly. Never in all the sordid entanglements of the story does he lose the power to distinguish black from white; never, though he displays them all, does he allow himself to become confused by the sundry shades of grey which overwhelm and foredoom his characters. To remove from the work this focus of clear vision is to extract from it its finest essence. . . [9]

Needless to say, the censor's assault on the manuscript was negated in this present text, every word of which is presented precisely as Shakespeare and Fletcher wrote it. On the final day of October 1611, Buc wrote on the last page, just beneath the author's fancy Latin *ffinis* and three playful stars:

> This second Maydens tragedy (for it hath no
> name inscribed) may wth the reformations bee
> acted publickely. 31. octob^{r} 1611.
> / G. Buc

Thus, with many of its characters still unnamed, and with a title invented by the censor, *Cardenio* entered the theatrical world officially censored for a court performance. From this point on, the manuscript play likely had the usual fold-over wrapper of the type used by nearly all acting companies. This wrapper probably identified the play as *Cardenio*. During the winter of 1612, the play was apparently readied for production. The player for each role was selected, the book-keeper provided each actor with his lines and cues, the music composed, and the entrances and exits designated.

In the margin of the book appears, in the stage prompter's hand, *Enter Mr/Goughe* (IV, ii, 1549), indicating the appearance on stage of the courtier, Memphonius, clearly played by Goughe. A few nineteenth century critics assumed that the stage entry alluded to was The Tyrant's, but, as The Tyrant was already on stage, indication of his entry would be superfluous; moreover, the next speech prefix is for Memphonius.

Robert Goughe or Goffe (died 1624) began his illustrious acting career when, as a youth, he played the roles of young ladies. The noted actor, Thomas Pope, who died in 1603, may have been his mentor. Pope left Goughe a legacy of half his wearing apparel and arms. In 1602 Goughe married Elizabeth Phillips, the sister of Augustine Phillips, another distinguished actor with the King's Men.

The second actor mentioned in the manuscript, in the prompter's hand, was Richard "Dickey" Robinson, as "Rich Robinõn," who played the role of "The Ladye." Robinson was born about 1597 and was about ten when Richard Burbage, Shakespeare's close friend and England's greatest actor, accepted him as a protégé. As Robinson matured, his roles matured with him, and he wound up playing male leads. When he played The Lady in 1513, Dickey was about fifteen and already a popular and renowned actor. Three or four years later, in his play, *The Devil is an Ass*, Ben Jonson wrote of Robinson:

> . . .there's Dickey Robinson
> A very pretty fellow, and comes often
> To a gentleman's chamber, a friend of mine. We had
> The merriest supper of it there, one night,
> The gentleman's landlady invited him
> To a gossip's feast: now he, sir, brought Dick
> Robinson
> Drest like a lawyer's wife, amongst 'em all:
> I lent him clothes. But to see him behave it,
> And lay the law, and carve and drink unto them,

> And then talk bawdy, and send frolics!
> It would have burst your buttons![10]

During England's Civil War, Robinson fought on the royalist side. He was captured, but immediately shot in the head by a Puritan zealot who was subsequently tried and hanged for murder by the Puritan army.

As it happens—or perhaps it was intentional on the authors' part—at the very time *Cardenio* was completed there was a unique opportunity for its presentation at Court.

In 1612-13 there were big festivities in progress at the royal palace in Whitehall. The king's daughter, Princess Elizabeth, only fourteen, was being married to the Prince Palatine, also fourteen. All sorts of celebrations were arranged far in advance to commemorate this momentous event that eventually took place on February 14, 1613. James I was a devotee of the drama. Of course, as king, he was unable, for security reasons, to attend performances at the Globe or at Blackfriars. The plays had to come to him. A special stage was usually erected in the palace for the King's Men. At least once a month they performed for the Court. In the earlier days of Queen Elizabeth I (before 1603), Shakespeare and his company, then known as the Chamberlain's Men, gave a total of 32 performances over the years for her majesty, but for James, a drama addict who doubtless yearned for new plays, Shakespeare's company, the King's Men, staged 177 performances, more than all the rival acting companies put together. King James's wife, Queen Anne, was equally drawn to the footlights. Early in James's reign, in a letter endorsed 1604, a courtier named Walter Cope wrote to Lord Cranborne at Court:

> I have sent and bene all thys morning huntying for players juglers and Such Kinde of Creaturs but fynde them harde to fynde. . .burbage ys come and Sayes ther ys no new playe that the queene hath not seene but they have revyved an olde one Cawled Loves Labore lost wch for wytt and mirthe he says will please her excedingly. And thys ys apointed to be playd to-Morowe night at my Lord of Sowthamptons. . . Burbage ys my messenger. . . Walter Cope.[11]

With the king and queen and their entourage eager for fresh entertainment, it is very likely that an exciting drama like *The Second Maiden's Tragedy,* prepared for production by the king's own acting company, would be presented before the royal audience at Whitehall during the Palatine nuptial celebrations. I studied carefully the list of plays performed and accounted for the title and the identity of every drama except the missing *Cardenio*, which suggests the strong probability that *Cardenio* is the title under which *The Second Maiden's Tragedy* was staged before his majesty.

Cardenio (also spelled *Cardenno* and *Cardenna*)[12] was performed twice at Court. The official entries in the Revels Accounts are thus recorded:

> Itm paid to the said John Heminges vppon the lyke warr^{t}: dated att Whitehall xxth die Maij 1613 for presentinge sixe severall playes viz one playe called a badd begininige [*sic*] makes a good endinge [*All's Well that Ends Well*]. One other called ye Capteyne, One other the Alcumist. One other Cardenno. One

> other The Hotspurr [*Henry IV, Part I*]. And one other called Benedicte and Betteris [Benedick and Beatrice—*Much Ado about Nothing]*. All played wth in the tyme of this Accompte viz p^{d}—ffortie powndes, And by the waye of his Ma^{ts} rewarde twentie powndes In all 1x^{li}.
>
> Itm paid to John Heminges vppon lyke warr^{t}: dated att Whitehall 1xth Die Julij 1613 for himself and the rest of his fellows his Ma^{ts} servanntes and Players for presentinge a playe before the Duke of Savoyes Embassadour on the viijth daye of June 1613 called Cardenna the some of vj^{li} xiij^{s} iiij^{d}.[13]

These are the only two contemporary mentions we have of *Cardenio*. The play does not appear on any later list of plays owned by the King's Men—nor, for that matter, does *The Second Maiden's Tragedy*. But forty years later both titles turned up, the property of Humphrey Moseley, an enterprising bookseller and distinguished publisher of Milton, Waller, Fletcher, Donne, Davenant, Vaughan and others. Among other literary works that appeared over Moseley's imprint were translations of Spanish and Italian romances. Moseley's shop was in St. Paul's Churchyard, a bookseller's mart once frequented by Shakespeare and Marlowe as they browsed in search of the latest literary works as well as volumes on the arcane and piquant—any books that might suggest or inspire a new play. A member of the Stationers' Company, an organization that controlled and authorized the printing of books, Moseley was interested in publishing old plays in cheap editions.[14] On 9 September, 1653, Moseley paid a fee of slightly more than a guinea (21 shillings and sixpence) to record forty-two plays in the Registers of the Stationers' Company, Liber E. His list of plays may have comprised the entire inventory of promptbooks that belonged to the King's Men.[15] Moseley recorded the two titles separately, *The History of Cardenio by Mr. Fletcher. & Shakespeare* and *The Maids Tragedie, 2d part*. It is my belief that these two titles represented the same play and *may* have been written on the same manuscript. Consider that for an additional sixpence Moseley could register both titles. Even if the original wrapper disintegrated or got lost, he could identify the play as the one he had registered. Six pennies was a trifling sum to lay claim to a play by Shakespeare.

Sir Walter W. Greg, who made a special study of the format of Elizabethan plays, noted that the title of a playhouse manuscript appeared on the cover wrapper, rather than on the manuscript promptbook itself. A lost or misplaced wrapper, Greg stated, might easily result in an untitled play. Further, Greg noted that in some cases the same play was entered twice in the Stationers' records under the same or a different title.[16]

Shakespeare and Fletcher might have chosen the censor's title (a most fortuitous one) on their final cover wrapper as a subtitle in order to prove conclusively that *Cardenio* had been officially licensed by Sir George Buc.[17] Further, retaining the subtitle of *The Maid's Tragedie, 2nd Part,* would add greatly to the audience appeal, since *The Maid's Tragedy* by Beaumont and Fletcher had only a year or two earlier been enormously successful. Shakespeare was certainly aware of the financial advantage of writing sequels to popular dramas. Witness his two parts of *King Henry IV*, followed by *The Merry Wives of Windsor,* mainly to exploit the character of Falstaff.[18]

The original manuscript of *The Second Maiden's Tragedy* has led an adventurous life, eluded many perils, narrowly escaped destruction, and miraculously survived to become a controversial literary document. The subject of its authorship has been an engrossing parlor game for the past one hundred and seventy years. After Moseley, the next recorded owner of *Cardenio* or *The Second Maiden's Tragedy* was John Warburton (1682-1759), who apparently purchased virtually all of Moseley's collection *en bloc*. An eccentric antiquarian and collector of rare books and manuscripts, Warburton was an author on heraldry and the Roman Wall. However, he is remembered today not for these scholarly accomplishments but for the doltish role he played in one of the greatest literary catastrophes of all time. Warburton allowed his cook, Betsy Baker (the name is palpably apocryphal, as no other facts are known about her), access to his superb archive of original manuscript plays, virtually all of them unpublished, straight from the files of Shakespeare's acting company. "Through my own carelessness and the ignorance of my servant," Warburton later wrote, "they were unluckily burned or put under pie bottoms."[19]

The eating of manuscripts, or such small portions as adhered to the bottom of pies, was a gastronomic pastime inadvertently much indulged in during the eighteenth century in England. One can imagine Warburton and his guests, a convivial group, imbibing their port and brandy, jesting merrily and devouring a large pie, unaware that they were eating Shakespeare's words.

They made no great matter of these
Books, &c: because they understood them
not, wch occasioned their servant maide
to wast about one halfe of them under Pyes,
& other like uses, wch when discovered,
they kept the rest more safe.

20th: August
1672.

E Ashmole

"They made no great matter of these Books, &c: because they understood them not, wch occasioned their servant maide to wast about one half of them under pyes, & other like uses, wch when discovered, they kept the rest more safe."

Further in evidence of this custom of using valuable documents and rare books under pies, I submit a manuscript note written by Elias Ashmole (1617-1692), an eminent antiquarian and founder of the museum at Oxford.[20] His note is dated August 20, 1692.

From memory Warburton drew up a list of all the plays used for pie-backing or starting fires during Betsy's holocaust. The cremated remains of Shakespeare, according to Warburton's list, comprised "Henry ye 1st, by Will. Shakespear & Rob. Davenport, Duke Humphery [by] Will. Shakespear"[21] [possibly *The Merry Deuill of Edmonton.*] In addition, there were allegedly fifty-six other plays that Warburton claimed had shared the fate of the four-and-twenty blackbirds, including "2^d. p^t. Maidens Trag. Geo. Chapman."[22] As we know, *The Second Maiden's Tragedy* survived, with two other plays and a fragment. Among the dramatists whose literary remains were incinerated were Massinger, Marlowe (*The Mayden Holaday)*, John Ford, Middleton, Thomas Dekker, and Cyril Tourneur (*The Nobleman*).

John Warburton died on May 11, 1759, and was buried in St. Benet's Church, Paul's Wharf, London. He left behind an enormous collection of books, manuscripts, and prints that was sold at auction. Many of his topographical manuscripts are in the Lansdowne collection in the British Museum Library.

The sale of Warburton's collections at Essex House by Samuel Peterson on November 19-24, 1759, was a major literary event. Lot 194 comprised the three survivors of the Betsy Baker holocaust. This lot, including *The Second Maiden's Tragedy*, was "knocked down" for only 14 shillings!

The buyer of Lot 194 was Philip Carteret Webb. Webb died in 1771, and his books were auctioned off later in the year. However, many of the choicest items, including *The Second Maiden's Tragedy,* were privately sold by his widow to the first Marquis of Lansdowne, then known as Lord Shelburne. After Lansdowne's death his manuscript collection was catalogued for sale (*Bibliotheca Manuscripta Lansdowniana*, 1807), but was purchased privately by a special parliamentary grant of 4925 pounds for the British Museum Library.[23]

The manuscript of *The Second Maiden's Tragedy* had been examined by such famed scholars as Edmond Malone and George Steevens during its sojourn in the library of the Marquis of Lansdowne, but it was not published until 1824, by which time the attribution to Shakespeare had been added to its wrapper. Other editions followed in 1875 (two editions), 1892, 1910, 1954 (unpublished Ph.D. thesis) and 1978. An amazing record for an anonymous play!

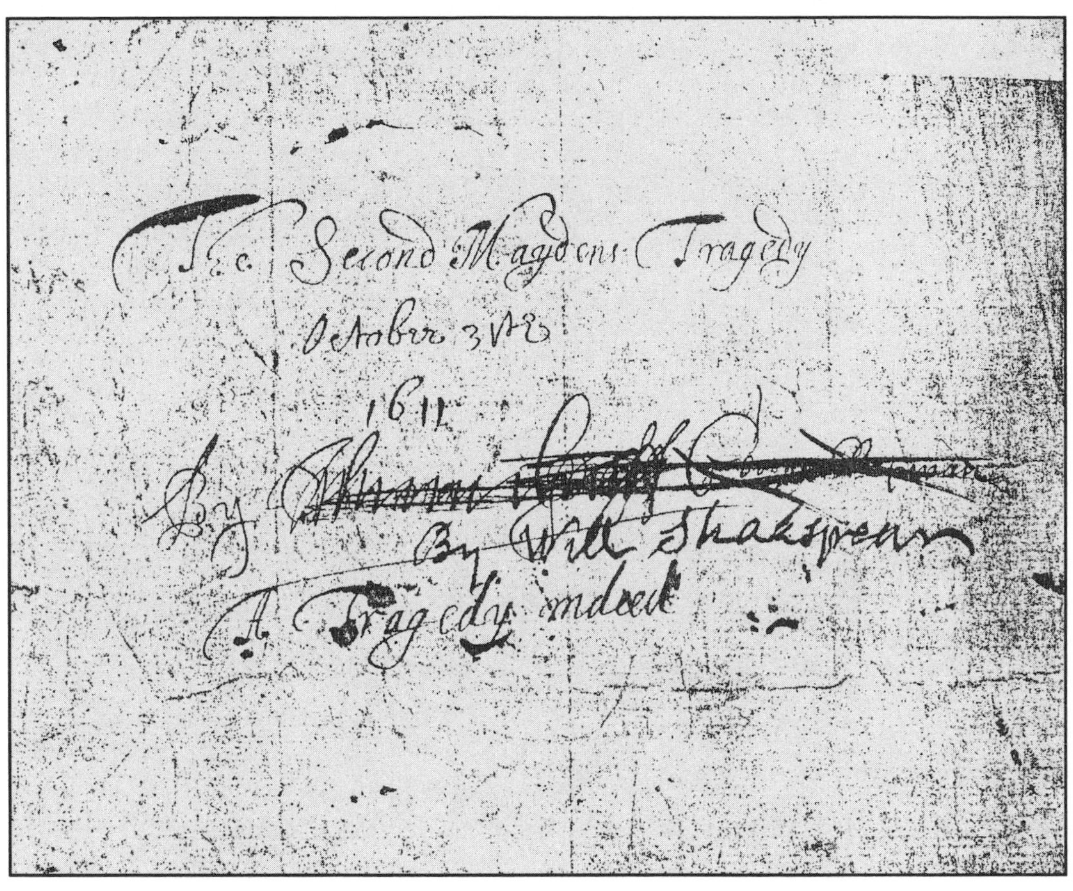
The Second Maydens Tragedy
October 31
1611
By
By Will Shakspear
A Tragedy indeed

Manuscript title page of *The Second Maiden's Tragedy* (British Museum Library, Lans. 807, fol. 56[a]).

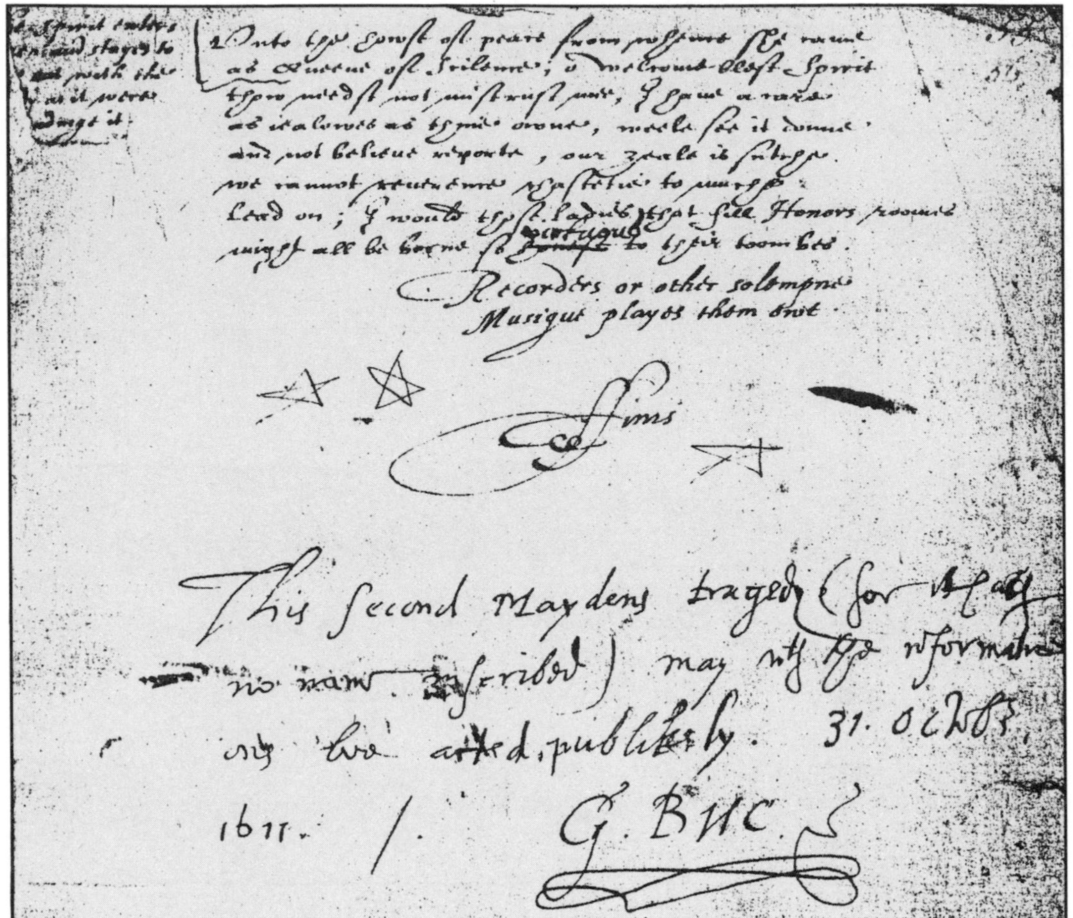

Unto the spirit of peace from whence shee came
as Queene of silence; o welcome blest spirit
thou needst not mistrust mee, I have a care
as iealous as thine owne, weele see it done
and not beleive reporte, our zeale is such
we cannot reverence chastetie too much.
Lead on; I would those ladies that fill Honors rownd
might all be borne so honest to their toombes.

Recorders or other solempne
Musique playes them out.

ffinis

This second Maydens tragedy (for it hath
no name inscribed) may wth the reformations
bee acted publikely. 31. octobr.
1611. / G. Buc.

Last page of the manuscript of *The Second Maiden's Tragedy,* with the concluding lines of the play in Shakespeare's beautiful script at the top, followed by an ornate *ffinis* and three stars, perhaps expressive of his delight at completing an arduous task. Beneath the stars appears Sir George Buc's censorship approval in which he improvises the title "second Maydens tragedy" for the play. (British Museum Library, Lans. 807, fol. 56[b]).

Frederick V (1596-1632), the Elector Palatine and his bride Princess Elizabeth (1596-1662). The bridal pair almost certainly witnessed a performance of *Cardenio* by the King's Men. (Engraved portrait by Renold Elstrack, c. 1613).

Two enthusiastic Shakespeare buffs, King James I and his wife Queen Anne (Engravings from John Speed's *A Prospect of the Most Famous Parts of the World*, 1631).

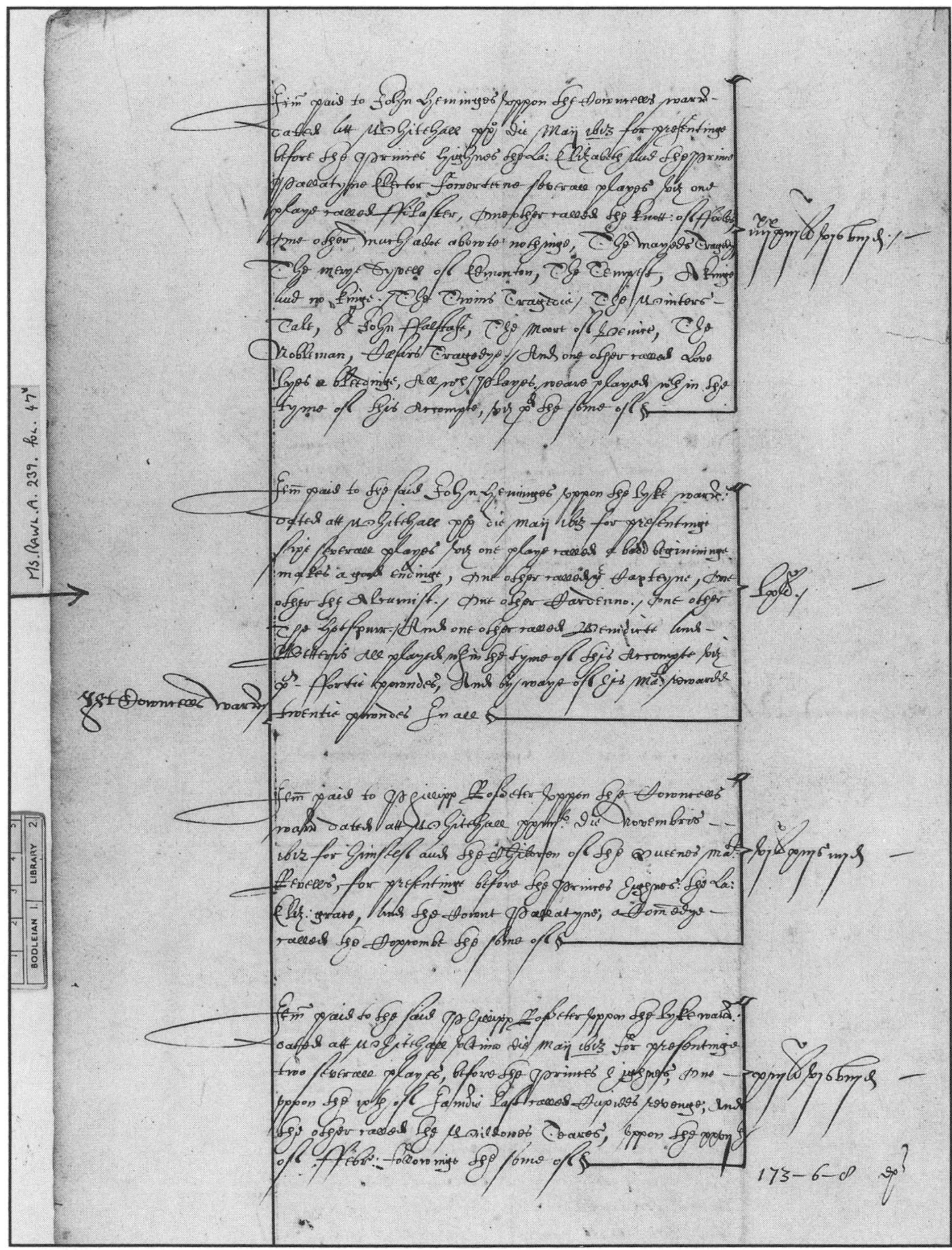

Item paid to John Heminges uppon the Cowncells warrant dated att Whitehall [illegible] die Maij 1613 for presentinge before the Princes Highnes the La: Elizabeth and the Prince Pallatyne Elector fowerteene severall playes viz one playe called ffilaster, One other called the knott of ffooles, One other Much adoe abowte nothinge, The Mayeds Tragedy, The merye dyvell of Edmonton, The Tempest, A kinge and no kinge, The Twins Tragedie, The Winters Tale, Sr John ffalstafe, The Moore of Venice, The Nobleman, Cesars Tragedye, And one other called Love lyes a bleedinge, All wch playes weare played wthin the tyme of this Accompte, viz pd the some of [illegible]

Item paid to the said John Heminges uppon the lyke warrant dated att Whitehall [illegible] die Maij 1613 for presentinge sixe severall playes viz one playe called a badd beginninge makes a good endinge, One other called the Capteyne, One other the Alcumist, One other Cardenno, One other The Hotspur, And one other called Benedicte and Betteris All played wthin the tyme of this Accompte viz pd ffortie powndes, And by waye of his Mats rewarde twentie powndes In all [illegible]

the Cowncells warrant

Item paid to Phillipp Rosseter uppon the Cowncells warrant dated att Whitehall primo die Novembris 1612 for himselfe and the rest of the Children of the Queenes Mats Revells, for presentinge before the Princes Highnes the La: Eliz: grace, and the Count Pallatyne, a Comedye called the Coxcombe the some of [illegible]

Item paid to the said Phillipp Rosseter uppon the lyke warrant dated att Whitehall [illegible] die Maij 1613 for presentinge two severall playes, before the Princes Highnes, One uppon the [illegible] of Januarie last called Cupids revenge, And the other called the Widdowes Teares, uppon the [illegible] of ffebr: followinge the some of [illegible]

173–6–8

Ms. Rawl. A. 239. fol. 47v

Page from the Revels Accounts (1613) in which *Cardenio* appears as *Cardenno*, together with several other plays by Shakespeare for which payment due on a Court appearance is authorized (Bodleian Library, Rawl. A 239, fol. 47v).

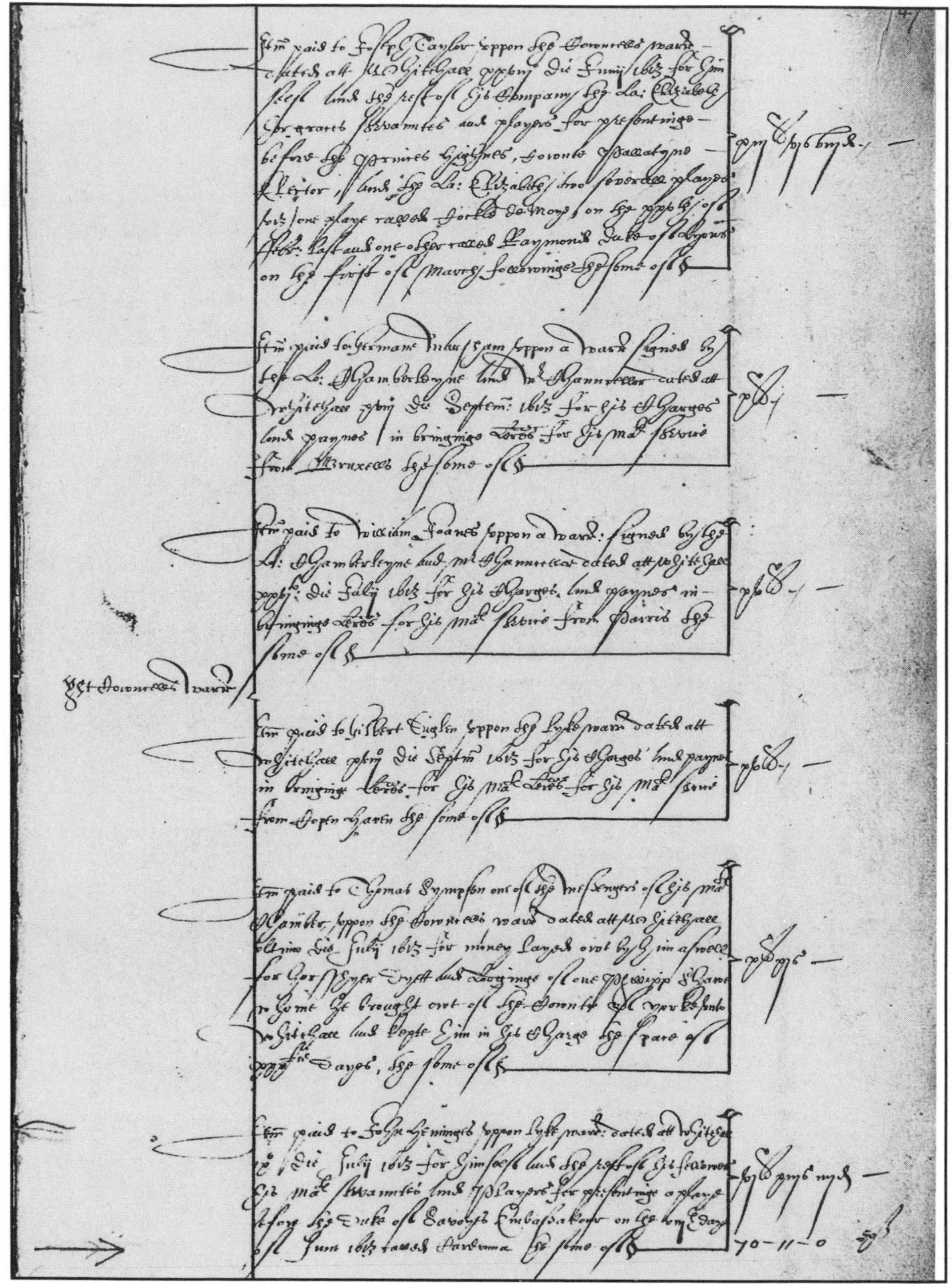

Page from the Revels Accounts (1613) in which *Cardenio* appears as *Cardenna* (bottom line) (Bodleian Library, Rawl. A 239, fol. 47[r]).

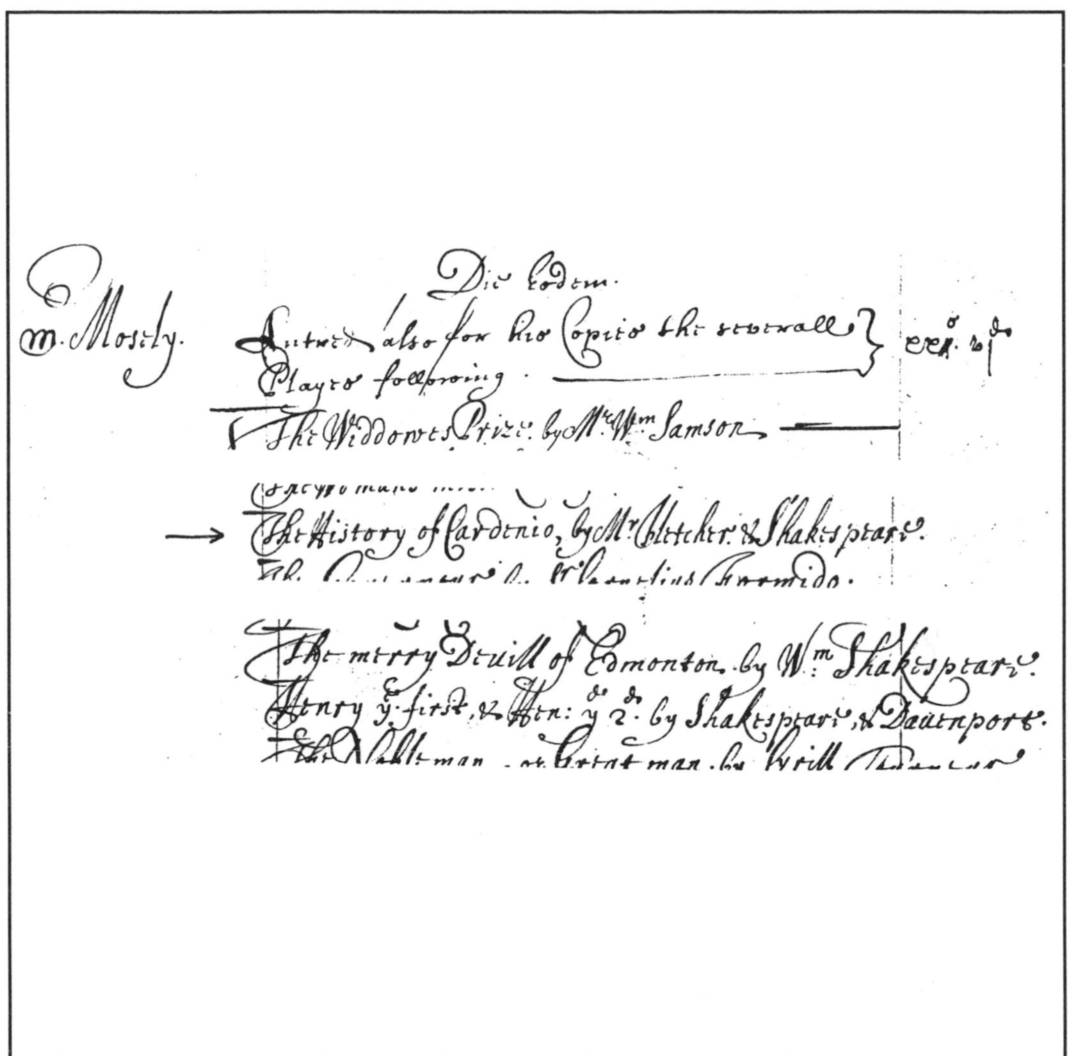

Die eodem.

M. Mosely. Entred also for his Copies the severall Playes following.

The Widdowes Prize: by Mr. Wm Samson

The History of Cardenio, by Mr. Fletcher. & Shakespeare.

The merry Devill of Edmonton. by Wm: Shakespeare.

Henry ye first, & Hen: ye 2d. by Shakespeare, & Davenport.

Cardenio by Mr. Fletcher. & Shakespeare, with two other plays attributed to Shakespeare (*Registers of the Stationers' Company,* September 9, 1653, Register E, pp. 855-56).

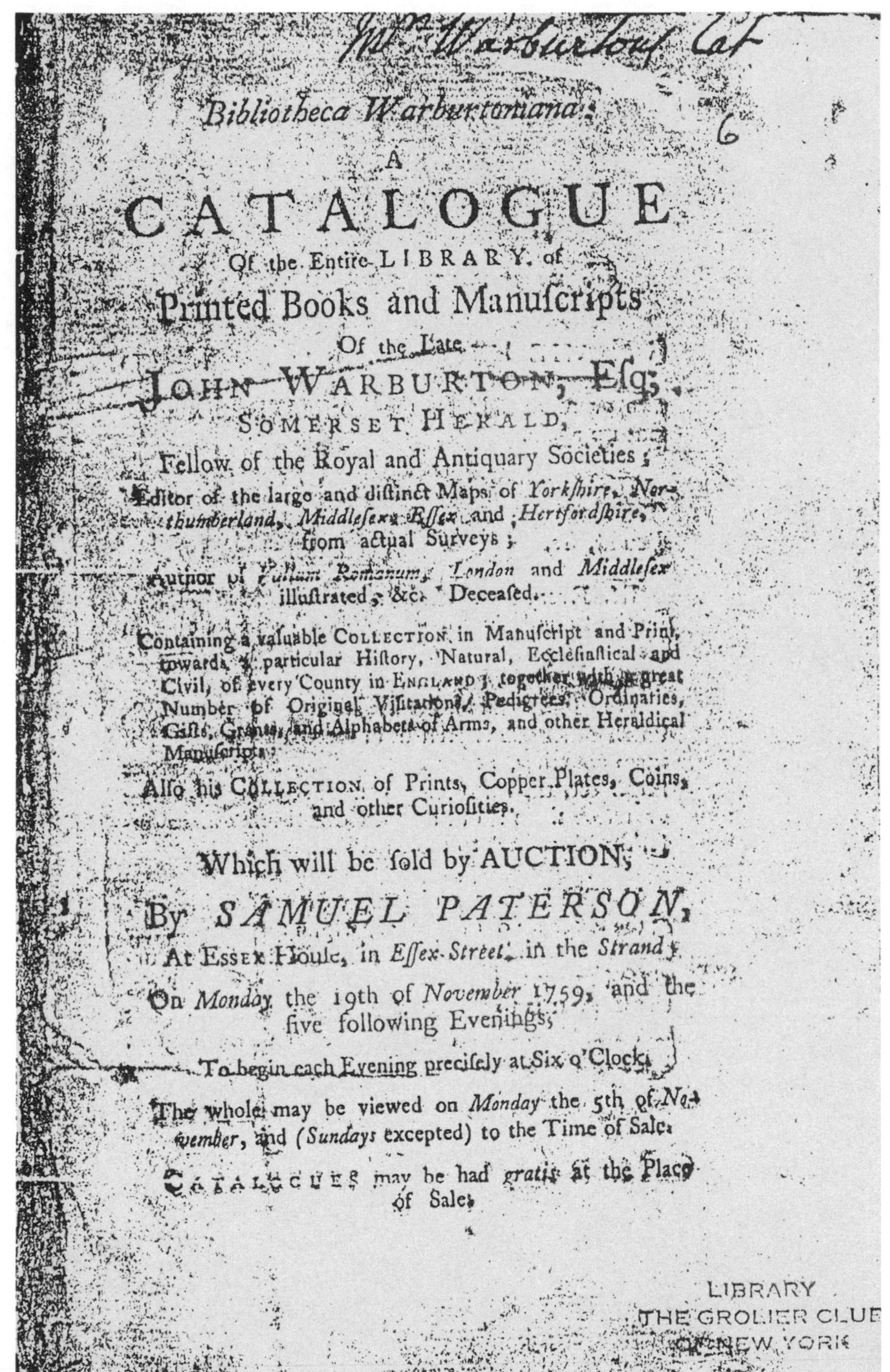

Mr. Warburton's Cat

Bibliotheca Warburtoniana:

A

CATALOGUE

Of the Entire LIBRARY of

Printed Books and Manuscripts

Of the Late

JOHN WARBURTON, Esq;

SOMERSET HERALD,

Fellow of the Royal and Antiquary Societies;

Editor of the large and distinct Maps of *Yorkshire*, *Northumberland*, *Middlesex*, *Essex* and *Hertfordshire*, from actual Surveys;

Author of *Vallum Romanum*, *London* and *Middlesex* illustrated, &c. Deceased.

Containing a valuable COLLECTION in Manuscript and Print, towards a particular History, Natural, Ecclesiastical and Civil, of every County in ENGLAND; together with a great Number of Original Visitations, Pedigrees, Ordinaries, Gifts, Grants, and Alphabets of Arms, and other Heraldical Manuscripts:

Also his COLLECTION of Prints, Copper Plates, Coins, and other Curiosities.

Which will be sold by AUCTION,

By *SAMUEL PATERSON*,

At ESSEX House, in *Essex-Street*, in the *Strand*;

On *Monday* the 19th of *November* 1759, and the five following Evenings;

To begin each Evening precisely at Six o'Clock.

The whole may be viewed on *Monday* the 5th of *November*, and (*Sundays* excepted) to the Time of Sale.

CATALOGUES may be had *gratis* at the Place of Sale.

Title page of the Warburton catalogue in which *Cardenio*, or *The Second Maiden's Tragedy* was put on the auction block, November 19, 1759 (Grolier Club Library, New York).

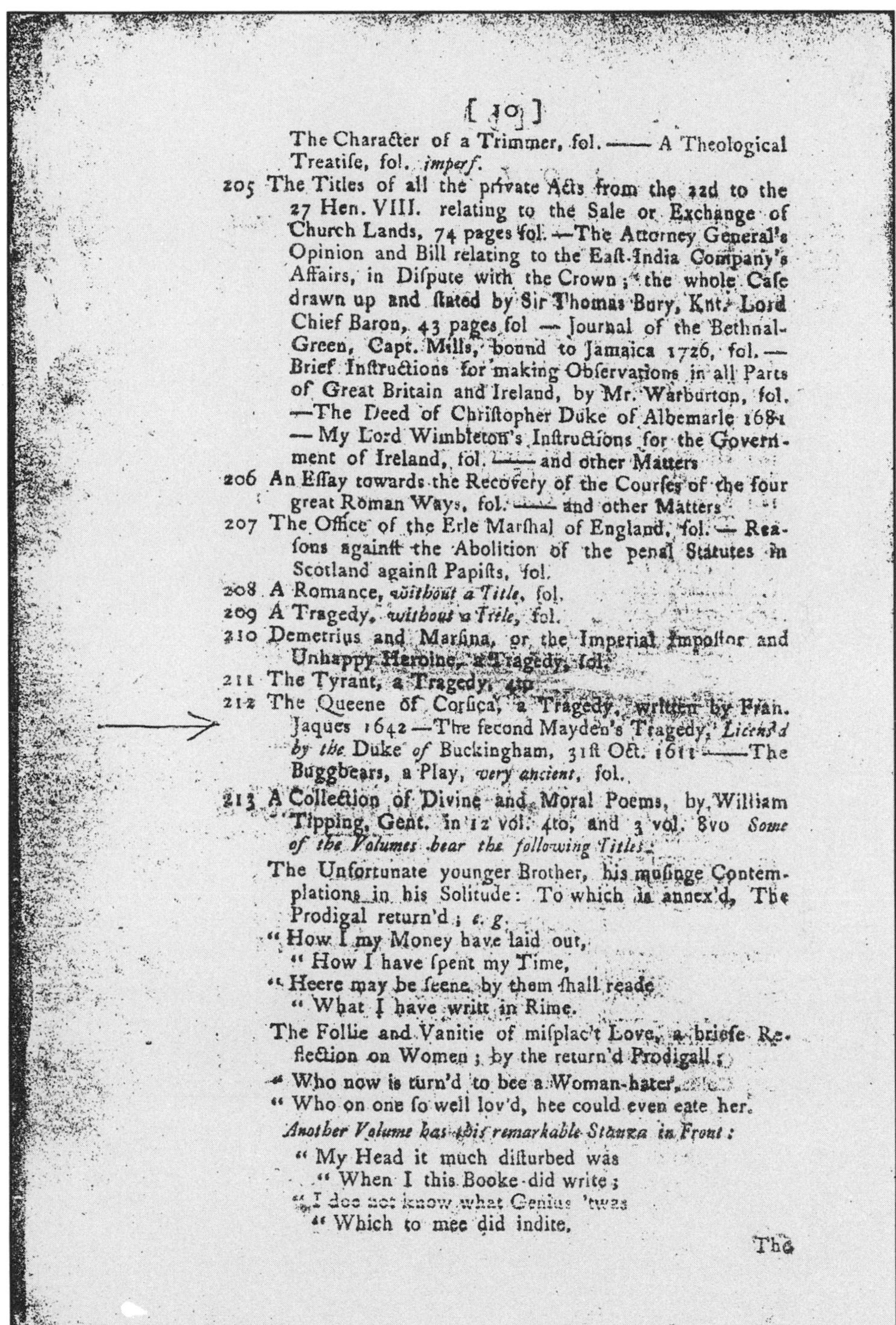

[10]

The Character of a Trimmer, fol. —— A Theological Treatiſe, fol. *imperf.*

205 The Titles of all the private Acts from the 22d to the 27 Hen. VIII. relating to the Sale or Exchange of Church Lands, 74 pages fol. —The Attorney General's Opinion and Bill relating to the Eaſt-India Company's Affairs, in Diſpute with the Crown; the whole Caſe drawn up and ſtated by Sir Thomas Bury, Knt. Lord Chief Baron, 43 pages fol — Journal of the Bethnal-Green, Capt. Mills, bound to Jamaica 1726, fol. — Brief Inſtructions for making Obſervations in all Parts of Great Britain and Ireland, by Mr. Warburton, fol. —The Deed of Chriſtopher Duke of Albemarle 1681 — My Lord Wimbleton's Inſtructions for the Government of Ireland, fol. —— and other Matters

206 An Eſſay towards the Recovery of the Courſes of the four great Roman Ways, fol. —— and other Matters

207 The Office of the Erle Marſhal of England, fol. — Reaſons againſt the Abolition of the penal Statutes in Scotland againſt Papiſts, fol.

208 A Romance, *without a Title*, fol.

209 A Tragedy, *without a Title*, fol.

210 Demetrius and Marſina, or the Imperial Impoſtor and Unhappy Heroine, a Tragedy, fol.

211 The Tyrant, a Tragedy, 4to

212 The Queene of Corſica, a Tragedy, written by Fran. Jaques 1642 —The ſecond Mayden's Tragedy, *Licens'd by the* Duke *of* Buckingham, 31ſt Oct. 1611 ——The Buggbears, a Play, *very ancient*, fol.

213 A Collection of Divine and Moral Poems, by William Tipping, Gent. in 12 vol. 4to, and 3 vol. 8vo *Some of the Volumes bear the following Titles*:

The Unfortunate younger Brother, his muſinge Contemplations in his Solitude: To which is annex'd, The Prodigal return'd; *e. g.*

"How I my Money have laid out,
" How I have ſpent my Time,
" Heere may be ſeene, by them ſhall reade
" What I have writt in Rime.

The Follie and Vanitie of miſplac't Love, a briefe Reflection on Women; by the return'd Prodigall;

" Who now is turn'd to bee a Woman-hater,
" Who on one ſo well lov'd, hee could even eate her.

Another Volume has this remarkable Stanza in Front:

" My Head it much diſturbed was
" When I this Booke did write;
" I doe not know what Genius 'twas
" Which to mee did indite.

The

Lot 212 in the Warburton Auction catalogue in which Sir George Buc, the licenser or censor, is erroneously alluded to by the cataloguer as "*The* Duke *of* Buckingham" (Grolier Club Library, New York).

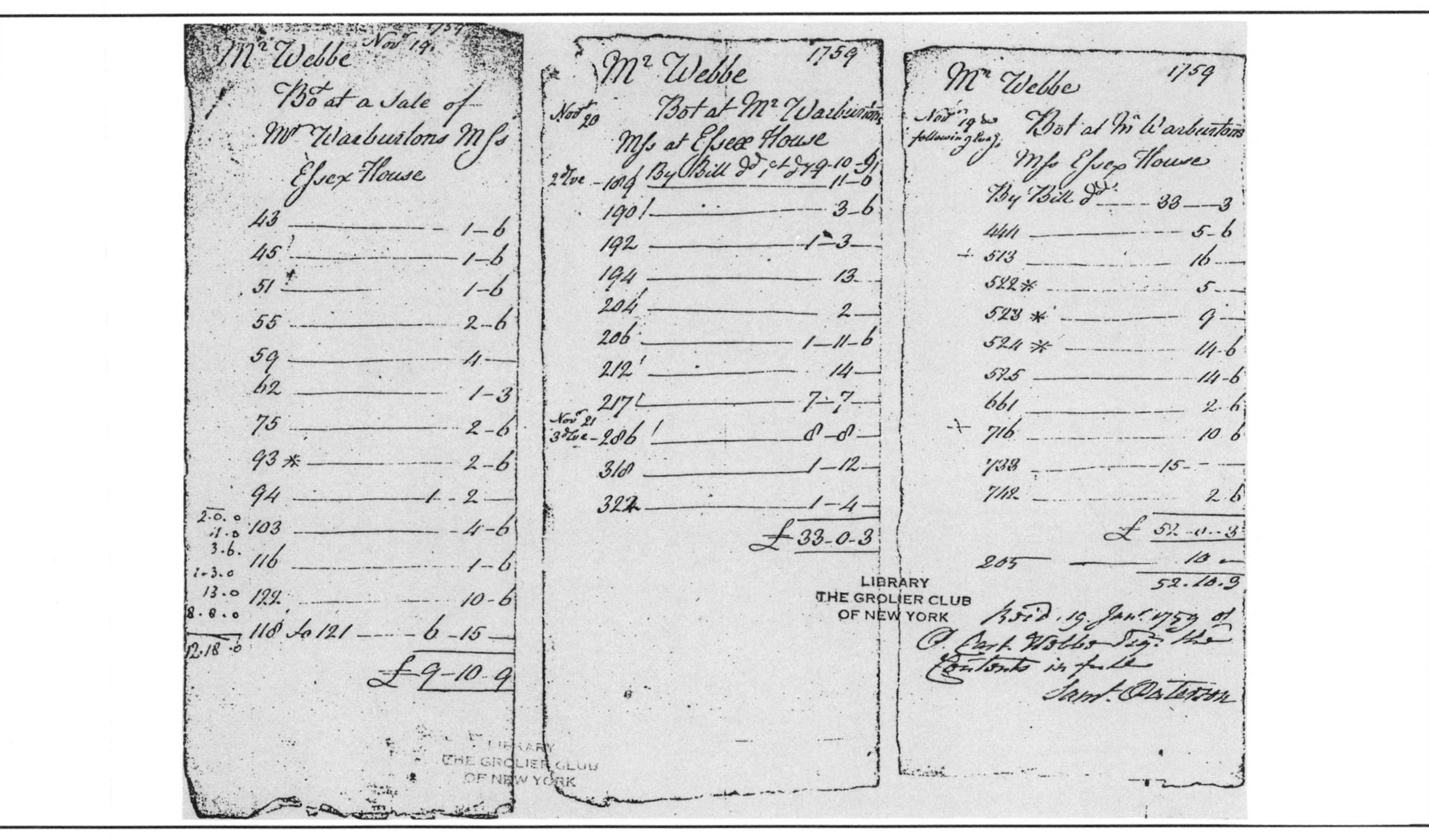

Mr Webbe Nov 14. 1759
Bot at a Sale of
Mr Warburtons Mss
Essex House

43	1-6
45	1-6
51	1-6
55	2-6
59	4-
62	1-3
75	2-6
93 *	2-6
94	1-2-
103	4-6
116	1-6
122	10-6
118 to 121	6-15-
	£9-10-9

2.0.0
11.0
3.6.
1.3.0
13.0
8.8.0
12.18.0

Mr Webbe 1759
Nov 20 Bot at Mr Warburtons
Mss at Essex House

2d Ove - 189 By Bill do, at £79-10-9	11-0
190	3-6
192	1-3-
194	13-
204	2-
206	1-11-6
212	14-
217	7-7-
Nov 21 3d Ove - 286	8-8-
310	1-12-
322	1-4-
	£33-0-3

Mr Webbe 1759
Nov 19 & following days Bot at Mr Warburtons
Mss Essex House

By Bill do	33-3
444	5-6
+ 513	16-
522 *	5-
523 *	9-
524 *	14-6
525	14-6
661	2-6
+ 716	10-6
738	15-
748	2-6
	£52-0-3
205	10-
	52.10.3

Recd 19 Jan 1759 of
P. Cart. Webb Esq. the
Contents in full
Saml Paterson

Bill for one of the biggest literary bargains of all time. Philip Carteret Webb buys the original manuscript of *Cardenio* or *The Second Maiden's Tragedy* for only fourteen shillings! See Lot 212 (Grolier Club Library, New York).

CHAPTER II

THE PALEOGRAPHIC EVIDENCE

Part 1. The Lodestar: Shakespeare's Will

The lodestar to all of Shakespeare's handwriting is his last will and testament. For many years it was assumed, upon no evidence whatsoever, that when Shakespeare decided to write his will, he sent for his attorney, Francis Collins. At Shakespeare's dictation, it was said, Collins or his clerk penned the will for the testator.[1] My repudiation of this venerable fiction is based upon the fact that Collins's script is in the modern round hand, much like we write today, and Shakespeare's will is in "the secretary hand," unreadable except to Renaissance paleographers. Collins was, however, called upon to witness the publishing, or announcing, of the will. As for Collins's clerk, believed by some scholars to have penned the will of Shakespeare's close friend, John Combe, as well as Shakespeare's will, his meticulous script is totally different from the handwriting in Shakespeare's will.

Shakespeare's will is, in fact, a rough draft that the dramatist never lived to recopy. It is written in two different scripts, both of them Shakespeare's. The entire three-page draft was first penned by the dramatist in a very legible, handsome hand at a time when, as Shakespeare stated, he was "in perfect health & Memorie." A few months later, Shakespeare decided to revise the will, still unsigned, possibly to disinherit his daughter Judith. During the rewrite, about two-thirds of the way down the first page, he apparently suffered a stroke, from which he later made a partial recovery. His subsequent script, enfeebled and tremulous, was written on the balance of page one, with two lines at the top of page two, and with some scattered interlinear additions.

Three distinguished medical experts, one of them Dr. Michael Baden, former chief medical examiner of New York City and world famous forensic pathologist who was in charge of the exhumation and examination of John F. Kennedy's body, studied the handwriting at my request. All three concurred that the writer had suffered a stroke while in the act of writing the will. These forensic experts were unanimous that the script, strong and firm at the start of page one, had, after about fifteen lines, begun a gradual deterioration until the words became smeary and broken, a jumble of blots, at which time the penman temporarily ceased to write. Dr. Michael Baden, who was told the identity of the writer, said to me: "The script of Shakespeare in his will follows precisely the pattern of poison or stroke victims. Such writing begins with vigor and full motor control and line by line disintegrates until it becomes smudged and illegible, at which time the writer is unable to continue. Later, as we see, Shakespeare made a partial recovery from his stroke and resumed writing. His subsequent additions to the will are very shaky and look almost like the handwriting of another person."

At the very conclusion of his will, Shakespeare wrote, *By me William Shakspear.* He may have written this signature (and two other almost indecipherable signatures on pages one and two of the will) on the day of his death. The terminal signature, a tiny, quavery scrawl, which rises at the end, tells us that the testator was writing while propped up in bed. As a forensic document examiner, I have studied and reported on thousands of documents every year, many of them disputed wills. Document experts agree that most signatures signed by bedridden testators move upwards in the final strokes because of the great difficulty the recumbent signer has in sustaining his arm or hand in the proper position to write horizontally.

The stark difference between the enfeebled signature at the end of the will and the bold handwriting of Shakespeare, written a few months earlier, just above it, has led a few paleographers to conclude that the handwriting in the body of the will and the signature at the end were penned by different individuals. A careful examination proves the contrary. Both handwritings are by the same individual.

If you are curious as to why a dying man who could barely write his name—the labor was so great that Shakespeare was unable to form the final letters of it—should preface his signature with *By me*, two apparently redundant words, each letter of which must have caused him much effort in the writing, it is because these two words are of great significance. According to legal experts, they indicate that the entire document is in the handwriting of the signer. During the course of my career I have handled over two million documents, many of which bore signatures preceded with *By me* or *Per me*, and I do not recall any document with those prefatory words that was not entirely in the hand of the signer. You will find other signatures of this type illustrated later in this chapter.

A few scholars have questioned the authenticity of Shakespeare's will on the grounds that the language is not that of a great poet, but is trite, repetitive, and apparently ungrammatical. The plain fact is that a will, like any other legal instrument, must follow a prescribed form and be indited in a prescribed language. Any deviation might delay probate indefinitely. Virtually all lawyers who have studied Shakespeare's will have pronounced it a document written with superb accuracy and precision, exactly as the law demands. Had Shakespeare waxed poetic and used some eloquent phrase such as "after I have departed for that undiscovered country from whose bourn no traveler returns" instead of "after my deceas [decease]," which even today is the legal term for *death*, his will might still be awaiting probate.

From the legal point of view, Shakespeare's will is expertly phrased, with correct terminology and accurate syntax. Permit me to offer in evidence a few remarks by one of the greatest legal minds of the nineteenth century:

> Lord Campbell, chief justice of the queen's bench and lord chancellor of England, wrote in 1859: "Among Shakespeare's writings, I think that attention should be paid to his WILL, for, upon a careful perusal, it will be found to have been in all probability composed by himself. It seems much too simple, terse, and condensed, to have been the composition of a Stratford attorney, who was to be paid by the number of lines which it contained. But a testator, without professional experience, could hardly have used language so appropriate as we find in this will, to express his meaning. . ." Lord Campbell praises Shakespeare's legal background, noting that the poet had "a deep technical knowledge of the law" and an easy familiarity with "some of the most abstruse proceedings in English jurisprudence." With regard to Shakespeare's "judicial phrases and forensic allusions," Lord Campbell observes: "I am amazed, not only by their number, but by the accuracy and propriety with which they are uniformly introduced."[2]

Some scholars have considered it unusual that Shakespeare made no mention of his books and literary property in his will. Why should he? Judging from the sources he is known to have used, his library contained mainly utility books that would be readily available and not prized for their rarity. Shakespeare was not a scholarly man. He was certainly not an avid bibliomaniac like his friend Ben Jonson, who at his death left a host of books bearing his diminutive signature, some of which still crop up on the rare book market from time to time. Consider, also, the possibility that Shakespeare may have left by oral bequest much or all of his library to his brilliant son-in-law, Dr. John Hall (who later refused a knighthood) or his close friend and *soi-disant* cousin, Thomas Greene, an amateur poet who had for some time lived in Shakespeare's home, New Place.

As for literary bequests, what did Shakespeare own that possessed any value? Nothing. It is believed by most scholars that prior to his death Shakespeare had disposed of his shares in *The Globe* and *Blackfriars*, the two playhouses with which he was associated. Of course, the rights to publish or perform Shakespeare's plays had always belonged to the King's Men, never to Shakespeare, and except as a stockholder, Shakespeare had no vested interest in them.

It is probable that Shakespeare received very few if any royalties from his poetry. He lived in the great age of patronage. Poets without a patron often faced starvation or were forced to seek hackwork on Grub Street. Shakespeare's patron was the youthful earl of Southampton. Both of Shakespeare's great narrative poems, *Venus and Adonis* (1593) and *The Rape of Lucrece* (1594) were dedicated to Southampton, who no doubt compensated the poet by a pouch of golden crowns or some other valuable gift. But that was two decades earlier. When Shakespeare wrote his will in 1616, both poems were long out-of-date classics with little or no commercial value. As for Shakespeare's *Sonnets* (1609), they were apparently printed without the poet's permission and quickly suppressed, judging from the great rarity of copies today.

Shakespeare's income at the time of his death was derived almost exclusively from his real estate holdings, and it was these properties that he dealt with in his will, a document largely slanted toward creating a male heir.

The three tremulous signatures on Shakespeare's will, plus three other widely known signatures of Shakespeare, all of them different, have inspired a few ridiculous speculations about the dramatist's lack of formal education. The truth is that the handwriting of many famous Elizabethans is so wretchedly indited that it may require hours for an expert paleographer to make out a single hard-to-decipher word, or pin down with certainty a hastily penned signature. The writing style of some noted individuals, such as Queen Elizabeth I and Francis Bacon, differed almost from document to document. In the section on the handwriting of Shakespeare and his contemporaries at the end of this chapter you will find numerous examples of erratic penmanship.

In accordance with the custom of his era, Shakespeare often varied his spelling, including the writing of his name—Shagspear (in his holograph marriage bond), Shakespeare, Shakespere, Shakespear, Shackspeare and so on. If we had more of the handwriting of Shakespeare's great contemporary, Christopher Marlowe, I am sure we would find the same range of spelling. He is mentioned in documents of his era as *Marlow* and *Marlin*, and in his only surviving signature he signs himself *Christofer Marley.* There was, of course, no standard way to spell *Shakespeare,* so it was up to the writer, whether the dramatist himself or a clerk, to devise a suitable phonetic rendition. The inconsistent orthography of Shakespeare has given hope and solace to the scholars who contend that Shakespeare was a semiliterate rustic who could not even spell his own name. This belief, based upon an egregious ignorance of the writing and spelling in the Elizabethan era, is untenable.

In connection with the anti-Stratfordians (those who disbelieve in Shakespeare's authorship) I cannot resist quoting a brilliant paragraph from one of the world's leading experts on Shakespeare, Professor S. Schoenbaum:

> In certain recurring features of anti-Stratfordian behavior we may discern a pattern of psychopathology. The heretic's revulsion against the provincial and lowly; his exaltation of his hero (and, through identification, himself) by furnishing him with an aristocratic, even royal, pedigree; his paranoid structures of thought, embracing the classic paraphernalia of persecution: secrets, curses, conspiracies; the compulsion to dig in churches, castles, river beds, and tombs; the autohypnosis, spirit visitations, and other hallucinatory phenomena; the descent, in a few cases, into actual madness—all these manifestations of the uneasy psyche suggest that the movement calls not so much for the expertise of the literary historian as for the insight of the psychiatrist. Dr. Freud beckons us.[3]

The work of the forensic document examiner is today considered a science in all courts of law. In fact, some judges and juries place more reliance on handwriting evidence than on fingerprint evidence. When testifying as a document expert in criminal cases, I have at times convinced a jury or judge that a careful handwriting analysis is more valid than opposition police eyewitness and fingerprint evidence that told a contrary story. The simple fact is that there is approximately the same possibility of finding two identical handwritings as there is of finding two identical sets of fingerprints.

One of the reasons—perhaps the most important reason—why all handwriting is different is because the format of a person's script is mainly determined by genes rather than chirographic training. Presume, for example, that one thousand individuals were educated to write in an absolutely identical fashion. Within a few months after their instructions ceased, their scripts would already have acquired obvious differences and personal touches. Certain tiny curlicues, quirks, and pen pressures would speedily develop, for a person's handwriting is inevitably as distinctive as his walk, facial structure, intellectual capacity, or voice box. Script, for an expert, is as easy to recognize as a voice. Frank Sinatra's handwriting (more varied than Shakespeare's) is distinctively his own, just like his voice. Enrico Caruso's script is as unmistakable as his golden tones. It would be impossible to counterfeit perfectly the handwriting or voice of either man.

In my earlier book about Shakespeare I demonstrated that Shakespeare's will was indited in his own hand by removing individual letters, or small parts of words, from a photocopy of the will and constructing from them replicas of the six undisputed signatures of Shakespeare.[4] This was a difficult task, because I had only two-and-a-half pages of Shakespeare's script in the will to work with, and part of this was written when the dramatist was near death and his scrawl was almost indecipherable. But I realized, as I hope you shall, that Shakespeare's will was a Rosetta stone that might lead us to hundreds of important discoveries about the life and work of the world's supreme poet. Other than in Shakespeare's will, and in a few other documents in the same hand that I subsequently identified and illustrated,[5] there was to the best of my knowledge no script in Stratford, or in Warwickshire, or in England, or in the entire world of Shakespeare's day, from which individual letters could be abstracted to reconstruct so successfully his six genuine signatures. The original signatures and reconstructions are illustrated in this chapter.

In the manuscript of *Cardenio* or *The Second Maiden's Tragedy,* written in the identical secretary script as his will, Shakespeare has also used two other styles of penmanship. There is the regular secretary hand for the body of the manuscript, italics for speech prefixes, songs and stage directions, and an ornate Latin italic lettering to designate the acts.

Shakespeare's pen lopes over the foolscap with an easy grace. His impatience to set down his thoughts leads to little errors in spelling, a fine disregard for punctuation, and, most disconcerting of all, a frequent delinquency in sharpening his quill. The dull nib causes his *a*'s and *o*'s and *e*'s to fill with ink. At other times, when the ink grows sparse in the nib and the hasting dramatist will not pause to dip his quill, his writing gets thin and anemic. Tiny portions of letters are transformed into gossamer threads.

In his edition of *The Second Maiden's Tragedy* Sir Walter W. Greg writes: "The manuscript is in the hand of a scribe who was an adept with the pen. . . The text, as we have it, is a fair copy of the author's rough draft."[6] For neither of these important assertions does Greg offer any proof or evidence. However, as Greg was, in effect, issuing a *promulgatio ex cathedra*, he expected his remarks to be accepted without question and with no supporting evidence. Accepted they were, and for more than eighty years they have passed as gospel. In fact, Sir Walter had reasons for his opinion. The handwriting is a handsome script and looks like what an amateur in chirography, as was Greg, might expect from a scribe. Further, it was not recognizable as any literary hand that Greg or any other scholar could recall. Finally, the textual emendations and deletions and additional bits of paper affixed to the manuscript led Greg to what undoubtedly seemed to him a valid conclusion—that the manuscript was a copy of a rough draft. To his initial reactions, Greg added: "The scribe's spelling is generally good; the punctuation, on the other hand, both deficient and irregular."[7]

Subsequent editors of *The Second Maiden's Tragedy* have endorsed Greg's remarks. Professor Anne Lancashire included a cautionary phrase: "The hand, no other extant examples of which have yet been found, is clear and professional. . . The scribe writes a beautiful, clear secretary hand, with Italian hand used for stage directions, speech headings, act divisions, songs and proper names within the text itself."[8] Another editor of the play, Harold L. Stenger, Jr., paid tribute to the beauty of the chirography: "The text of the play is written in a cursive English secretary hand remarkably free from eccentricity, while the stage directions, and such special portions as the two interpolated songs are done by the same scribe in an Italian hand of singular exquisiteness. The two songs. . .give almost the effect of copperplate engraving."[9]

Greg faced an interesting problem with the *Cardenio* manuscript. He was puzzled that the textual corrections were in the same "scribal" hand as that of the entire manuscript. He found it impossible to reconcile the creative nature of the changes, all of which admittedly improved the play, with the menial function of a scribe. However, Greg refused to admit that the script was authorial since he could not identify the writer. On the other hand, Stenger was convinced that the manuscript corrections merely indicated that the scribe had been inept. He noted that "the evidence points almost inevitably to the conclusion that this manuscript represents a scribal copy. . ."[10] and he cites "certain verbal misreadings. . .which a creative writer could not possibly make,"[11] such as errors in stage directions and spelling like *discontedly* for *discontentedly*, *shame* for *same* and others similar. From my own experience, after examining thousands of original manuscripts of authors, I have concluded that the usual marks of a creative writer in a fine frenzy are deletions, misspellings, and failure to punctuate properly, if at all. Heminges and Condell, who may have submitted Shakespeare's original manuscripts to the printer without recopying them, wrote of the dramatist in their preface to *The First Folio*: "His mind and hand went together, and what he thought, he uttered with that easyness that we have scarce received from him a blot in his papers."[12] As you look at the original pages and writing of Shakespeare illustrated in this chapter, please notice that even after the mauling and corrections made during the transformation of his manuscript into a prompt copy, his pages are clean and fresh and beautiful to behold, precisely as described by Heminges and Condell (and Ben Jonson, also, many years later).

The invention of an inspired scribe who made corrections that improved the play was forced upon Greg and other scholars who insisted that *Cardenio* or *The Second Maiden's Tragedy* is in a clerical hand. The corrections, both interlinear and marginal, are clearly authorial, and it logically follows that the entire manuscript is in the hand of the author. To attribute highly important textual changes, all of which improved the play, to a clever scribe is an easy way to avoid taking a position on the author's identity. This sort of unscholarly solution was also attempted in the case of the celebrated Langleat page that contains an illustration from *Titus Andronicus*. A few experts in drama, apparently eager for an answer to the *raison d'être* of the page, sought to explain it as the work of an inspired playgoer who dashed off two lines of blank verse to provide a transition for a disjointed text he had allegedly taken down during a performance of *Titus*. My own view is that the fragmented text and detailed drawing were prepared to suggest the stage set and costumes for a possible production of the play.[13]

One factor that eased a comparison between the handwriting in Shakespeare's will and the handwriting in *Cardenio* is that the documents were written only about five or six years apart. Despite the will's brevity, I was able to find at least one example of every letter in the alphabet for comparison with the words in the play manuscript. There were some minor difficulties. The vocabulary in the play is literary; the vocabulary in the will is legal. This curtailed the number of similar words for comparison. Also, Shakespeare's habit of writing with a blunt-nibbed quill eliminated as prospects for comparison a number of similar words and letters that might otherwise have been suitable, since an unsharpened quill (or a very sharp quill) often alters the visual appearance of handwriting.

From a strictly scientific point of view, there is powerful evidence against the supposition that there could be two identical handwritings in the world. The famous American astronomer and professor of mathematics at Johns Hopkins University, Simon Newcomb (1835-1909), devised a formula for determining the mathematical probability for recurrence of events, such as the recurrence of idiosyncrasies in scripts: "The probability of concurrence of all the events is equal to the continued produce of the probabilities of all the separate events." Scientists have recently applied this formula to the twelve elementary procedures used by most forensic document examiners: movement, embellishment, terminal and initial strokes, writing skill, size of writing, slant, shape, spacing, shading (important in quill penmanship), speed, connective strokes and overall form. The result? They found that the probability of discovering these twelve distinctive characteristics as they exist in Shakespeare's handwriting in the handwriting of another individual is one chance in 241,140,625. However, if we add another twelve procedures, such as many forensic document experts employ, including myself, the probability of Shakespeare's will and *The Second Maiden's Tragedy* being written by two separate individuals, instead of the same individual (in this case, Shakespeare) is one chance in 55,844,879,025,390,625. For more particulars, see Albert S. Osborn's *Questioned Documents* (2nd ed., Albany: 1929, pp. 226-27, 350.).

Based upon a careful comparison of the handwriting in the will of Shakespeare and the handwriting in *Cardenio* or *The Second Maiden's Tragedy,* I am convinced beyond all doubt that both documents were written by the same individual and that individual was William Shakespeare.

There are, besides Shakespeare's, three other early handwritings in the manuscript promptbook of *Cardenio*. One hand is clearly that of the stage assistant who wrote directions for the actors and musicians in the margin. Another is that of the censor, George Buc. The fourth hand may be that of another stage assistant.

Shakespeare's will. The bottom half of the first page, revealing Shakespeare's powerful, clear script at the top, the breakdown of the handwriting and, finally, near the center, the smeary, blotted script that marks his stroke. Beneath this blotted portion appears Shakespeare's handwriting after his stroke, shaky and far more difficult to read. The quill does not seem to obey the writer's commands. During the writing of this quarter of a page in Shakespeare's enfeebled script, the writing gradually degenerates and the final two lines on the page are extremely difficult to decipher.

The stage assistant's marginal directions are boldly penned in a hand that looks very much like that of Ralph Crane, a professional scribe. I am indebted to *William Shakespeare: a Textual Companion*, a most useful work by Stanley Wells and Gary Taylor, for their interesting account of Crane and his variant scripts.[14] A comparison of Crane's script in the illustration that appears in *William Shakespeare: a Textual Companion* with the script in the margins of *Cardenio* shows that the size, slant, pen pressure, ink flow and many letters are very similar.[15]

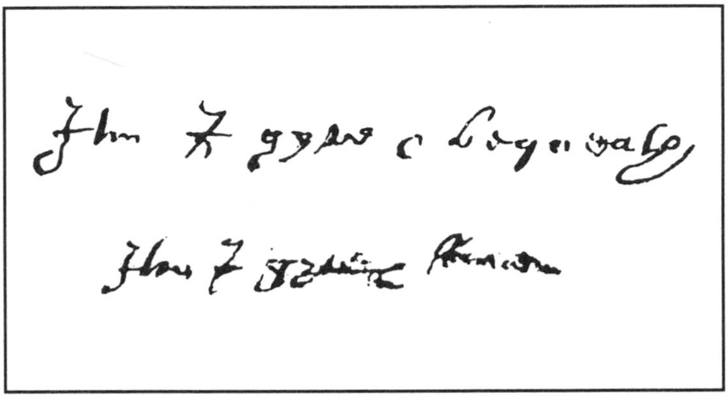

Shakespeare's script before and after his stroke. The standard legal phrase, *It [e]m I gyve & bequeath*, often repeated in the dramatist's will, was (at top) written in a very clear "secretary hand" when Shakespeare had perfect motor control (page two, line seven). The bottom line (last five words on page one) was written after Shakespeare's stroke. The ampersand, which looks like the letter *C*, is joined to the word *gyve* and the word *bequeath* is virtually indecipherable. (Both exemplars actual size.)

Third (and last) page of Shakespeare's will. This final page of Shakespeare's will was penned when he was in good health, but the interlinear note between lines eight and nine, "Itm I gyve unto my wief my second best bed with the furniture" is the same enfeebled script as his signature, affixed when he was bedridden, possibly on the day of his death.

Handwriting of Francis Collins compared with the script in Shakespeare's will.

(a) Francis Collins's name as it appears twice in Shakespeare's will, penned in the dramatist's secretary hand.

(b) Notation, "witness to the publishing hereof," in Shakespeare's enfeebled hand, identical with the after-stroke script in the will. The deceptive visual resemblance between Shakespeare's notation and Collins's signature is caused by the similarity in ink intensity. Very possibly Collins used Shakespeare's quill. Collins's signature indicates that he could not have written the easy, flowing first draft of Shakespeare's will or the fragmented, broken almost illegible interlinear additions. Collins's script is in the modern round hand, with every letter (except the faded *a* in *Fra*: and the faded terminal *s*) very legible, whereas Shakespeare's five-word note is in the secretary hand and unreadable to those who have not studied Renaissance paleography.

(c) Early signature of Francis Collins. Observe that the lawyer's script here, as on the will, is much easier to read than the "old-style" secretary hand used by Shakespeare. The poet employs the antiquated *ff* for *F* and the secretary *C* that looks like a dolled-up *O* or *D*. The minuscule letters are also different, especially the *y* in *Collyns*. Collins swings the tail of his *y* to the left, as in modern writing, and Shakespeare swings it to the right, as in the *By me* that appears with his signature at the end of the will. Collins uses the modern *r* and Shakespeare prefers the secretary *r* that resembles a *u* or a *v*. Collins's terminal *s* is modern. Shakespeare uses the secretary terminal *s* that looks like an *o* with a little tongue of ink flickering upward from its top.

(d) Early signature of Francis Collins, showing his abbreviated given name, *Fra*, also used in his signature on the will.

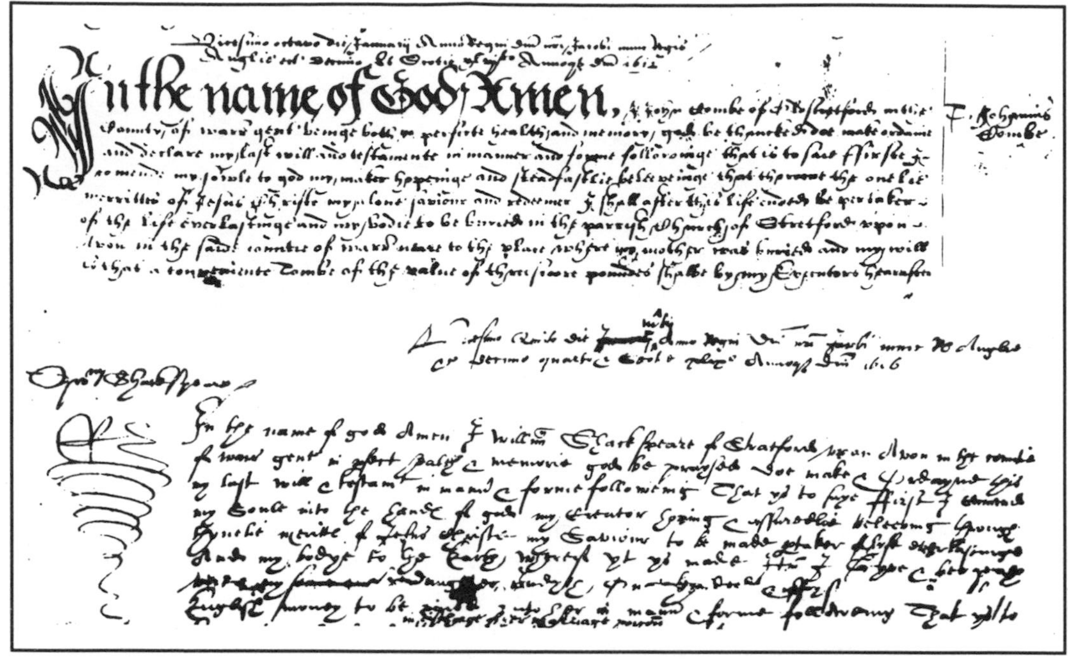
In the name of God Amen,

The writing in John Combe's will compared with the writing in Shakespeare's will. (Top) Latin exordium and first eight lines of John Combe's will, penned, so scholars say, by Francis Collins's clerk. (Bottom) The Latin exordium and first eight lines of Shakespeare's will, written in the dramatist's hand.

The nine-page will of John Combe is in the script of a professional scrivener, fastidiously penned. It contains no spelling or chirographic irregularities and no corrections. The script is totally different from Shakespeare's. The scribe who penned Combe's will wrote out the word *and*, with a *d* very different from Shakespeare's. The poet, in writing his will, used an ampersand instead of *and*. The key word *the* in the two scripts is also completely different.

Comparison of handwriting from John Combe's will, written by Collins's clerk, and Shakespeare's will, written in Shakespeare's hand.

(Top) Four lines from the manuscript of John Combe's will, allegedly by the clerk who also wrote Shakespeare's will. Combe's bequest of five pounds to Shakespeare is mentioned and Shakespeare's full name occurs as the first two words of the third line. I have examined a photocopy of the will, dated January 28, 1613, now in the Public Record Office, London, Prob. II/126, formerly in Somerset House, catalogued as *118 Wood* or *118 Rudd*. It bears no corrections of any kind and is a fair copy penned by a fluent scrivener. The sheets are numbered at the bottom in a modern hand.

(Bottom) Four lines from Shakespeare's will in which the dramatist's name appears (last word of the top line and first word of the second line). The handwriting in Shakespeare's will is completely different from that in John Combe's. Compare the writing of the name William Shakespeare (first two words of line three) as it appears in Combe's will with the poet's name in his own will.

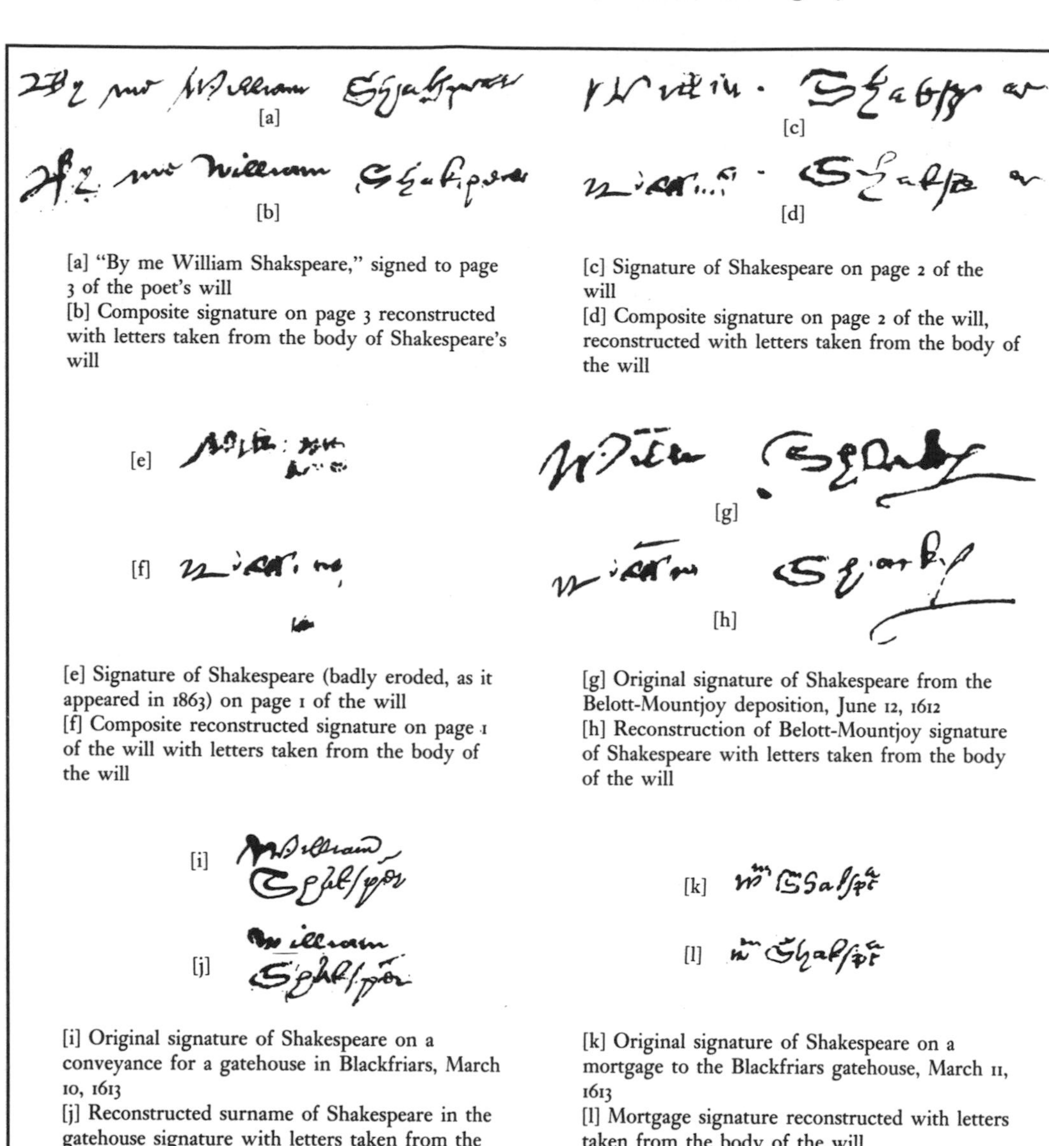

[a] "By me William Shakspeare," signed to page 3 of the poet's will
[b] Composite signature on page 3 reconstructed with letters taken from the body of Shakespeare's will

[c] Signature of Shakespeare on page 2 of the will
[d] Composite signature on page 2 of the will, reconstructed with letters taken from the body of the will

[e] Signature of Shakespeare (badly eroded, as it appeared in 1863) on page 1 of the will
[f] Composite reconstructed signature on page 1 of the will with letters taken from the body of the will

[g] Original signature of Shakespeare from the Belott-Mountjoy deposition, June 12, 1612
[h] Reconstruction of Belott-Mountjoy signature of Shakespeare with letters taken from the body of the will

[i] Original signature of Shakespeare on a conveyance for a gatehouse in Blackfriars, March 10, 1613
[j] Reconstructed surname of Shakespeare in the gatehouse signature with letters taken from the body of the will

[k] Original signature of Shakespeare on a mortgage to the Blackfriars gatehouse, March 11, 1613
[l] Mortgage signature reconstructed with letters taken from the body of the will

Shakespeare's authentic signatures duplicated. The top signature of each vertical pair is an undisputed signature of William Shakespeare. Beneath each of these six known-to-be-genuine signatures is a reconstruction taken from letters and words in the body of Shakespeare's holograph will. Because of the volatility and variety of Shakespeare's authentic signatures, it is impossible that such an accurate reconstruction could be made from any other known Elizabethan handwriting.

Modern variant handwriting. Clearly the random usage of variant signatures was not confined to the Elizabethan era. For example, consider the following: The five signatures above were all signed by Harvard-educated John Kennedy, who rarely signed his name the same way twice. Shakespeare's signatures are less capricious and more legible than Kennedy's! Even more baffling are the signatures of Richard Nixon. Below are a few from official documents bearing his signature as president.

Manuscript page from *Cardenio* or *The Second Maiden's Tragedy* (IV, iv, 1708-62). Disclosed here is Shakespeare's method of writing speech prefixes, introducing scenes, his handsome secretarial script, and his Italian hand. All of the handwriting on this page is Shakespeare's except for the marginal note, *Enter Lady/Rich Robinson,* which is probably in the hand of a stage assistant.

and of all that

in his would by

to is in no so

can bodie for go

Words from Shakespeare's will compared with words from *Cardenio* or *The Second Maiden's Tragedy*. The top word of each vertical pair was taken from Shakespeare's holograph will. The bottom word was taken from the text of *Cardenio*. Note the almost identical placement of *i*-dots in the words *in* and *is*. The position of *i*-dots in certain commonly used words is regarded as of paramount importance in forensic document examination.

A A a b b C c d d e e

F (ff) f g h I i k l m

n o p q r r S s sh ss

st T t th u v w x y z

Shakespeare's alphabet in his holograph Will (1616) compared with *Cardenio* alphabet (1611). The top letter of each vertical pair was removed from words in Shakespeare's two-and-one-half page will. The bottom letter of each pair was removed from words in the original manuscript of *Cardenio*. Variant letters are included. According to Professor Simon Newcomb's classic laws of probability, the mathematical odds against two different individuals having a script with this high degree of similarity are astronomical.

88. The witch

Hec. Put-in againe

1. the Juice-of Toad: the oile of Adder

2. those will make the yonker madder.

Hec. Put in: ther's all. and rid the stinch.

Fire. nay heere's three ounces of the red-haird wench.

all Round: around: around &c. /

Hec. so: so: enough: into the vessell with it

there 't hath the true perfection: I am so light

at any mischief: there's no villanie

but is a tune me-thinkes

Fire. A tune: 'tis to the tune of damnation then: I warrant

you: and that song hath a villanous Burthen.

Hec. Come, my sweet Sisters: let the Aire strike our tune

whilst we show reverence to yond peeping Moone. — here they Daunce ye witches Dance & Exit.

Scena 3a. Enter L. Governor, Isabella, Antonio, Florida, Francisca, Abberzanes, Gaspero, Hermio:

Is. My Lord, I have given you nothing but the truth

of a most plaine, and innocent intent.

My wrongs being so apparant, in this woman

(a Creature that robbs widdowhood of all comfort)

were

Manuscript page transcribed by Ralph Crane from Thomas Middleton's *The Witch* (1619-27). Bodleian Library, Ms. Malone 12, 88.

Similarity between stage directions in Ralph Crane's transcript of *The Witch* and in *Cardenio* or *The Second Maiden's Tragedy.*

At top: Three lines of stage directions in the hand of Ralph Crane, c. 1619-27. Bottom: Four stage directions from the holograph manuscript of *Cardenio* or *The Second Maiden's Tragedy.*

Although approximately a decade separates these two script exemplars, and the top exemplar was likely penned leisurely at a desk and the bottom one probably in the bustle of a stage rehearsal, there is a distinct similarity in the handwriting.

In the bottom exemplar, compare the *A* in *A florish* with the *A* of *Abberzanos* at top (line two, word three). Compare the *lori* of *florish* with the *lori* in *Florida* at top (line two, word one). Compare the *n* and *r* of *Enter Lady/Rich Robino* at bottom with the *n* and *r* in *Enter* at top (line one, word three).

Further, compare the *b* of *Robino* with the *b*'s in *Abberzanos* at top (line two, word three). They are identical. Compare the *a* in 4^a at top (line one, word two) with the *a* in *Lady* in *Enter Lady* at bottom. Other letters that are similar in both exemplars are *S* and *u*.

Finally, note the terminal downward flourish in *musick* (last word in the bottom line) and the terminal stroke on the *z* in *Abberzanos* at top (line two, word three). They are the same in pressure and curve.

THE PALEOGRAPHIC EVIDENCE

Part 2. Handwriting of Shakespeare and His Contemporaries

Handwriting speaks to us eloquently. Let parchment and paper be wrinkled, crinkled, faded, torn, stained, even brutalized by vulgar fingers, it is still the most powerful entry we have into the past. A few scribbles on paper often outlast marble and brass, and letters and documents are the cohesive forces that pull all knowledge together to recreate an era for us.

The vast array of handwriting presented here will help you, should it be your pleasure, to become acquainted with the varieties and vagaries of Elizabethan scripts. By comparing anonymous manuscripts with the exemplars in this section, you may be able to discover the identity of the writers.

In gathering exemplars over the years, I was able to ferret out many names that will be familiar only to lovers of arcane Elizabethan literature. Here you may examine the penmanship of scores of authors, great and small, whales and minnows. Like as not, you will find your favorites. Some there are, like John Lyly, rough sailing even on a breezy day, and others, like Thomas Dekker, often a bosom companion of my evenings when I had world enough and time to explore the underbelly of London with him. Many outstanding names are absent from the roll—Francis Beaumont, Robert Greene, Cyril Tourneur, and John Webster. We have no undisputed exemplars from their quills, so we must rest content with those writings we now possess until others are discovered. Until about two decades ago, there was not a pen scratch of Marlowe known to exist, but now we have a youthful signature. I have reconnoitered this signature a thousand times and tried to match its curlicues and twirls to whatever unsigned Elizabethan scribble was at hand. No luck yet, but I shall keep at it.

For all who wish to probe deeply into the Elizabethan and early Jacobean eras, this assemblage of handwritings, the largest and most complete ever formed, will be of great value. It will prove especially useful to all Shakespearean scholars who seek to look behind the scenes and search out fresh and exciting data on the great age of English drama. Of importance, too, are the multiple exemplars of leading personalities, like Shakespeare, Bacon, Sidney, Raleigh, Jonson, and others whose extraordinary achievements and intriguing personalities continue to lure new scholars. In every great archival collection in the world are masses of unexplored documents awaiting the inquisitorial eye of the youthful researcher.

These picturesque handwritings, were you to confront the original scripts, would present a wonderful variety of colors such as golden brown, grey, yellow, red, black, all from inks fabricated with rainwater and gum arabic, plus galls from the stately oaks of England, or perhaps gunpowder, soot from the chimney, fireplace or lamp, or rusted iron scraped from old halberds or swords. An infinite variety of inks with which the swashbuckling Elizabethans might set down their thoughts! All penned with goose or turkey quills on foolscap with a dazzling gallery of watermarks—dunce caps, royal insignias, bells.

Quill strokes cannot be duplicated by modern pens. Notice in these old handwritings the beautiful shading as the writer deftly rotates his quill as he writes, cutting swaths as thick as poinards or spinning spidery lines that trail away like cobwebs. Such is the beauty of these old handwritings that many philographers esteem the artistry of the document above the message in it.

Only in the context of his era can we understand Shakespeare's handsome penmanship. It reflects his superb taste and excellent education (once ridiculed by fellow dramatist, Ben Jonson). Shakespeare's handwriting tells us that he was a cultured gentleman who could deftly touch the quill to paper and turn out beautiful italics, a sweet-flowing secretary script, or an elaborate court hand.

Shakespeare was under no chirographic obligation to write his name in any particular way. His spelling, too, varied with his mood, and, since he was creative and original, he ever let his fancy roam. His frequent variation in spelling his name is important to note, because amateurs who bumble into the field of Elizabethan spelling sometimes make the ludicrous presumption that if a writer does not spell his name the same way every time, a secretary or forger must have signed it.

Among the examples of old handwriting presented in this chapter, you will notice that some are receipts from the account books of Philip Henslowe, theatrical manager who, with Edward Alleyn, built the famous Fortune playhouse in London. These receipts present a bewildering variety of spellings of Henslowe's name—imaginative creations by dramatists who exercised the right of all Elizabethans to spell phonetically. The variant spellings are a delectable foray into the vagaries of Elizabethan orthography.

Henslowe's first name is variously spelled *Philip, Phillip,* and *Phillipp;* his surname, with perpetrator: *Hynchlow* (Thomas Dekker); *Henchlowe* (Henry Porter); *Hensloe* (Robert Wilson); *henslow* (Charles Massey); *hinslowe* (Michael Drayton); *henchloe* (Samuel Rowley); *hinchlow* (William Birde). Only his agent, whose handwriting is not represented here because he was not a dramatist, spelled it *Henslowe,* as we spell it today.

In reading the receipts made out to Henslowe, you will note that in each case when a writer precedes his signature with the words *per me* or *by me,* the document is holographic, or entirely in the hand of the signer. Documents signed in this manner are, in effect, more binding legally because they also act as a validation by the writer of his signature. In signing his name "By me William Shakspear" at the end of his will, the dramatist was certainly aware that the addition of these two very short words gave a legal ratification to his final testament.

Should you have any doubt about the handwriting in *Cardenio* or *The Second Maiden's Tragedy* being Shakespeare's, and think that perhaps it might be Middleton's or Fletcher's, you can easily study it here and satisfy yourself that the script in *Cardenio* matches perfectly the handwriting in Shakespeare's will.

It is significant that there is no known playwright or poet of the Elizabethan era whose handwriting looks like Shakespeare's.

Fifteen Who Would Be Shakespeare

The critics who claim that William Shakespeare was an untutored rustic and hence could not have written the plays that bear his name all have their special candidate for authorship. Foremost among the "claimants" are Sir Francis Bacon (Lord Verulam) and Edward De Vere (seventeenth earl of Oxford), whose candidacy is impaired by his death in 1604, eight years before Shakespeare ceased to write. Both claimants were deficient in poetic skills. Bacon wrote a little jingle called "Life" that is remembered not for its merit but because he wrote it. Despite the fact that "Life" is trite and unimaginative, the Victorian anthologist, Sir Francis Palgrave, included it in his best-selling anthology, *The Golden Treasury*, and thus gave impetus to Bacon's "claim" to be the "real Shakespeare." However, Bacon was no more a poet than Albert Einstein, whose impromptu verses are delightful, but merit preservation only because the great physicist wrote them. Edward De Vere, a quarrelsome courtier, was little more than a parlor versifier (also included in Palgrave's anthology!). De Vere's surviving verses—he wrote court plays that are lost—suggest such a modest talent that, like Bacon, his candidacy would be strengthened if he had not left behind the pleasant but pedestrian rimes that reveal the limitations of his literary ability.

Christopher Marlowe, who was dirked to death in 1593 and quickly became a legend, undoubtedly had the genius to write the plays and poems of Shakespeare—he would have been a formidable rival to the Stratford bard had he lived—but to validate his candidacy requires an elaborate resurrection. William Stanley, sixth earl of Derby, whose initials at once capture our attention, is said to have written comedies, none of which survives. Queen Elizabeth I, who, like her successor on the throne, James I, wrote occasional verses and aspired to be a poet, had only a modest talent. Sir Walter Raleigh, who spelled his name *Ralegh* or *Rauley* but never *Raleigh*, was a courtier, adventurer, historian, and poet, a man of extraordinary ability. Raleigh is certainly a more viable candidate than Bacon or De Vere. His surviving poems entitle him to be included among the notable poets of his era.

Roger Manners, fifth earl of Rutland, copied out a song by Shakespeare, "Farewell, dear love," the manuscript of which was discovered among his family papers and naturally led to his candidacy. Henry Wriothesley, third earl of Southampton, was Shakespeare's patron, a distinguished soldier and courtier and intimate friend of Lord Essex. Southampton had ample opportunity to collaborate with Shakespeare and is alleged by some to have aided Shakespeare in writing the sonnets and a few of the comedies.

Mary Herbert, countess of Pembroke, sister of Sir Philip Sidney, was a close friend of Spenser and Ben Jonson and the patron of Samuel Daniel. She was a skilled translator and collaborated with her famous brother in writing psalms, a fact that has suggested to some critics that she may have dashed off the plays of Shakespeare during her spare hours. Robert Cecil, earl of Salisbury, was a distinguished English statesman and a close associate of James I. His claim to authorship was once frequently touted but has faded badly in recent decades. Edward Dyer, an intimate friend of Sidney, inherited a part of Sidney's library and was in his own day acclaimed as "a master of elegy." No evidence to substantiate this claim has survived.

Charles Blount, earl of Devonshire and eighth Lord Mountjoy (died 1606) commanded the fleet that defeated the Spanish Armada and was a brilliant scholar as well as a great military leader. His arcane knowledge has led a few persons to acclaim him as the true Shakespeare.

Anthony Bacon, brother of Sir Francis Bacon, was a diplomat with some literary attainments. A few scholars have contended that he wrote Shakespeare's sonnets. The romantic, colorful Robert Devereux, second earl of Essex (beheaded for "treason," 1601) was a favorite and lover of Elizabeth I. Essex wrote many beautiful sonnets, but his early death debars him from serious contention for the crown of the world's greatest dramatist and poet. John Florio, an Italian-English scholar and, like Shakespeare, a protégé of Southampton, translated Montaigne's *Essays* into English. Shakespeare may have dipped into Florio's translation when writing *The Tempest*. There is in the British Museum a copy of Florio's *Montaigne* with a bogus signature of Shakespeare in it. This amateurish forgery is excoriated in my book, *In Search of Shakespeare* (pp. 242-46), but before anyone had ever studied Shakespeare's handwriting, the forgery helped to substantiate the claim that Florio wrote the plays of Shakespeare.

Fifteen Who Would Be Shakespeare

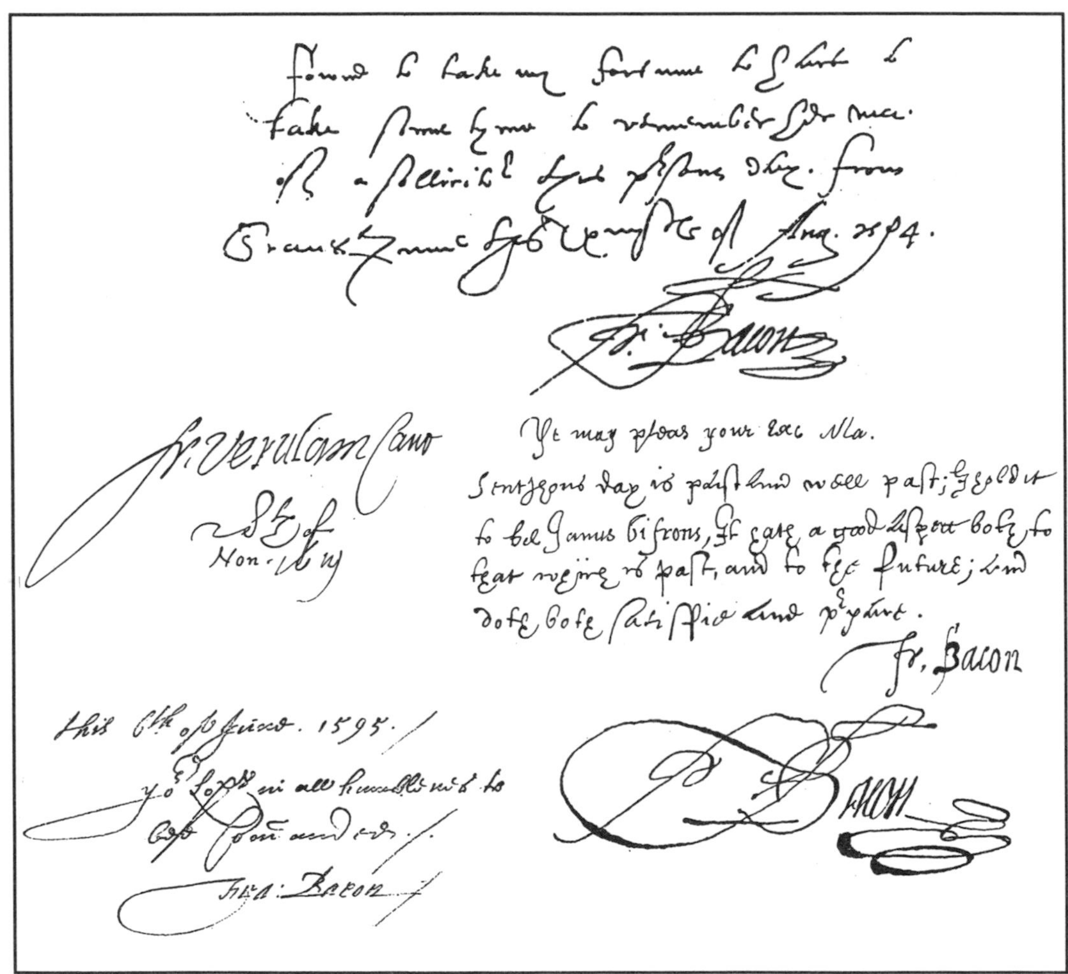

Sir Francis Bacon, Lord Verulam (1561-1626). Variant handwritings and signatures.

I must not forget to geve yowre Lordship hise thankes which ar due to yow. for this yowre honorable dealinge to her Maiestie in my behalf. whiche I hope shall not be wythout effect.

yowre Lordships. assured.

Yowre most assured and lovinge Brother.

Edward Oxenford

Edward Oxenford

Edward De Vere, seventeenth earl of Oxford (1550-1604). Two variant handwritings, with signatures.

Christofer Marley

Christopher Marlowe (1564-93). A unique signature, discovered two decades ago.

Thanks good Uncle for your kynd remembrance and writinge to your postscript I will cum to be a suter to her Majestie my selfe, who am not a lyttle Joyfull to understand of her gratyousnes so hyghely to favor my wyff and me and thus though satisfyed yet not without salutinge you with these few unworthy hasty lynes I doe cease restinge alwayes

Your Lovinge Nephew and trew frend

Will Derby

Will Derby

William Stanley, sixth earl of Derby (1561-1642). Handwritten note signed, with additional signature.

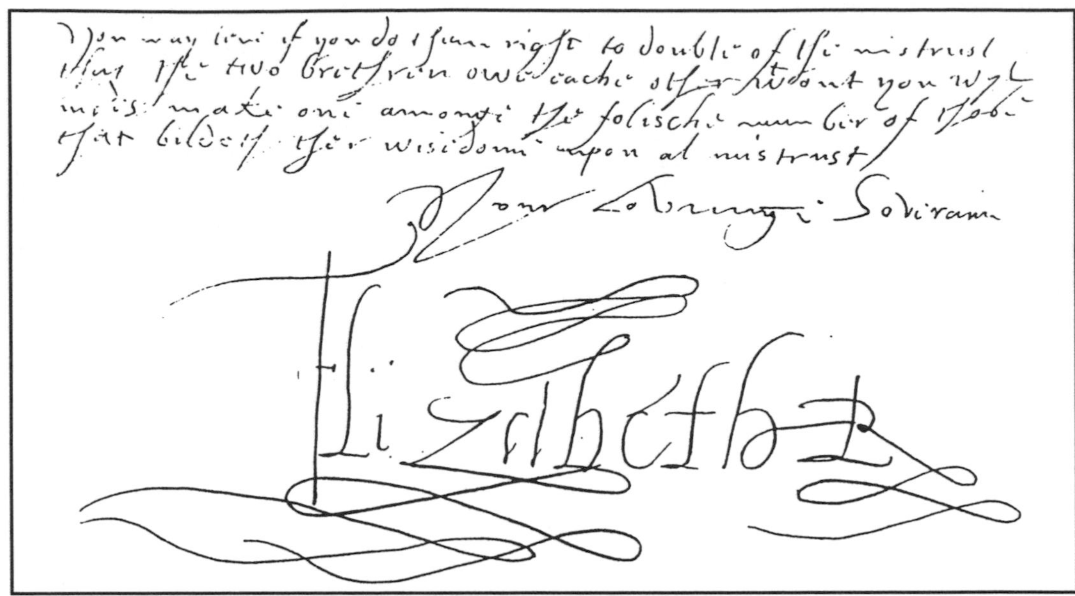

Yow may see if you do it sum right to doubte of the mistrust that the two brethren owe eache other without you wyl misse make one amongst the folische number of those that bildes ther wisidome upon al mistrust

Your lovinge Soveraine

Elizabeth

Elizabeth I (1533-1601). Portion of a handwritten letter with signature.

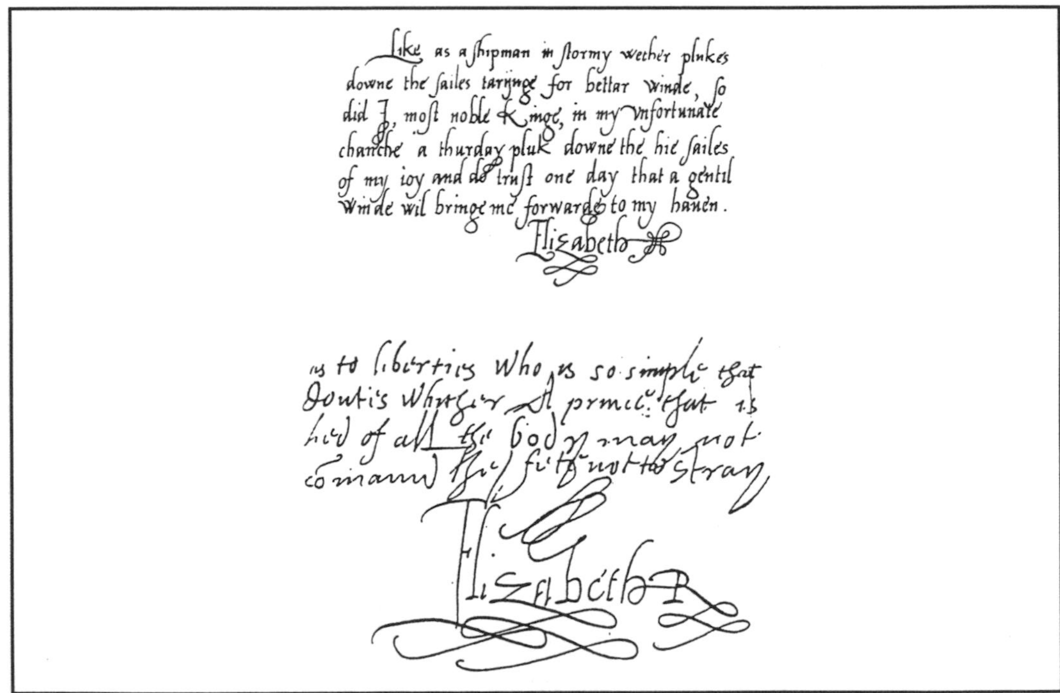

Like as a shipman in stormy wether plukes downe the sailes tarijnge for bettar winde, so did I, most noble Kinge, in my vnfortunate chanche a thurday pluk downe the hie sailes of my ioy and do trust one day that a gentil winde wil bringe me forwarde to my hauen.

Elizabeth

as to liberties who is so simple that doutes whether a prince that is hed of all the body may not comaund the fete not to stray

Elizabeth

Elizabeth I. Two variant signatures and handwritings.

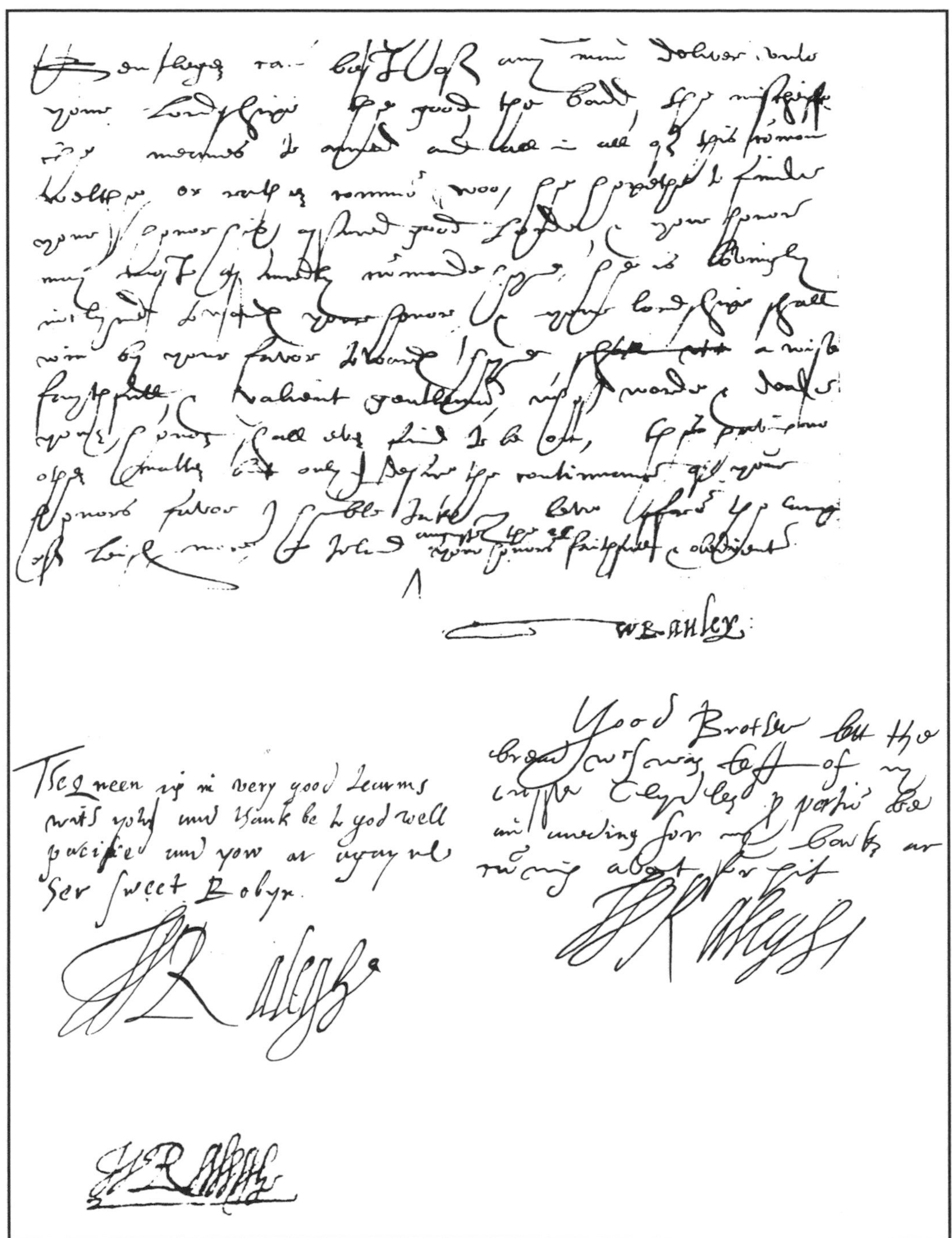
The Queen is in very good termes with you and thank be to god well pacified and you ar agayne her sweet Robyn.

Sir Walter Raleigh (1552?-1618). Variant handwritings and signatures. The writing and signature (*W. Rauley*) at top is an early script.

My singuler good Ladie and mother my ductie most humbly remembred vnto your Lpp: May it please yow to vnderstand that I am in verie good health I thanke god and verie sorie that my brother Frauncis his iorney hither was letted by reason of the weather, and verie glad that my brother George his ague is gone but most of all sorie that my sweete sister hath caught the ague, for which my Ladie Wharton and my Cosens are verie sorie, as well as my selfe: I make no doubte but your Lpp: heareth from her how she and my Cosens doe by this messenger. Thus humblie craving your blessing I humblie take my leave this 23 of februarie 1590.

Your Lpps most dutifull and obedient sonne.

Roger Rutland

Roger Manners, fifth earl of Rutland (1576-1612). Handwritten letter signed to his mother, penned in a fine italic script.

To the right honorable my verry good Lo: the Ld. Keeper of the great Seale of England

I have sent you herewith a petition delivered vnto mee in the behalf of certayne poore men dwellinge at Gosport who have been hardly vsed by Winter

I rest

your assured frend H. Southampton

...the 17 of Octob

Henry Wriothesley, third earl of Southampton (1573-1624). Shakespeare's patron and dedicatee of Shakespeare's *Venus and Adonis* (1593) and *The Rape of Lucrece* (1594). Handwritten letter signed.

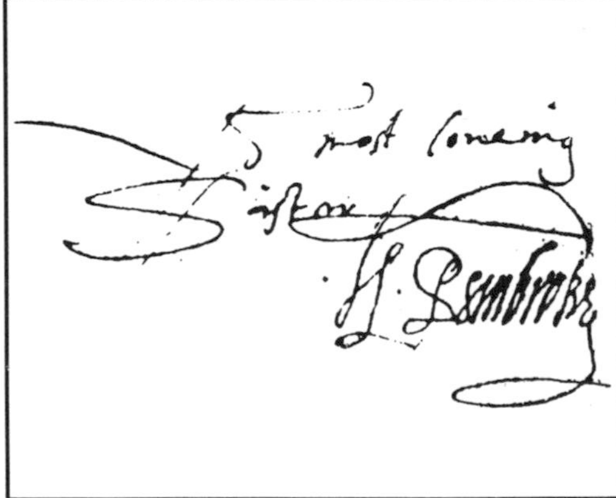
Your most loving Sister

M. Pembroke

Mary Herbert, countess of Pembroke (1561-1621). Conclusion of a handwritten letter signed.

That it pleased you, (a great Prince) to vouchsafe me thanks for such a Tryfle you shew how neare you are to Cæsar, who preferred Presents of Pleasure, before Gyfts of valew

R Salisbury

Robert Cecil, earl of Salisbury (c. 1563-1612). Handwriting and signature as earl of Salisbury.

The q. doth in all honorable sort use those Embassadours, And the E. of Marr rides abroade with her

Ro: Cecyll

Robert Cecil, earl of Salisbury. Handwriting and signature as Robert Cecil.

Edward Dyer (d. 1607). Last line of a handwritten letter signed.

Edward Dyer

Iff I with all thatt I have may stopp
the gullfe off theas wars, by throwinge
my sellfe to bee swallowed upp thearin, I
shall dye a happye and a contented
Curtius,

June, 1600

Mountjoye

Charles Blount, earl of Devonshire and eighth Lord Mountjoy (d. 1606). Conclusion of a handwritten letter signed "Mountjoy."

Your merely assured to
use Anth: Bacone

Anthony Bacon (1558-1601). Conclusion of a handwritten letter signed.

Upon wensday I meane to goe to the Camp wch I do
humbly desire you to further for as you will know
yt is not now fitt for me to tarry heere
from Yorke house at midnight this 29th of July. 1588

Essex

Robert Devereux, second earl of Essex (1566-1601). Conclusion of a handwritten letter signed.

faccio voto di essere vostro sincerissimo
et affettion.mo amico et servitore J Florio

John Florio (1553-1625). Conclusion of a handwritten letter signed.

And for that wee cannot herein without beeing too tedious deſcribe our proiect more fully, nor ſhew in particular, how acceptable to Almighty God, how comfortable to ſo many blinde ſoules, that liue and die in ignorance for want of light, how profitable to this whole land, and beneficiall to euery one of vs, this enterpriſe (by Gods bleſſing) may in ſhort time ſhew and manifeſt it ſelfe; we haue alſo ſent you annexed hereunto, ſome few of our Printed Bookes, which by reading and diuulging the ſame among your friends, will further enforme you of each particular.

And whereas you ſhall therein reade, that we purpoſe to maintaine and carry all in a Ioynt ſtocke for ſeuen yeares, and then to deuide the lands, &c. Yet we thought it meete to let you know, that the Stocke and Marchandize which ſhall ariſe from thence, we purpoſe ſooner and ſo often as the greateneſſe of it ſhall ſurmount the charge, to make a Diuident and diſtribution thereof to euery man according to his Bill of Aduenture.

And further wee doe aſſure you, that it is no way our purpoſe or meaning, to enforce or cauſe any man, hauing once aduentured to aduenture or ſupply any more, except of his owne motion and willingneſſe he ſhall bee ſo diſpoſed, neyther ſhall hee looſe his former aduenture, for we doubt not (by Gods helpe) but after the ſecond returne from thence, to haue ſufficient matter returned to defray all charges of new ſupplies, and to giue ſatisfaction to men that haue aduentured

And ſo leauing it to your wiſe and beſt aduiſed conſideration, when we ſhall receiue your aunſwere, which wee pray with your conuenient expedition may be returned to Sir *Thomas Smith* in Phil-pot Lane in London, Treaſurer for the Colonie, you ſhall then finde vs ready to performe in what we may, to your beſt content.

Signature page of the prospectus of the Virginia Company, organized to colonize Virginia, signed by Shakespeare's patron, the earl of Southampton (upper left) and at right, William, Lord Pembroke (1580-1630), sometimes identified as the dedicatee, *Mr. W.H.*, of Shakespeare's *Sonnets* (1609). It was in 1609 that the Virginia Company sponsored the voyage of the *Sea Adventure*, a ship that became separated by a tempest from the other vessels en route to Virginia. The battered and leaking *Sea Adventure* was driven ashore in Bermuda, where the officers and crew survived for ten months. The exciting tale of their experiences may have inspired Shakespeare's play, *The Tempest*.

Shakespeare and His Contemporaries

William Shakespeare (1564-1616). English dramatist and poet. Page of the manuscript of *Cardenio* or *The Second Maiden's Tragedy* (Act III, lines 1064-1111), penned in Shakespeare's beautiful, meticulous script.

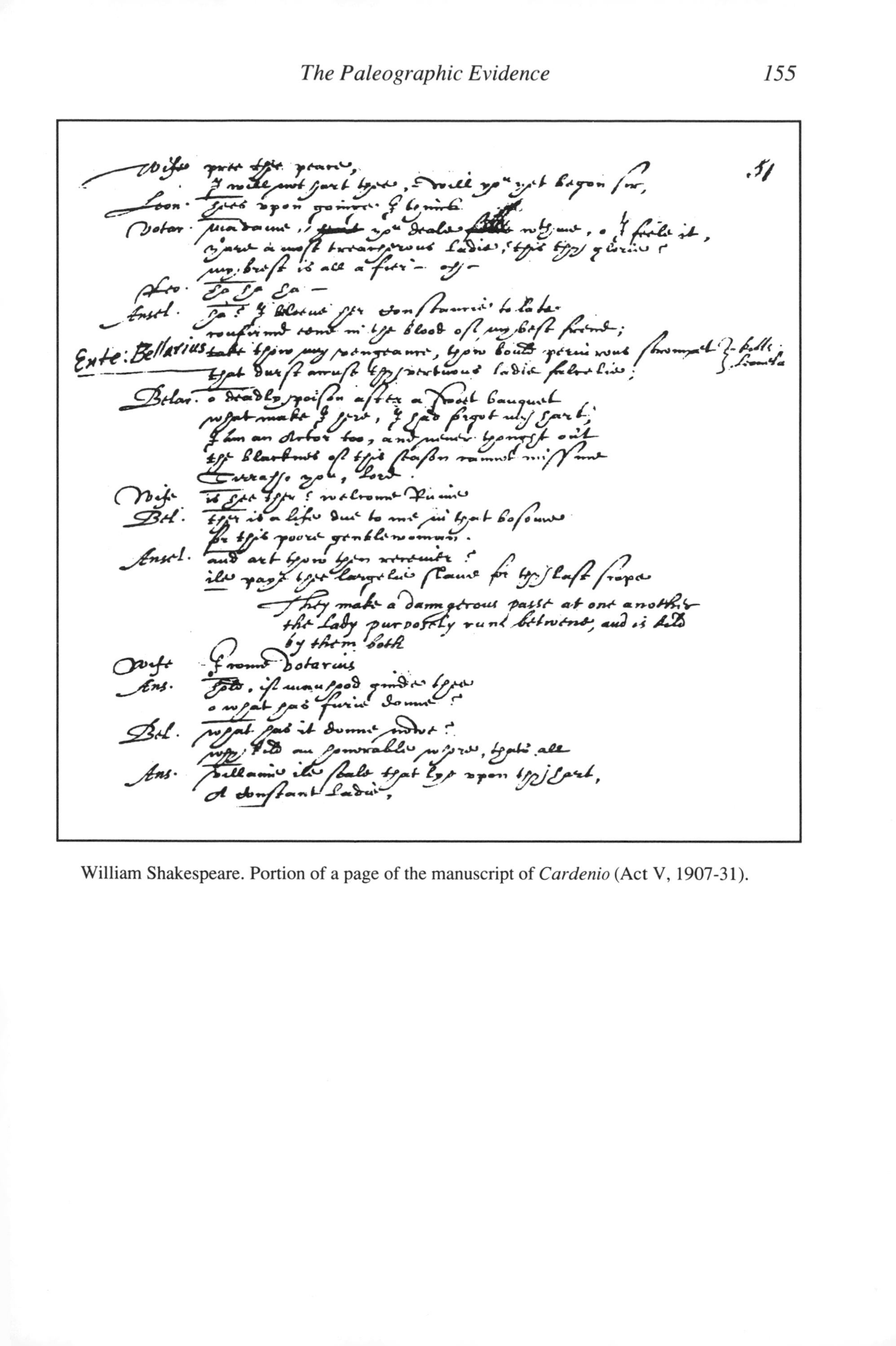

William Shakespeare. Portion of a page of the manuscript of *Cardenio* (Act V, 1907-31).

Govianus kneeles at the Toomb wondrous passionatly. His Page singes

The Songe

If euer pitty were well plac'st.
on True Desart, and virtuous Honor,
It could nere be better grac'st:
freely then bestowe it vpon hir,
Neuer Lady earnd hir fame
In Vertues warr with greater strife,
To preserue hir constant name
she gaue vp beauty, youth and life
There shee sleepes
and here he weepes
The Lord vnto so rare a wife
Weep weep and mourne lament,
you virgins that pass by hir
For if praise come by death agen,
I doubt few will lye nye hir

Manuscript poem from the text of *Cardenio,* written in Shakespeare's fine italic hand (Act IV, iv, 1714-31).

On a sodayne in a kinde of Noyse like a Wynde the dores clattering, the Toombstone flies open and a great light appeares in the midst of the Toombe; His Lady as went out, standing iust before hym all in white, Stuck with Jewells and a great crucifex on hir brest

Actus Quintus

William Shakespeare. Stage directions from the manuscript of *Cardenio* in Shakespeare's italic script (Act IV, iv, 1746-51). With Act Five in Latin.

Five lines of blank verse with a speech prefix, from *Cardenio* or *The Second Maiden's Tragedy*. The signature was abstracted from the first line of Shakespeare's holograph will.

John Fletcher (1579-1625). English dramatist; close friend and collaborator with Francis Beaumont and William Shakespeare. Six holograph lines from a dedicatory epistle signed. For an account of the discovery of Fletcher's handwriting, see Chapter IV.

Thomas Middleton (c. 1570-1627). English dramatist. Five lines in Latin, with his signature. Many scholars regard Middleton as the author of *Cardenio* or *The Second Maiden's Tragedy*, but there is not the slightest similarity between Shakespeare's script and Middleton's.

Receaved by me George Chapman for a pastorall
ending in a Tragedye in part of payment the
summ of fortye shillings, this xvijth of July
Anno 1599

By me George Chapman

George Chapman (1559-1634). English dramatist. Handwritten receipt signed. The words *By me* that precede Chapman's signature indicate that the entire document is in his hand. Some experts have considered Chapman to be the author of *Cardenio* or *The Second Maiden's Tragedy*, but the manuscript is not in his handwriting.

my humble desyer
is that it would please your honor to open my
estate unto her in such manner as she may
know I am poore & yet thankfull, if she
have compassion

Foulk Grevill

Fulke Greville, Lord Brooke (1554-1628). English poet and dramatist; biographer of Sir Philip Sidney; wrote two Senecan tragedies. Five lines from a letter, signed.

Poetry, my Lord, is not borne with every man; Nor every day: And,
in her generall right, it is now my minute to thanke your Highnesse,
who not only do honor her with your eare, but are curious to examine
her with your eyes, and inquire into her beauties, and strengths.

By the most trew admirer of your Highnesse Vertues, Ben: Jonson.

Famae et honori eius
Servientiss.
imo addictissimus
Ben: Jonsonius

Victurus Genium debet habere liber.

Ben Jonson (1572-1637). English dramatist; close friend of Shakespeare. Jonson used several variant hands, of which two are illustrated here.

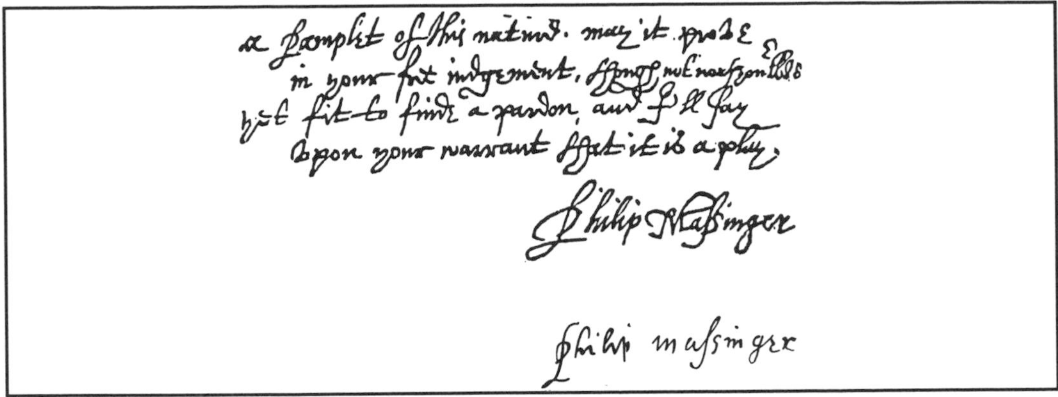

a Pamphlet of this nature may it prove
in your fit iudgement, though not necessarie
yet fit to finde a pardon, and I'll say
Upon your warrant that it is a play.

Philip Massinger

Philip massinger

Philip Massinger (1583-1640). English dramatist. Handwritten quatrain signed, with variant signature.

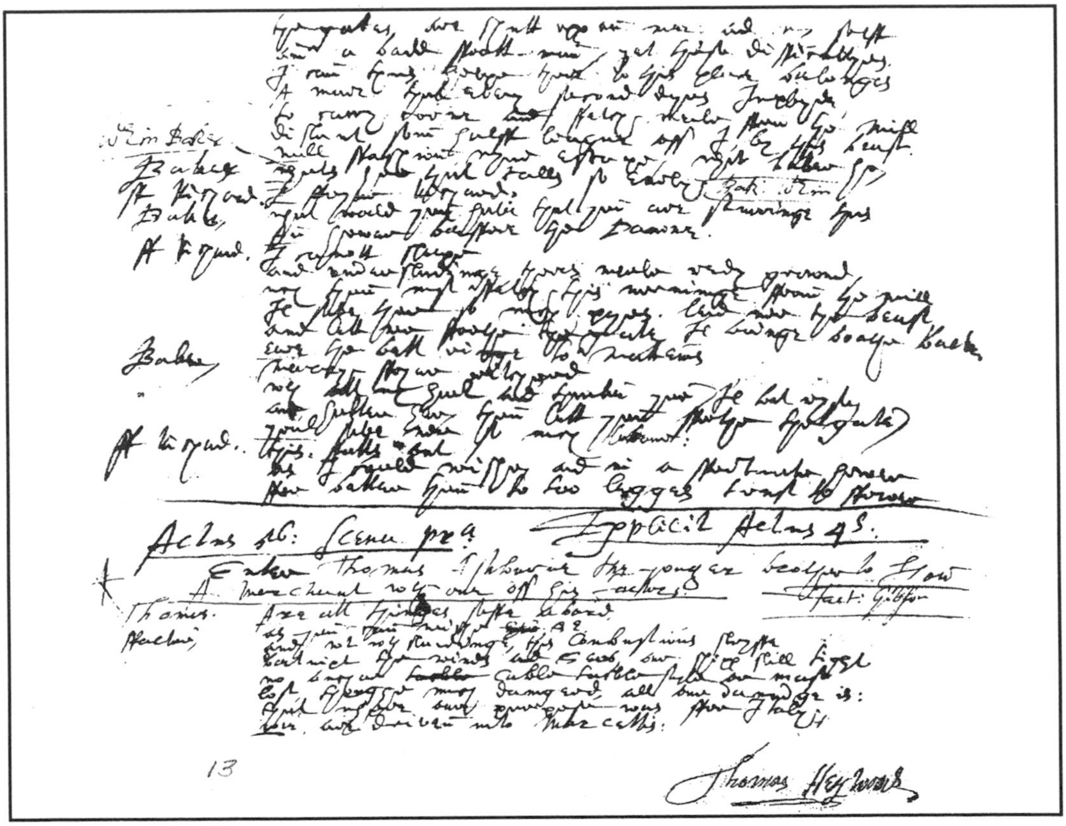

Thomas Heywood (1574-1641). English dramatist and poet; wrote *A Woman Killed with Kindness*. Portion of a page from a play in his hand, with signature.

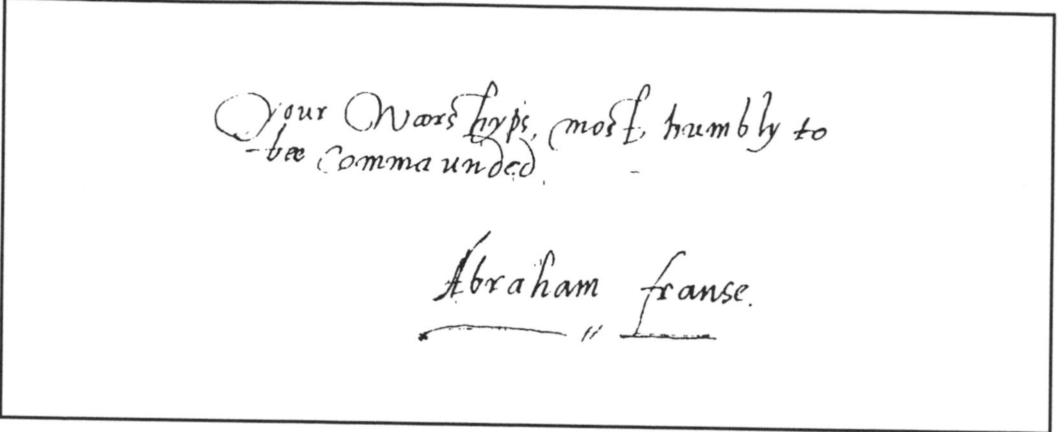

Your Worshyps, most humbly to
bee Commaunded.

Abraham Franse.

Abraham Franse or Fraunce (1560?-1633). Shropshire poet; known for his adept hexameters. Two lines and signature.

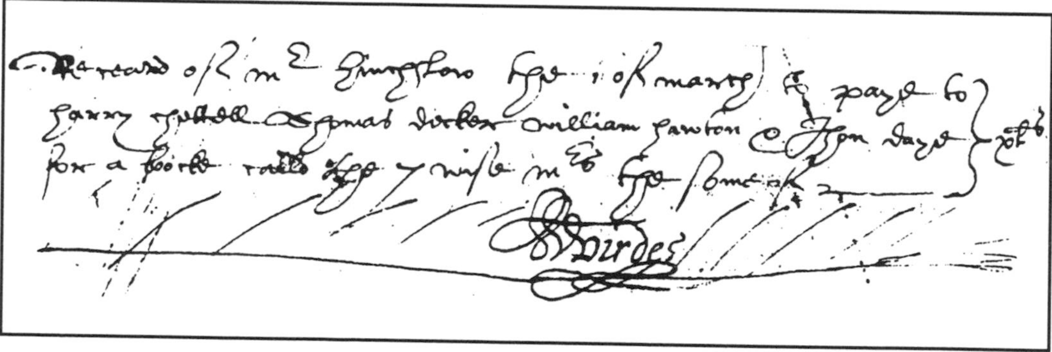

Receaved of mr Henslowe the 1 of marche to paye to
harry chettell thomas decker william hawton & John daye } xls
for a boocke called the 7 wise mr the some of

W Birde

William Birde or Borne. English dramatist. Handwritten receipt signed.

Be it knowne unto all men that Henry
Porter do owe unto phillip Henslowe
the some of xxs of lawfull money of England
wch I did borrowe of him the 26 of
maye ao dom 1599

Henry Porter

Henry Porter (1573-1628). English dramatist. Handwritten receipt signed, 1599.

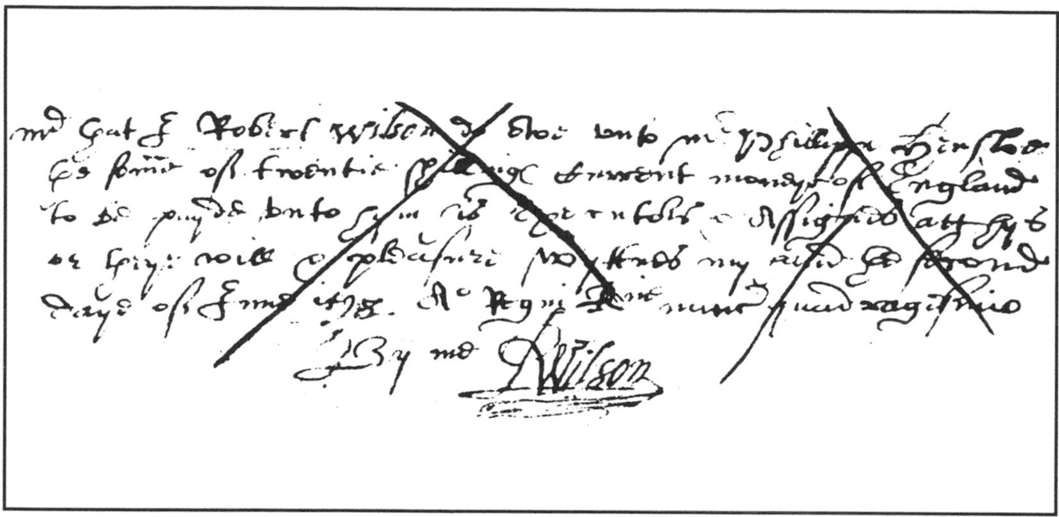

Robert Wilson (1579-1610). English dramatist; collaborated with Michael Drayton. Handwritten receipt signed "By me R. Wilson."

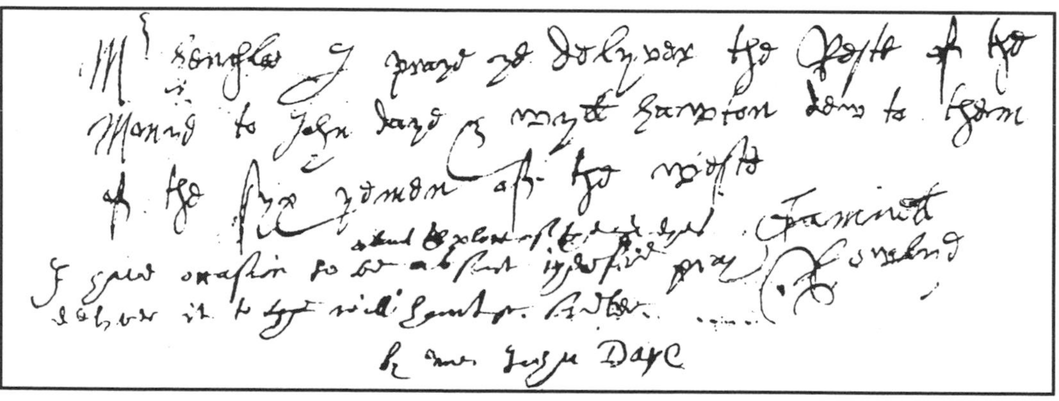

Samuel Rowley (d. 1633?). English dramatist; wrote two extant plays. Handwritten note signed, written above a receipt by John Daye.

John Daye (c.1575-c.1640). English dramatist; educated at Cambridge; wrote *The Blind Beggar of Bethnal* Green (1600). Handwritten receipt signed "by me John Daye" at bottom of receipt by Samuel Rowley.

Nathaniel Field (1587-1633). English actor in Shakespeare's company; dramatist; collaborated with Massinger. Conclusion of a handwritten letter signed.

Robert Dayborne. English dramatist; collaborated with Massinger, Tourneur, and possibly Fletcher. Handwritten note signed at bottom of "Nat" Field's letter.

Robert Dayborne. Last line of a handwritten letter signed.

Richard Burbage (1567-1619?). English actor; close friend of Shakespeare's; played in roles created for him by Shakespeare; stockholder in Globe Theater. Signature.

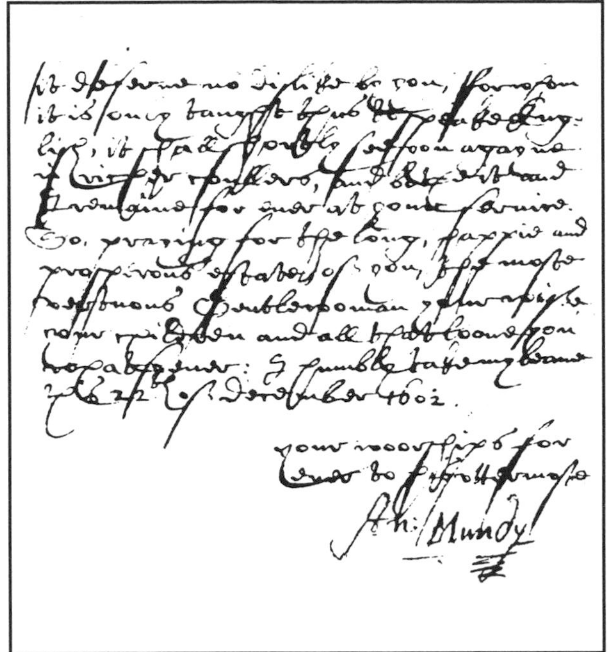

John Heminges (1556?-1630). English actor and close friend and business associate of Shakespeare's; co-edited *The First Folio* (1623). His name is spelled various ways, including Heming and Hemminge. Signature.

Anthony Munday (1560-1633). English dramatist and actor; wrote plays about Robin Hood and Sir John Oldcastle; rival of Ben Jonson. Conclusion of a handwritten letter signed.

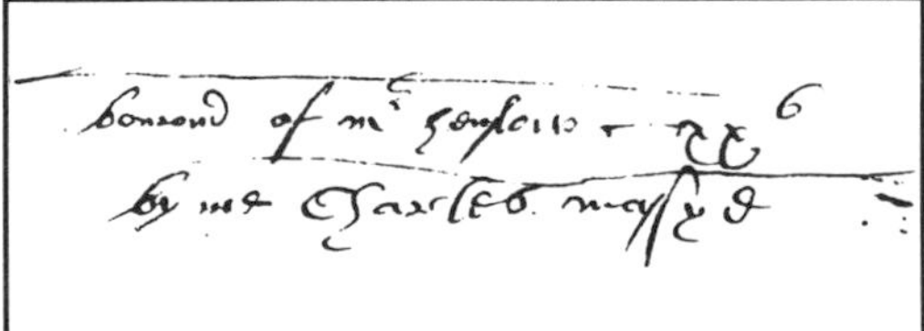

Charles Massey. English dramatist. Handwritten receipt signed "by me Charles Massye."

Richard Hathaway. English dramatist; collaborated with Dekker. Signature.

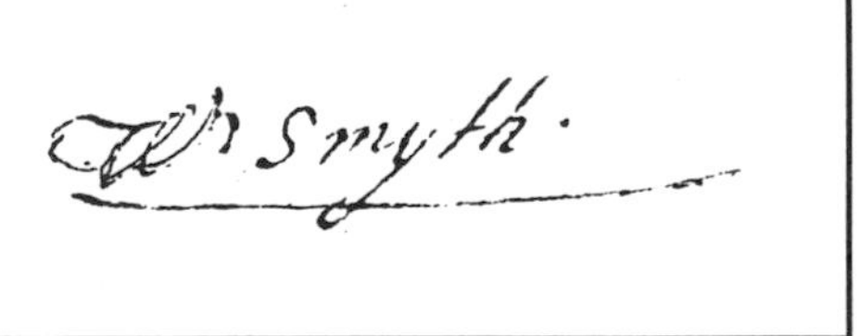

William Smith. English dramatist; collaborated with Dekker and John Webster. Signature.

Anthony Wadeson. English dramatist. Signature.

Howbeit if some outcast Ismael for want or of his owne dispose to lewdnes, haue wth pretext of dutie or religion, or to reduce himself to that he was not borne vnto by enie waie incensd yor Lp to suspect me, I shall beseech in all humillitie & in the feare of god that it will please yor Lp but to censure me as I shall prove my self, and to repute them as they ar in deed Cum totius iniustitiæ nulla capitalior sit quam eorũ, qui tum cum maxime fallunt id agunt vt viri boni esse videantur for doubtles even then yor Lp shalbe sure to breake

their lewde designes and see into the truthe, when but their lyves that herin haue accused me shalbe examined & rypped vp effectually, soe maie I chaunce wth Paul to live & shake the vyper of my hand into the fier for wch the ignorant suspect me guiltie of the former shipwrack. And thus (for nowe I feare me I growe teadious) assuring yor good Lp that if I knewe eny whom I cold justlie accuse of that damnable offence to the awefull Matie of god or of that other mutinous sedition towrd the state I wold as willinglie reveale them as I wold request yor Lps better thoughtes of me that never haue offended you.

Yor Lps most humble in all duties

Th Kydde

Thomas Kyd (1557?-1595). English dramatist; wrote *The Spanish Tragedy*. A"missing" play about Hamlet, known as the *Ur-Hamlet*, has often been attributed to Kyd, but is, in my opinion, an early play (c. 1592-94) by Shakespeare, subsequently published in 1603 and known as a "bad quarto." Shakespeare's revised and very popular *Hamlet* was published in 1604 and marks a vast improvement over the earlier version. Kyd's name is spelled in various ways, the most often encountered of which are *Kid* and *Kidd*. My study of the script in this letter reveals that it was entirely written in the hand of the signer. Last page with signature.

The umbllest servant
of yo'r sacred majesty
John Marston

John Marston (1575?-1634). English dramatist; wrote *Eastward Ho* with Jonson and Chapman (1605). Conclusion of a handwritten letter signed.

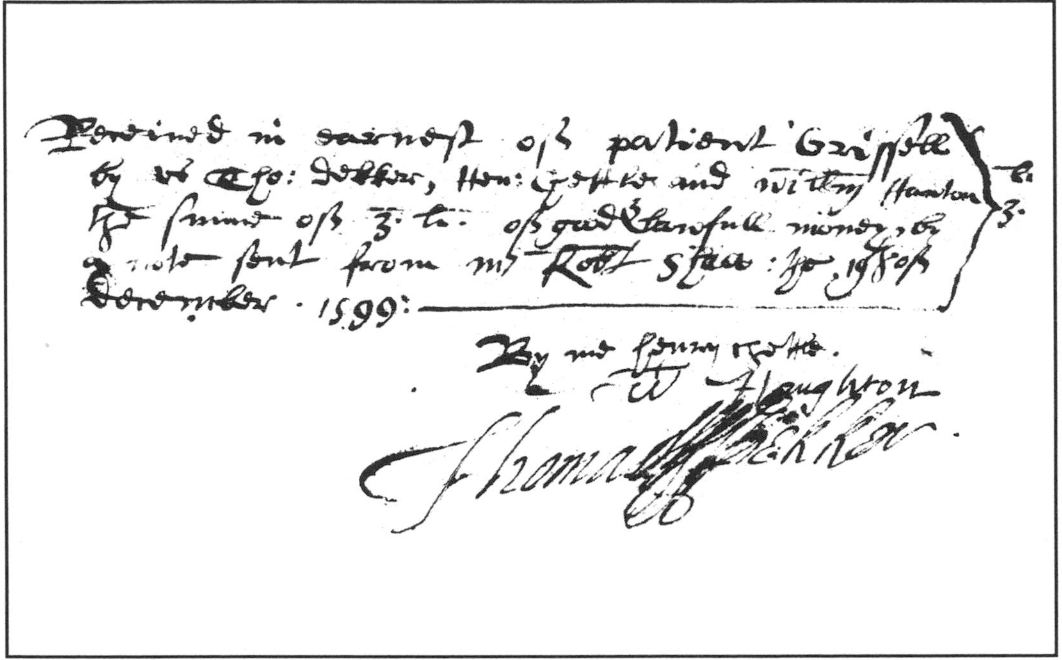

Henry Chettle (1560?-1607). English dramatist; wrote thirteen plays. Handwritten document signed "by me henry chettle." Also signed by co-authors William Haughton, a minor dramatist, and Thomas Dekker.

Thomas Dekker (1572?-1632). English dramatist; poet and pamphleteer; wrote *The Shoemaker's Holiday*, *The Roaring Girl* (with Middleton) and *The Gull's Hornbook*, a delectable satire. Handwritten receipt signed, 1599.

Edmund Spenser (1552-1599). English poet; wrote *The Faerie Queene*. Handwritten document signed. Like many other writers, Spenser wrote his signature in a larger and more ornate hand than his usual script.

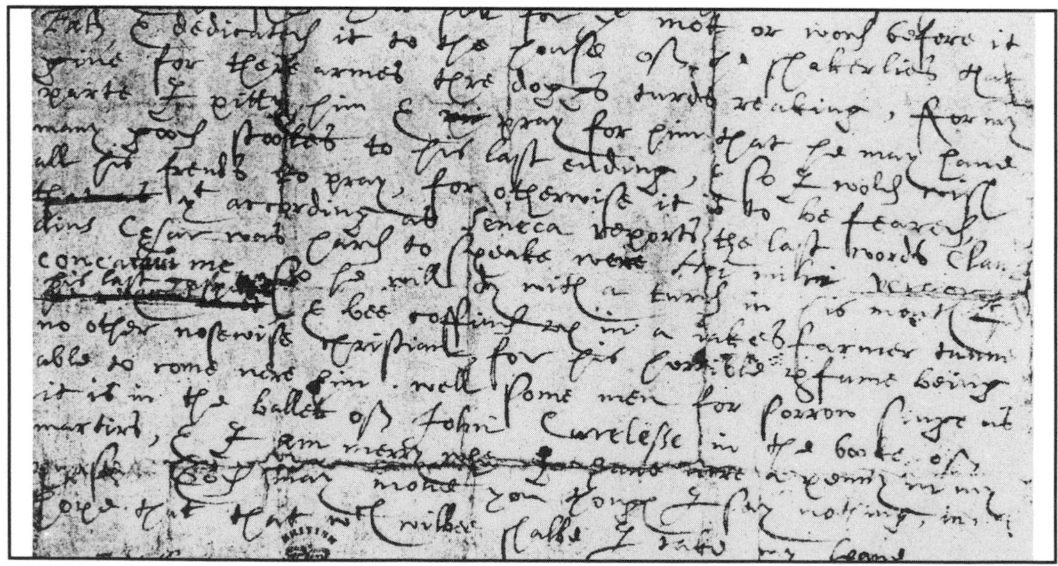

Thomas Nashe (1567-1601?). English dramatist; wrote controversial *Ile of Dogs* (1597), and was imprisoned. Unsigned handwritten letter to William Cotton.

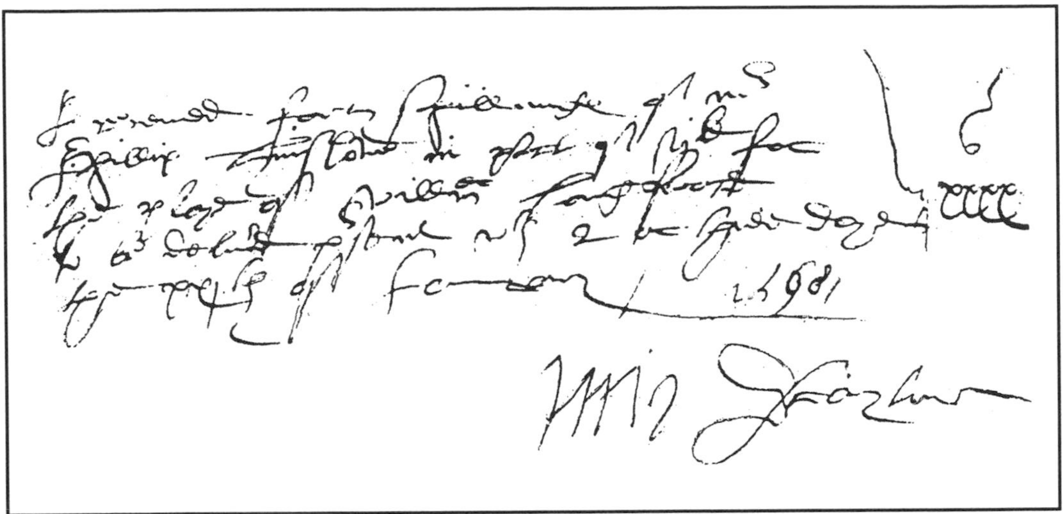

Michael Drayton (1563-1631). English poet; probably a close friend of Shakespeare's. Handwritten document signed.

I can but besech of god that the hous do not
mislike her: that is my cheif care: the rest shalbe
performed with that good hart: as I am sure yt
wilbe accepted. But yf her h. had tarried but on
yere longer: we had ben to to happy. but gods will
and hers be doon. 4 Julij 1577. yr Lo. humble to comaund

T. Dorset. T. Buckehurst

Thomas Sackville, first earl of Dorset and Baron Buckhurst (1536-1608). English dramatist; wrote *Gorboduc,* the first English tragedy (1561), with Thomas Norton. Conclusion of a handwritten letter signed.

John Lyly (c. 1554-1606). English dramatist; wrote comedies for boys to perform at Court; may have influenced Shakespeare. Conclusion of a handwritten letter signed.

Samuel Daniel (1562-1619). English dramatist; may have influenced Shakespeare. Signature.

George Peele (1556-96). English dramatist; may have collaborated with Shakespeare. Conclusion of a handwritten letter signed.

Phineas Fletcher (1582-1650). English poet and pastoral playwright. Signature.

Giles Fletcher (1549?-1611). English poet; uncle of John Fletcher; wrote a sonnet sequence. Signature.

Right honorable

Although I am resolued that your approued iudgement is such that you respect not men as they comply, but as they loue and deserue, yet because it is a receaued opinion in this world that the best meanes of entertaining great mens fauour is by wrighting, and they are esteemed vnworthy Honorable respect that neglect to entertaine it wth officious letters, I haue thought good in thes few lines to acknowledg my loue and deuty to your Honner by whose meanes I haue not only reposed my Country, but my peace and quietnes in the same. To you I ascribe all my good fortunes. and in way of gratuity sacrifice all my vnfurnished seruice, being addressed to exemplifie it when soeuer you shall command: Now find I your worthines euen in your absence, because your Honner so nobly preuented my dangers by your prouidence at your being heare, that whilst I liue I am bound to reverence and serue you. I haue no newes to entertaine you Honnor wth synce this place is but barren in offering signal occurrents, and to let you know that Oliuer the Phisition is dead and Coreate the fooles booke is vppon the press is but triuiall and vnworthy your eares. When Seneca speaketh good English as I hope he shortly shall I will send him ouer into France to attend your Honnor. his newes will best content you who is replenished wth all morral wisdome. I am affraid to be to tedious and therfore will cancell vpp thes complements wth both myne owne and my wifes humble commendations to your Honnor and my worthy Lady. praying god continually that He will bless and enable you both in this life and hearafter crowne you wth Eternity.

17 January 1610

Your Honnors euer
bounden

Thomas Lodge

Thomas Lodge (1558-1625). English dramatist and poet; translated Seneca; collaborated with Robert Greene. Handwritten letter signed.

Noted Elizabethan Authors

Right honorable my very good Lorde. I am bolde to troble your L. withe these few wordes. humbly to crave your Lps favour so farr unto me, as that it will please you to lett me understande, whether I may withe your Lps. leave, and that I may not offende in wante of my service, remaine absente frome the courte this Christmas tyme.
Frome wilton this 16th of December 1577

Philippe Sidney.

Unto your good opinion, my selfe preste at yo[ur]
I humblie ende. Frome Oxforde this xxvith of
Februarie A° 1569

Yours in all humble sorte
as your owne

Philip Sidney

Joh. Wiero S.
Mi Wiere vem vem. Valde te
cupio, de vita periclitor. aut vivus,
aut mortuus non ero ingratus.
Sed festinus oro. Plura non possum.

Tuus Ph. Sidney.

Ph. Sidney

Monsieur. Jay receu vos lettres
Et vous remercie infiniment pour
m'avoir este liberall, de vostre
cognoissance et amitie.

Ph. Sidney

Sir Philip Sidney (1554-86). English poet; mortally wounded in battle. Variant handwritings and signature.

Thomas Chaloner "The Younger" (d. 1615). English statesman and poet. Handwritten note signed to Robert Cotton.

Arthur Golding (1536?-1605). English poet; translator of Ovid; his work was familiar to Shakespeare. Handwritten acknowledgment of a loan, 1590, signed "By me Arthur Golding." Golding's signature also appears in the first line.

Joseph Hall (1574-1656). English prelate and poet; wrote satires and treatises. Conclusion of a handwritten letter signed.

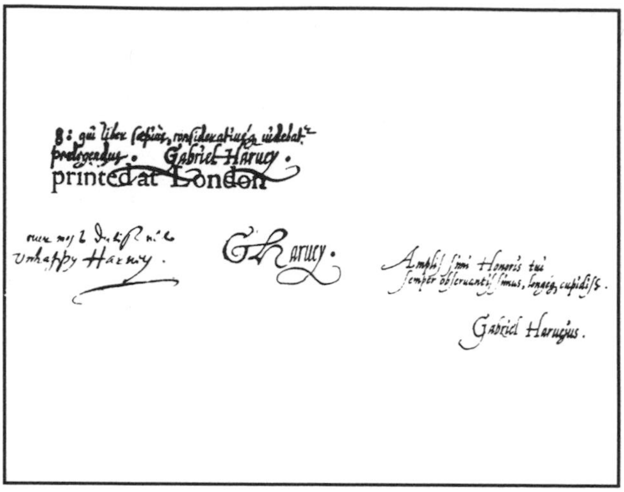

Gabriel Harvey (1545?-1630). English poet; friend of Spenser; claimed to be "the father of English hexameter;" center of many literary storms. Three variant exemplars of his handwriting and signature.

William Drummond (1585-1649). English poet; interviewed Ben Jonson. Signature, with Latin abbreviation of given name.

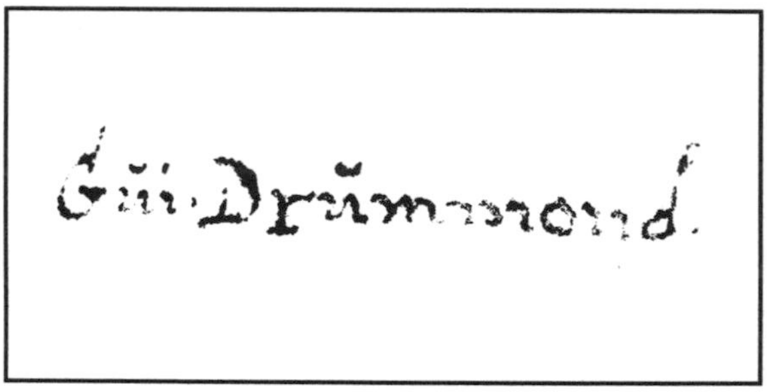

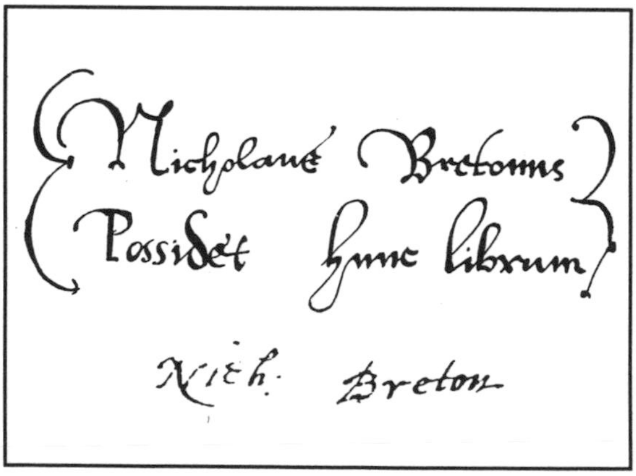

Nicholas Breton or Britton or Brittaine (1551?-1623). English poet; wrote pastorals. Two variant signatures.

Sr as afore so now I entreat you
to pay to mr Adrian marius the
accustomed summe 10 li acknowledging my
self and all my endevours to bend to you
and to my virtuous Lady for whome
I doe and will entreate to blesse you
with more then an ordinarie happinesse.

my Herrick
everlastingly
R Herrick

Robert Herrick (1591-1674). English poet; wrote "Gather Ye Rosebuds. . . ." Handwritten letter signed.

To the right Honorable:
Sr Francis Walsyngham
att
Barne Elmes

L. Andrewes

Lancelot Andrews (1555-1626). English pulpit orator; helped translate King James version of the Bible. Handwritten address signed, from a letter to Walsingham.

send me by this bearer and lend
it me for some tyme. the
Liger booke of Bentli
priorie
Joh. Haryngton

John Haryngton

Sir John Harington (c. 1561-1612). English satirist; wrote *Commonwealth of Oceana*. Handwritten note signed, with a variant signature.

William Byrd (1543-1623). English composer; may have written songs for Shakespeare's plays. Signature.

Pardone I pray you (Sir Camden) this breache of my promise in that I have holden your booke some fiue dayes above the tyme.
yours, in the Lorde, William Lambarde
29. Jul. 1585.

William Lambarde (1536-1601). English lawyer and antiquarian; probably a friend of Shakespeare's. Handwritten letter signed.

from my prison in my Chamber 20 febru: 1601
J Donne

John Donne (c. 1572-1631). English poet and preacher. Handwritten note signed "from my prison in my Chamber, 1601."

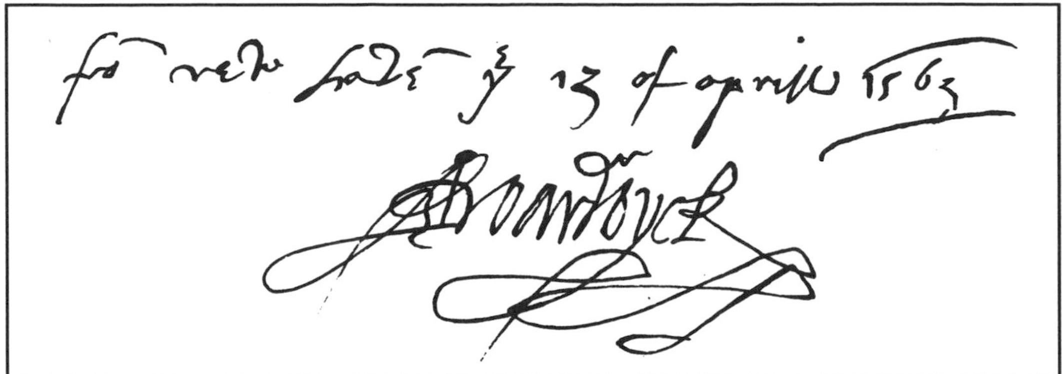

Ambrose Dudley, earl of Warwick (1528-1590). Brother of earl of Leicester; favorite of Queen Elizabeth; patron of an acting company, whose performances in Stratford Shakespeare may have attended in his youth; died of a wound received in battle in 1589. Conclusion of a handwritten letter signed.

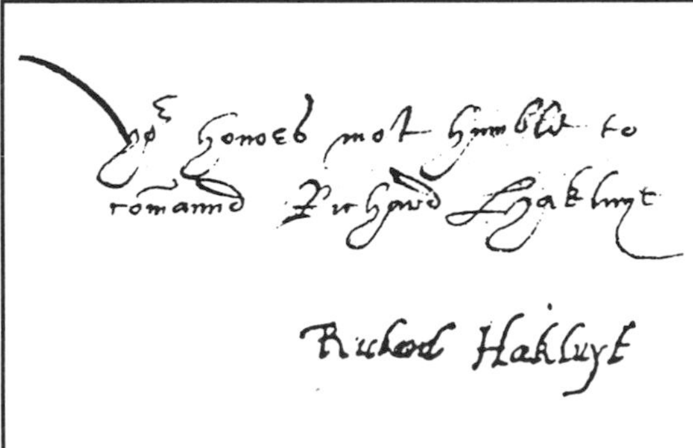

Richard Hakluyt (1552?-1616). English geographer; compiled a famous collection of voyages, probably used by Shakespeare. Conclusion of a handwritten letter signed, with variant signature in italic hand.

Sir Thomas Bodley (1544-1613). Founded Bodleian Library. Conclusion of a handwritten letter signed.

Roberti Cottoni liber ex dono doctissimi Patricii Young generosi

Sir Robert Cotton (1571-1631). English author and book collector; founded Cottonian Library in British Museum Library. Handwritten identification signed in a book from his library.

from Venice this 22. of June 1609 stile of the place

Henry Wotton

Henry Wotton (1568-1639). English statesman and poet. Conclusion of a handwritten letter signed.

John Stowe (c. 1525-1605). Topographer; wrote *Survey of London*. Conclusion of a handwritten letter signed.

Sir Edward Coke (1552-1634). English jurist; prosecuted Essex and Raleigh, both of whom were beheaded. Conclusion of a handwritten letter signed.

Alexander Nowell (1507?-1602). English clergyman and author. Conclusion of a handwritten letter signed.

John Speed (1552-1629). English cartographer; produced fifty-four pictorial maps of England. Conclusion of a handwritten letter signed.

Your Maiesties
most humble Subiect,
& devoted Servant,
Josuah Sylvester.

Joshua Sylvester (1563-1618). English poet and translator. Conclusion of a handwritten letter signed.

Sir Francis Drake (c. 1540-1596). English navigator and buccaneer. Five lines signed from a handwritten letter, with two variant signatures.

George Buchanan (1506-82). Scottish historian. Concluding lines from a handwritten letter signed.

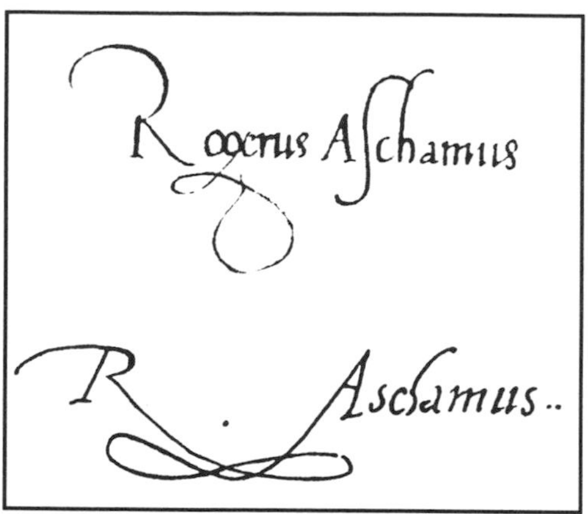

Roger Ascham (1515-68). Handwriting expert; wrote treatise on toxophilia (archery); handwriting teacher of Queen Elizabeth and often credited with introducing the italic style of writing into England. Two variant signatures.

My very good ffriend, Mr Camden
Coventry . 25 . August . 1609
Ph . Holland

Philemon Holland (1552-1637). English scholar; translator of Livy and Pliny the Elder, both used by Shakespeare. Conclusion of a handwritten letter signed.

Most Gratious Soveraine Lady, The God of heaven and earth, (Who hath mightilie, and evidently, given unto your most excellent Royall Maiestie, this wunderfull Triumphant victorie,) be allwaies thanked, praysed, and glorified;
A Dni: 1588: John Dee

John Dee (1527-1608). Mathematician; astrologer and magician. Handwritten letter signed to Queen Elizabeth.

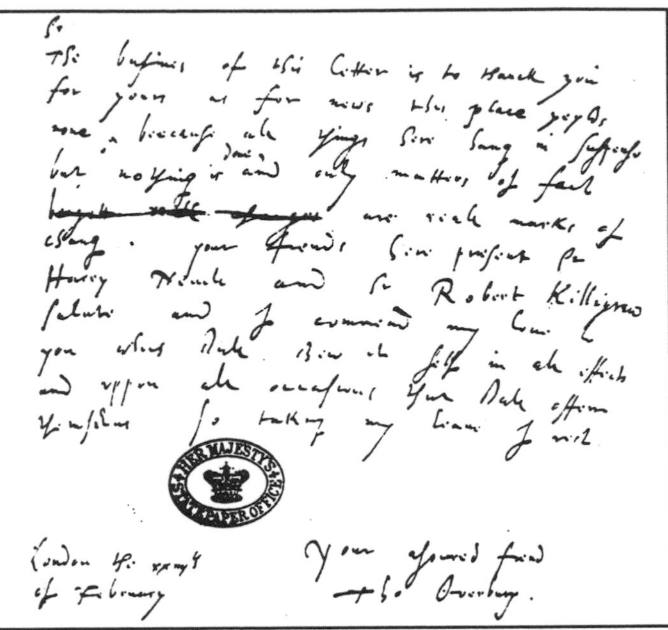

Sir Thomas Overbury (1581-1613). Courtier and poet; murdered in Tower of London. Handwritten letter signed.

Henry Howard, earl of Northampton (c. 1539-1614). Instigated the murder by poisoning of Sir Thomas Overbury. Handwritten note signed.

Sir Francis Walsingham (c. 1530-1690). Elizabethan statesman; expert at deception and espionage. Conclusion of a handwritten letter signed.

Celebrated Heralds of Shakespeare's Day

Like most of his contemporaries, Shakespeare was keenly interested in heraldry. The various heralds in the College of Heralds were regarded as personages of great importance.

Right worthy Syr. That in my solitarines here
I maye avoide the deadly sinne of Slouth, I
am now an humble suitor to you that you
would send me by Willm Holland my servant
the Booke of Heraldry, if you have bound
it vp. or as it is. Or some other booke or
Papers wch you shall think fitting my studies
or delighte.

Willm Camden Cl

William Camden (1551-1623). English antiquarian; expert in heraldry; appointed Clarenceux king-of-arms in 1597; friend of Shakespeare and probably helped Shakespeare to obtain a family coat of arms. Handwritten letter signed.

Nich: Charles
Lancaster

Nicholas Charles (died 1613). Lancaster herald. Signature.

Paddy Lancaster herald, a pson (were he well knowne
vnto your Lps) not able to execute the same,
your Ho: in all dutie bounde
Ra: Brooke: Yorke: Herald.

Ralph Brooke (c. 1560-1625). York herald; tried to block Shakespeare's application for a coat of arms on the grounds that the design had been used previously. Conclusion of a handwritten letter signed.

My wholle contynuall travayle my Lo: is, in finishinge the worke of the tresures of Englande which I have brought unto Henry ye fourthe: and hoope to finishe before Easter next, untill which I onlye make use of yor Lo: yt some staye maye be made of bestowinge those offices untill I have fynished yt booke

December 1593.

Francis Thynne

Francis Thynne (d. 1611). Lancaster herald in the College of Heralds from 1602 until his death. Conclusion of a handwritten letter signed.

Sir William Dethick (d. 1612). Garter king-at-arms; helped Shakespeare to obtain a coat of arms. (The application was made for John Shakespeare, William's father.) Handwritten note signed.

I have sent you verses prynted in Tubinge where that Lo Spencer was entretayned with many Honors and Orations by the Rator and Learned of that Universite:

1608.

Sr Willm Dethick

I pray you lend me your Book of Buralls in the Minories that was Mr Camdens.

Augu: Vincent

Augustine Vincent (d. 1626). Windsor herald. Handwritten note signed.

Noted Statesmen of England

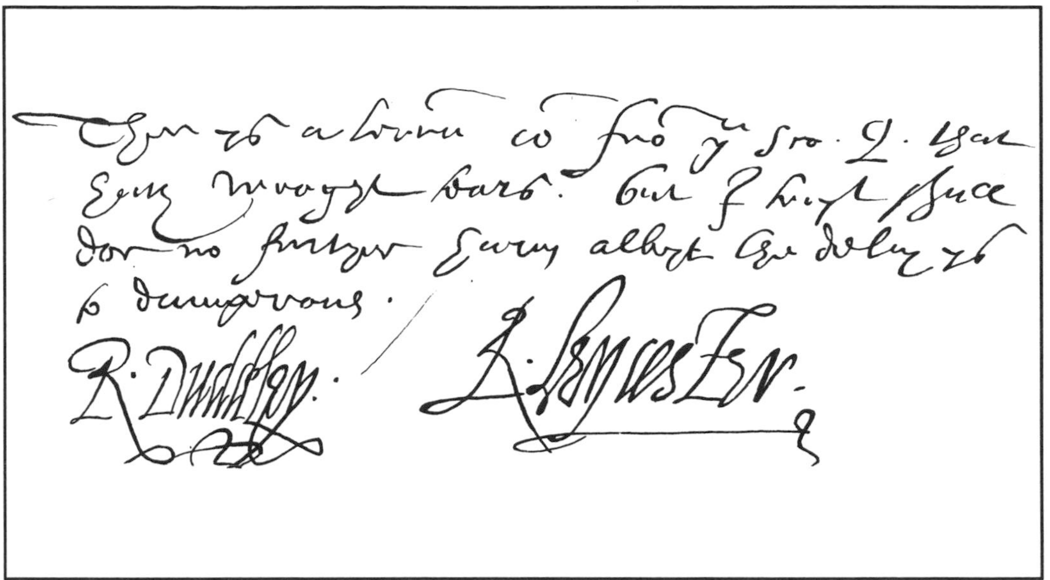

Robert Dudley, earl of Leicester (c. 1552-1588). Courtier and favorite of Elizabeth I; lived near Stratford; his acting company was led by James Burbage, and Shakespeare may have joined Leicester's men while still in his teens. Handwritten note signed, with variant signature as *R. Dudley*.

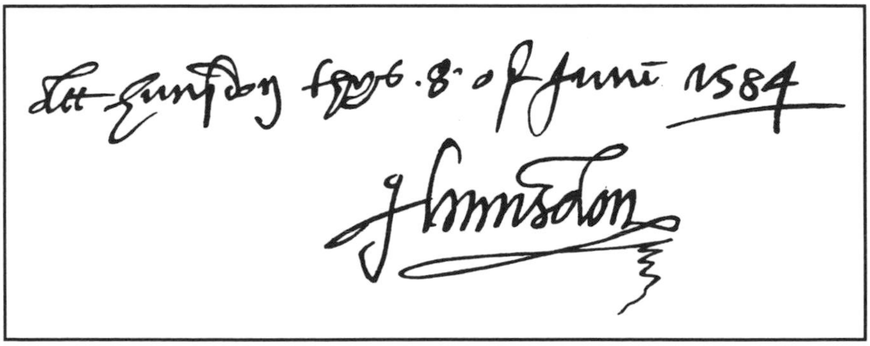

Henry Carey, first Lord Hunsdon (c. 1524-96). English courtier; lord chamberlain; organized Lord Chamberlain's Men, an acting company that included Shakespeare (1594). Signature and date.

William Cecil, Lord Burghley, with signature as *W. Cecil.*

King James I and the Royal Family

James I (1566-1625). King of England. Handwritten letter signed.

So kissing your handes
I remaine she that will euer loue
you best
Anna R.

Anna of Denmark (1564-1619). Queen of England; wife of James I; also known as "Queen Anne;" an enthusiastic playgoer who especially enjoyed the dramas of Shakespeare. Conclusion of a handwritten letter signed.

Henry

Prince Henry (1594-1612). Prince of Wales; son of James I. Signature.

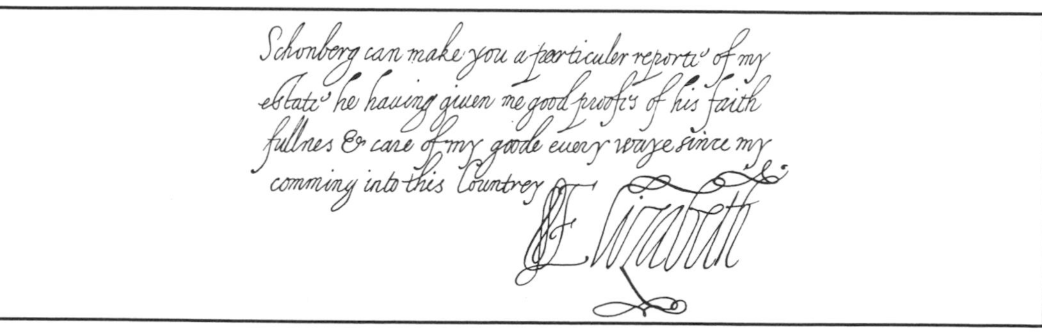
Schonberg can make you a perticuler reporte of my
estate he having giuen me good proofes of his faith
fullnes & care of my goode euery waye since my
comming into this Countrey
Elizabeth

Elizabeth, queen of Bohemia (1596-1662). Daughter of James I. Her marriage to Frederick V, palatinate elector, was a festive occasion in 1613, during which the new play by Shakespeare and Fletcher (*Cardenio)* was performed at least twice. Handwritten note signed.

Vous priant me continuer l'honneur de vos bonnes graces
comme a celuy qui sera pour tousjours
Vostre bienhumble et tres
affectione cousin
Monsieur mon cousin
Frideric Electeur Palatin

Frederick V (1596-1632). Husband of Princess Elizabeth of England; king of Bohemia (1619-20). Conclusion of a handwritten letter signed.

CHAPTER III

SHAKESPEARE AND CERVANTES: COLLABORATORS

Shakespeare and Cervantes never met.[1] They lived a thousand miles apart and spoke and wrote in different languages. Shakespeare was handsome and rich and full of honors, welcomed at court and saluted as a great dramatist and poet. John Fletcher, too, was a "golden boy," raised in affluence, educated at Cambridge, and launched into the world as a gentleman. Cervantes, crippled and pain-wracked, his left hand mangled at the Battle of Lepanto, failed as a playwright and expended most of his luckless existence in a fierce, ever-losing struggle against poverty. Yet, in a strange gesture, the Dark Man sought out Shakespeare and Cervantes on the same day. Both died on April 23, 1616.[2] Aside from this remarkable coincidence, what did these two great writers have in common that eventually, near the end of their lives, made them collaborators?

There is little parallel in the lives of Shakespeare and Cervantes. And, to speak plainly, there is a vast disparity between their literary talents, with Shakespeare far outshining his Spanish counterpart. It is in their Renaissance minds and souls that they are in bright accord.

Shakespeare was brought up in a middle-class family in the town of Stratford. He was handsome, clever, pleasant, and scion of an uneducated father and mother who claimed at least a few noted antecedents. Despite his apparent inability to write his name, Shakespeare's father, John, became the bailiff (or mayor) of Stratford. It is probable that his son, William, received the usual education at the Stratford Grammar School. Most scholars are in agreement that young Will remained in school until he was fourteen and received an excellent classical education, despite Ben Jonson's snide remark that he had "small Latin and less Greek." If you are not familiar with the school system of the time, you might dip into George A. Plimpton's *The Education of Shakespeare*.[3]

Shakespeare was a distinguished dramatist and poet by the time he was thirty. At forty, he was wealthy in a modest way. He sported a coat of arms that proclaimed him a gentleman, was acquainted with the king of England, and widely recognized for his literary genius. A generous fate had bestowed upon him the honors he deserved.

But it was a niggardly fate that presided over the destiny of Miguel de Cervantes Saavedra. The exact date of Cervantes's birth at Alcalá de Menares was not recorded and must be inferred from the date of his baptism, but it was probably October 7, 1547. Cervantes's life was as colorful as the stories in his books. He left a trail of official documents that makes it easy for biographers to follow his exciting career. In 1569, at twenty-two, Cervantes contributed six poems, including a sonnet and an elegy, to an anthology published by his Madrid schoolmaster. Unable to find other employment, Cervantes entered the army as a private in 1570 and the following year was on board a vessel in the armada of Don John of Austria during the famous battle of Lepanto. Although ill with fever, Cervantes joined his comrades in the engagement. He was hit three times with bullets, twice in the chest and once in the left hand, a wound that permanently maimed him and won him the colorful sobriquet, *El Manco de Lepanto* (The Handless One of Lepanto). After convalescence, Cervantes returned to the army. In 1575 he and others were captured by Barbary pirates and sold into slavery. An effort by his parents to ransom him failed and Cervantes tried to escape. His case became a *cause célèbre.* Three times he tried to get away. Three times the Viceroy of Algiers threatened to kill him but finally, so the story goes, admitted that "so long as I have the maimed Spaniard in safekeeping, my ships and city are secure." Eventually, a ransom of five hundred gold ducats, raised by Spanish officials, got him out of the hands of his master and back to Spain.

Cervantes began writing for the stage, but although the long list of his dramas swelled, his coffers remained as empty as ever. Despite a few modest successes, he was never able to support himself by writing plays. In 1584, Cervantes made a bid for fame with his novel *Galatea.* By his own admission, this work "proposes something and concludes nothing." Even the dowry of his wife was meager. It comprised five vines, an orchard, a few household items, four beehives, forty-five hens and chickens, one cock, and a crucible.

Beset by poverty and with his literary career going nowhere, Cervantes in 1587 became a provisioner for the famed Spanish Armada that was to fail miserably in the attempted conquest of England the following year. In 1592, he was briefly imprisoned for unknown reasons. By 1597, he was again in jail, this time for failure to pay the exchequer officials. Most biographers accept as a true statement Cervantes's remark in the prologue of his masterpiece, *Don Quixote*, that the book reveals "what might be begotten in a jail." This suggests that he started to write *Don Quixote* during one of his prison sojourns.

The first part of *Don Quixote*, published in 1605, was a phenomenal success. Despite its great length and verbal flatulence, it proved to be a perfect long-winter-nights book. Pirated editions cascaded from presses all over Spain. Cervantes found himself famous, but as poor as ever. A promised second part of *Don Quixote* was delayed by Cervantes's persistence in writing unproducible dramas. Finally, when a rival author turned out a sequel to *Don Quixote* with a preface deriding Cervantes's physical infirmities and imprisonments, Cervantes buckled down and finished his masterpiece with a second part (1612) that brought him additional renown but sparse profit. He continued to write feverishly on a new book until four days before his death in Madrid.

Cervantes wrote dozens of plays, of which fourteen survive, mostly unsuccessful then and unproducible now. For twenty years Cervantes sought vainly for a producer. The reason he could not find one is obvious. Cervantes never understood the demands of the stage. On the other hand, Shakespeare and Fletcher were both masters of the theater and knew precisely what would amuse, delight, frighten, or hold enthral their audience.

The first edition (so designated by literary historians) of *Don Quixote* (Part I) in English was published in London by William Stansby in 1612 "for *Ed. Blount* and *W. Barret.*" And, as already indicated, Sir George Buc had finished his censorship task on *Cardenio*, or *The Second Maiden's Tragedy* on October 31, 1611. Shakespeare and Fletcher may have had access to the proofs, or manuscript of the translation, or else, as is more likely, read the book in the original Spanish, or possibly in a Brussels edition (1607). In his admirable essay, "An Elizabethan Bookseller,"[4] Sir Sidney Lee discusses in detail the friendly rapport that existed between Blount and Shakespeare and Fletcher. Blount published works by both Shakespeare and Cervantes, and was perhaps the main sponsor of Shakespeare's *First Folio*. Sir Sidney writes: "Blount's literary taste was always catholic, and, doubtful of reaping a large harvest out of the products of native genius, he scanned with eagerness the literature of foreign lands. In 1605, the first part of *Don Quixote* appeared at Lisbon. Blount had no hesitation in presenting his readers with the romance in an English dress. As early as 1606, Thomas Shelton had begun work on his famous rendering. On January 19, 1611, Blount, while still in partnership with Barrett, entered on the *Stationers' Register* "A booke called the Delightfull History of the Witty Knighte Don Quishote. . ."[5] As we know from many of Fletcher's other dramas, he was very familiar with *Don Quixote* and other works by Cervantes. Almost certainly he could read Spanish. However, both Fletcher and Shakespeare liked Blount, who was born in 1564, the same year as Shakespeare. Blount had been a close friend of Christopher Marlowe and Shakespeare's Italian friend, John Florio, a fellow protégé of the earl of Southampton. Apparently, Blount and Shakespeare had once tiffed over Blount's unauthorized publication of a poem entitled, "A Poeticall Essaie on the Turtle and Phoenix" to which Blount affixed Shakespeare's name. But that was a decade earlier, in 1601, in a little volume called *Love's Martyr;* or, *Rosalind's Complaint,* and no doubt Shakespeare and Blount had almost forgotten the incident. Certainly, either Shakespeare or Fletcher or both might have had access to the manuscript or unpublished proofs of Thomas Shelton's translation of *Don Quixote*.

In the dedication of his spirited translation, Thomas Shelton explains to his patron, Lord Howard de Walden, that he had translated Cervantes's work from Spanish into English five or six years previously for "a very dear friend." Shelton did not use the original Spanish edition, but the Brussels imprint of 1607. Later, in 1616, Shelton translated the second part of *Don Quixote*. His racy rendition is today regarded as a classic, and when first published was an enormous success.

One of the most popular tales within a tale was "The History of Cardenio" that Cervantes used to break the monotony of Don Quixote's peregrinations. At the time *Don*

Quixote burst upon a delighted public and made merry England merrier than ever, Shakespeare and Fletcher had already completed their play, *Cardenio* or *The Second Maiden's Tragedy*, but had not yet affixed a title to it or named all their characters. Overnight, the picaresque heroes, Don Quixote, Sancho Panza, Cardenio, and Luscinda became household fixtures, and their names and deeds were known to every literate person. For Shakespeare and Fletcher, who had already used portions of *Don Quixote* for their main and subplots, it required only a few words of instruction to the stage prompter to change orally the names of the characters to match the names of their prototypes in the Cardenio tale. Cervantes related the "history" of Cardenio so that it actually comprises a story within a story. There is the lengthy story of Cardenio, his frustrated love and subsequent adventures, and within that story is told another story (not relevant to the Cardenio tale), "The Tale of the Curious Impertinent,"[6] which I shall discuss in the next chapter. Both stories were utilized by Shakespeare and Fletcher in *Cardenio* or *The Second Maiden's Tragedy.*

Everyone knows about Don Quixote's tilt with the windmills, but that is only one escapade of many in Cervantes's classic. Certainly, the dominant story, one that requires about two hundred pages to relate, is "The History of Cardenio." After a few adventures and misadventures, including the loss of Sancho's ass, which inexplicably reappears later in the tale, Sancho and Don Quixote find a rotting portmanteau containing a heap of gold crowns, together with a memo book, a sonnet about the writer's despair over his lost love, and other papers. Don Quixote and Sancho decide to search for the owner of the gold coins, which, by the way, they never return. They discover the owner, Cardenio, a strange individual who leaps from rock to rock and tuft to tuft in the Sierra Morena. Cardenio's legs and feet are bare and his tawny, velvet breeches are in shreds. He lives in the hollow of an old cork tree. In addition to cavorting like a goat, this mountain creature also howls and rants. As he dissolves from one violent fit of madness to another, Cardenio screams his hatred of Don Fernando. Don Quixote, "the Knight of the Rueful Visage" and his sidekick Sancho finally calm down Cardenio, "the Ragged one of the Sorrowful Countenance." Cardenio then relates the tale of his ill-starred love for the rich and beautiful Luscinda. He had received from Luscinda a letter hinting that she would accept his proposal of marriage. Certain impediments bar the way. Cardenio asks his noble friend Don Fernando to arrange the wedding. The highborn, rich Don Fernando has but recently seduced a beautiful maiden named Dorotea, whom he promised to marry, but upon meeting Luscinda he falls for her charms and jilts Dorotea. At this point, Cardenio interrupts his story to tongue-flay his betrayer with a castigation mightier than Cicero ever laid upon Cataline. Here it is, in the original Elizabethan spelling of Thomas Shelton:

> O ambitious Marius. O cruell Cataline. O facinorous [atrociously evil] Quila. O treacherous Galalon. O trayterous Vellido. O revengefull Iulian. O covetous Iudas. Traytor, cruell, revengefull, and couzening, what indeserts [injuries] did

> this wretch commit, who with such plaines [frankness] discovered to thee the secrets and delights of his heart? What offence committed I against thee? What words did I speake, or counsel did I give, that were not all addrest to the increasing of thine honour and profite? But on what doe I of all wretches the worst complaine, seeing that when the current of the starres doth bring with it mishaps, by reason they come downe precipitately from above, there is no earthly force can with-hold, or humane industry prevent or evacuat them? Who would have imagined that Don Fernando, a noble Gentleman, discreet, obliged by deserts [favors], and powerful to obtaine whatsoever the amorous desire would exact of him, where and whensoever it seazed on his heart, would (as they say) become so corrupt, as to deprive me of one onely sheepe (little lamb), which yet I did not possesse?[7]

In order to pull off his scheme to steal Luscinda from the still unsuspecting Cardenio, Don Fernando dispatches Cardenio on a fool's errand (the ideal type of errand for Cervantes's Cardenio). Several days later, upon receipt of a letter from Luscinda containing the news that Don Fernando has double-crossed him ("Sir, you shall understand, that he hath demaunded me for his wife; and my father borne away be the advantages of worthes. . .hath agreed to his demand"),[8] Cardenio rushes back to his "own Citie" and seeks out Luscinda.

Cardenio continues:

> . . . as soone as Luscinda perceived me, shee said, Cardenio, I am attired in my wedding garments, and in the Hall doe waite for me, the traitor Don Fernando, and my covetous father with other witnesses, which shall rather be such of my death, then of mine espousal; bee not trubled deare friend, but procure to be present at this sacrifice, the which if I cannot hinder by my perswasions and reasons, I carry hidden about me a poynard secretly, which may hinder more resolute forces, by giving end to my life, and a beginning to thee, to know certain the affection which I have ever borne, and doe beare unto thee. I answered . . .Sweete Ladie, let thy workes verifie thy words for if thou carriest a poynard to defend thy credit, I doe heere likewise beare a sword wherewithall I will defend thee, or kill my selfe, if fortune proove adverse and contrary. . .[9]

Cardenio conceals himself behind a tapestry to watch the wedding:

> Luscinda came out of the Parlour, accompanied by her mother and two waiting maides of her owne, as richly attired and deckt, as her calling and beautie deserved, and the perfection of courtly pompe and bravery could affoord: my distraction and trouble of minde lent me no time to note particularly the apparell shee wore, and therefore did onely marke the colours, which were carnation, and white; and the splendour which the precious stones and Iewels of her Tires, and all the rest of her garments yeelded: yet did the singular beauty of her faire and golden tresses surpasse them so much, as being in competencie with the precious stones, and flame of foure linkes that lighted in the Hall, yet did the

> splendour thereof seeme farre more bright and glorious to mine eies. . .as they thus stood in the Hall, the Curate of the Parish entred, and taking them both by the hand, to do that which in such an act is required at the saying of, 'Will you Ladie Luscinda take the Lord Don Fernando, who is heere present for your lawfull Spouse, according as our holy mother the Church commands?' I thrust out all my head and neck out of the tapistry, and with most attentive eares and a troubled mind, settled my self to heare what Luscinda answered; expecting by it the sentence of my death, or the confirmation of my life. . . .
>
> The Curate stood expecting Luscinda's answer a good while ere she gave it: and in the end, when I hoped that she would take out the Poynard to stab her selfe, or would unloose her tongue to say some truth, or use some reason or perswasion that might redound to my benefit, I heard heere in stead thereof, answer with a dismaied and languishing voice the word, 'I will': and then Don Fernando said the same, and giving her the Ring, they remained tyed with an indissoluble knot. Then the Bridegroome comming to kisse his spouse, she set her hand upon her heart, and fell in a trance betweene her mothers armes.[10]

At this awful turn of events, which he had espied from his hiding place, Cardenio was filled with conflicting emotions. Finally he mounted his donkey and rode out of town. He traveled "at random" for three days, eventually finding a few goatherds who fed him.

This portion of the Cardenio tale which, except for the wedding ceremony, Shakespeare appropriated for his main plot, reveals the serious flaws of Cervantes as a writer. Cervantes's story, full of wit and clever observations, is marred by one literary lapse after another. There is no confrontation between Luscinda and her pandering father and there is no confrontation between Cardenio and the double-crossing Don Fernando, either before or after the wedding. Perhaps most unforgivable of all, the exciting scene at the wedding fizzles out after Cervantes had set the stage for raw thrills. Forced by her pandering father to wed the lecherous, treacherous Don Fernando, the beautiful Luscinda goes to the ceremony with a dagger concealed in her wedding gown. Now, when a distraught maid, armed with a bare bodkin in her bodice, confronts the villain of the piece, the laws of drama require that she use that bodkin, either to stab herself or the villain, or to have the weapon wrested from her in a suspenseful struggle. To permit her to faint is a cheap trick. It is the same shabby device used by otherwise reputable writers of the last century (Thomas Hardy, for example) who, in a concession to Victorian prudery, would "draw the curtain of charity" over any scene that promised to be delectably prurient.

Cervantes's melodrama now disintegrates as Cardenio, smoldering with hatred for Don Fernando, turns into a crag-bounding lunatic. Luscinda also runs away and Don Fernando pursues her. More than a hundred pages later, relieved by interesting interludes like Don Quixote's fierce sword battle with the giants that leaves the cellar floor covered with blood (the giants turned out to be wine bags and the blood turned out to be wine), and "The Tale of the Curious Impertinent," Dorotea, who has also escaped from Don Fernando with the aid of a faithful servant whom she later shoves over a cliff because he makes improper advances, joins Cardenio, Don Fernando, and Luscinda, and all the loose ends are gauchely tied by Cervantes. Instead of skewering Don Fernando, Cardenio meekly accepts his apology and is reunited with Luscinda. (Cervantes had obviously forgotten that Luscinda and Don Fernando were legally married.) The penitent Don Fernando finally ends up with Dorotea.

Cervantes's characterizations of Don Fernando, Cardenio, Luscinda, and Dorotea are limned in black and white. They are men and women whittled of wood and move only when the author prods them into action. If there is a character change, it comes with the startling, sudden effect of a bucket of cold water in the face. In the last scene of the Cardenio tale, Cervantes violates every law of creative writing with a rash of bowing and scraping and apologies when there should be oaths and anger and the clash and flash of good Toledo steel. The wild Cardenio, who fled from his native Andalusia rather than confront the man who had stolen his beloved, is suddenly hit with a desire to cross swords with his foe. Of course, he does not, for Cervantes never follows through on an obligatory scene. Instead, Cardenio and Don Fernando shake hands. The seduced and betrayed Dorotea, described elsewhere by Cervantes as "so beautiful, modest, wise and virtuous that no one who knew her could decide which of those qualities she most excelled in," this elegant lady who had pushed her devoted servant over a cliff and never bothered to find out whether he died in agony from compound fractures or was instantly killed, melts into the arms of the seducer, liar, sneak and double-crosser, Don Fernando, whose frank admission that he was a cheat and deceiver presumably patches up his contemptible character and renders him loveable. In this scene Cervantes puts the willing suspension of disbelief to its ultimate test.

Despite the fact that William Lyon Phelps called *Don Quixote* "a colossal bore," adding that "the Don tilted against windmills; hence I wish he had tilted against the author of his being, who was one of the greatest windmills of all time,"[11] I found the lunacy that was afoot on every highway and in every hostelry rather delightful. Most of the characters are a little zany; some, like the Don himself, are downright pixilated. Occasionally, without the slightest motivation, villains become heroes and heroes become villains. Still, this is a great book of adventure, rich in proverbs and memorable expressions, among which I might cite: "plain as the nose on a man's face," "let's not mince matters," "looked before he leapt," and "made a laughing stock of himself."

I feel quite sure that what appealed to Shakespeare in *Don Quixote* was the clever way in which Cervantes ridiculed and helped to depopularize the knight-errant romances of the Middle Ages. Cervantes himself tilted against the preposterous conventions of the past. His great book is also a mighty blow against injustice. The crazy Don is, in fact, a new type of hero, one who seeks truth in the realm of the imagination, who mixes common sense with insanity. In spite of his cultural pretenses, Don Quixote speaks in the vernacular. His idiom belongs to the common people, and this is one of his universal appeals. There is a wild wisdom in Don Quixote that probes into the inner nature of man. In the aging Don's lunacy lies the essence of his age: the war against hypocrisy and evil, the quest for the underlying truth of reality. Cervantes's Don Quixote was blood kin of Hamlet. Both characters were obsessed with finding out the truth; both abhorred lies and pretense; and both were trapped in an inexorable flow of destiny. Hamlet had his Horatio and Don Quixote his Sancho. Each sidekick was a sounding board for the inner thoughts and doubts that plague all reasoning men.

Cervantes and Shakespeare shared another bond. As Renaissance men, their quest for worldly wisdom led them to draw their characters out of royal chambers and bawdy houses. They delved into every realm of life. It is easy to find parallels in their work because they reasoned alike.

An average critic, reading the Cardenio tale in Cervantes, will marvel that Shakespeare and Fletcher could pry a sparkling plot out of it. But ferreting out plots was one of Shakespeare's *métiers*. Although George Bernard Shaw was forever castigating Shakespeare for his ill-developed plots, one is always astonished that the great dramatist from Stratford could take a few paragraphs of pedestrian prose and transform them into an exciting, believable play. The ability of Shakespeare (and Fletcher had the identical knack, to a lesser degree) to espy a plot lurking in a few lines of pedestrian exposition is one of the many wonders of his genius. In their highly original book, *Shakespeare Alive!*, Joseph Papp and Elizabeth Kirkland encapsulated this sparkling facet of Shakespeare's talent:

> The variety of [Shakespeare's source] material alone is impressive and has intrigued professors and scholars for decades. But even more amazing is what Shakespeare did with his sources. No matter how dull the material he started with, his finished product was always an exciting, funny, or gripping drama.
>
> This is because Shakespeare approached his sources, not as a scholar, but as a playwright. Although he had plenty of facts at hand, his goal was dramatic truth. Everything he read, everything his absorbent mind took in, was shaped and molded to the needs of the theater. The question at the back of his mind as he flipped through Samuel Harsnett's *Declaration of Egregious Popish Impostures,* or Thomas Lodge's *Rosalynde* or Raphael Holinshed's *Chronicles* was always the same: what will work on the stage?
>
> In the process of answering this question, Shakespeare often took extraordinary liberties with his sources—changing names, settings, and centuries; rearranging events; compressing or extending time; and cutting and inventing characters. He made tragedy out of biography, comedy out of pastoral, and "pastoral-comical, historical-pastoral, tragical-historical, and tragical-comical, historical-pastoral" (as Polonius might have said) out of everything.
>
> To comprehend how amazing his transformations were, just imagine *Romeo and Juliet* without the nonstop patter of the Nurse; *As You Like It* without Touchstone's wit and Audrey's country simplicity; or *Henry IV Part I* without the fiery prominence of Hotspur. All of these colorful characters were either nonexistent or very minor figures in the sources Shakespeare borrowed from. From the historian Raphael Holinshed's brief comment in the story of Richard II that the Duke of York "communed with the Duke of Lancaster," Shakespeare

> fashioned the powerful scene between York and Bolingbroke in Act 2 of *Richard II*. Here, the playwright brings family relationships, power games, and conflicting loyalties to a dramatic climax—all from a historian's short reference.[12]

For the play of *Cardenio* or *The Second Maiden's Tragedy,* Shakespeare borrowed from Cervantes for the main plot the events leading up to the wedding ceremony of Luscinda and Don Fernando and from them created a whole series of dramatic confrontations between the characters (to use Cervantes's names) Luscinda and her father, and Luscinda and Don Fernando, Cardenio and Luscinda's father and Cardenio and Don Fernando. The final scene with Luscinda is handled with skill. Shakespeare and Fletcher jettison the frustrating marriage ceremony and create immense excitement by having the lusting Don Fernando (The Tyrant) dispatch soldiers to seize Luscinda (The Lady). Unlike the fainting Luscinda in Cervantes's tale, The Lady learns that soldiers are on their way to arrest her and take her to Don Fernando's bed, so she asks Cardenio to draw his sword and slay her. She explicitly tells him to thrust the blade into her bosom. At this point, Shakespeare's audience must have held its collective breath. Was Cardenio really going to plunge his sword into the woman he loved? Had he slain her, as Shakespeare and Fletcher knew, the rules and regulations of Elizabethan drama would have required that he then commit suicide and the curtain would fall and whatever was left of the play would be anticlimactic. The dramatists deftly solved the problem and at the same time astonished and horrified their audience. Cardenio, with naked sword pointed at his beloved's bosom, rushes at her, but the murderous task is too much for him and he falls in a dead faint at Luscinda's feet. With the soldiers pounding at the door, Luscinda picks up the sword and thrusts it into her breast. Her courageous suicide (which Cervantes had neatly sidestepped) sets the course for this morality romance in which Luscinda's dead body and ghost will both play a decisive role. With the story background provided by *Don Quixote*, Shakespeare and Fletcher now hurl Cervantes's characters into the midst of an intrigue that sweeps them, all of them, towards an inevitable climax of murder, retribution, and final triumph.

Miguel de Cervantes. Engraved by Hinchcliff after a portrait by Vandergucht.

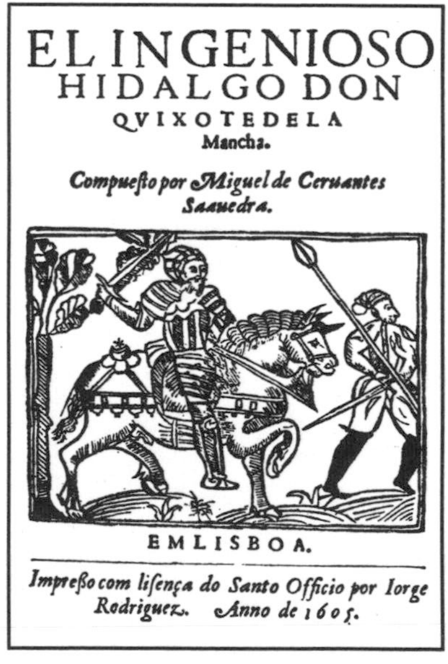

EL INGENIOSO
HIDALGO DON
QVIXOTE DE LA
Mancha.

Compueſto por Miguel de Ceruantes Saauedra.

EM LISBOA.

Impreſſo com liſença do Santo Officio por Iorge Rodriguez. Anno de 1605.

Title page of the first Portuguese edition of *Don Quixote*, Lisbon, 1605.

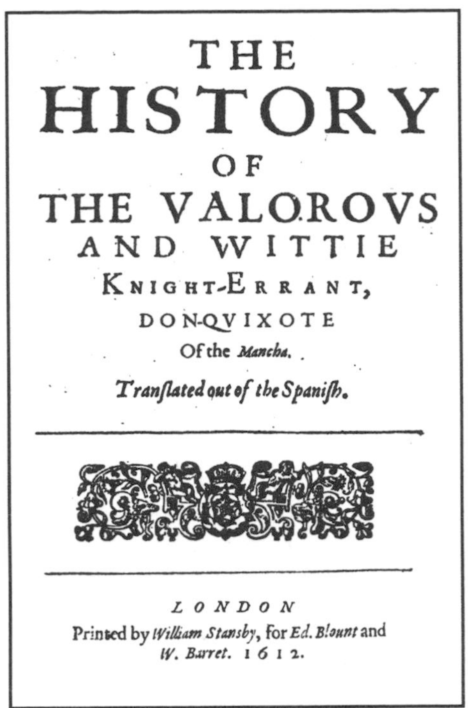

THE
HISTORY
OF
THE VALOROVS
AND WITTIE
KNIGHT-ERRANT,
DON-QVIXOTE
Of the *Mancha*.

Translated out of the Spanish.

LONDON
Printed by *William Stansby*, for *Ed. Blount* and
W. Barret. 1612.

Title page of the first English edition of *Don Quixote (Part I)*, London, 1612.

Title page of a very early English edition of *Don Quixote, The first part*, 1612.

CHAPTER IV

SHAKESPEARE AND FLETCHER

In 1611 Shakespeare was forty-six years old. For nearly two decades he had turned out an average of almost two plays a year. Now semiretired and spending much of his time at New Place, his beautiful home in Stratford, Shakespeare had given up acting and was on his way to becoming the playwright emeritus of Blackfriars and the Globe. Shakespeare was tired. To absorb part of his continuing labors for the King's Men, he turned to a young collaborator for help. His choice was John Fletcher, an energetic, skilled dramatist, a genius in his way, only thirty-two, but with a long line of credits. Fletcher could turn out a middling subplot, fill in sparkling dialogue, dash off an entertaining scene or a whole act.[1] He was also easy to work with, if we are to judge from the numerous collaborators he had during his career—Beaumont, Shakespeare, Cyril Tourneur, John Ford, Massinger, and several others, some say even Ben Jonson. Most important of all, Fletcher was an accomplished mimic. He could play the sedulous ape to the style of his collaborator.

John Fletcher (1579-1625) was the son of Richard Fletcher, D.D., minister of Rye, Sussex, a former fellow of Corpus Christi College, Cambridge, who later, as dean of Petersborough, disgraced himself as the spiritual tormenter of Mary Stuart during her last moments of life. By this improper act, Fletcher's father won the favor of Queen Elizabeth and became not only the Queen's chaplain, but successively bishop of Bristol, Worcester, and London. John Fletcher was only seven when his father again disgraced himself, this time by espousing, as Swinburne put it in a most genteel euphemism, "a lady of such character as sometimes too frequently figures on the stage of his illustrious son."[2] The bishop, who is said to have died as a result of heavy smoking, left all his books to John.

The tales of John Fletcher's youth and education are mostly apocryphal. Some biographers aver that he became bible-clerk at Cambridge when only fourteen and went on to complete his education at Cambridge. Around 1607, Fletcher and Francis Beaumont met and began their famous collaboration. Their first play may have been *The Woman Hater*, entered on the *Stationers' Register* on May 20, 1607. Some critics claim the play was entirely written by Fletcher; others insist that Beaumont wrote it all—clear proof that even in their first drama their individual styles were almost indistinguishable.

John Aubrey, the English Suetonius, dug up some interesting scuttlebutt about Beaumont and Fletcher: "There was a wonderful consimility [similarity] of fancy between them. I think they were both of Queen's College in Cambridge. I have heard. . .that [Beaumont's] main business was to correct the overflowings of Master Fletcher's wit. They lived together on the Bankside, not far from the [Globe] playhouse, both bachelors; lay together, etc.; had one wench in the house between them, which they did so admire; the same clothes and cloak, etc., between them."[3]

Aside from his three collaborations with Shakespeare, Fletcher's most significant contributions to English drama are four great plays written with Beaumont: *The Maid's Tragedy, Philaster, A King and No King*, and *The Knight of the Burning Pestle*. Fletcher is credited with twenty-seven plays sans a collaborator. During the great plague of 1625, according to Aubrey, "a knight of Norfolk or Suffolk invited him [Fletcher] into the country. He stayed [in London] but to make himself a suite of cloathes, and while it was makeing fell sick of the plague and died."[4]

Fletcher was an enormous help, a crutch almost, to the semiretired Shakespeare. The Shakespeare-Fletcher dramas to which Fletcher may have contributed a generous share, perhaps more than a generous share, are *Henry VIII* (accepted by Heminges and Condell as Shakespeare's and included in *The First Folio*), *The Two Noble Kinsmen,* and *Cardenio* or *The Second Maiden's Tragedy.*

For more than one hundred and fifty years scholars have known that the subplot in *Cardenio* is based upon Cervantes's "Historie of the Curious Impertinent" in Sheldon's translation of *Don Quixote*.

In reading the curious-impertinent tale in Sheldon's translation, we are struck by its frivolous tone. As the plot begins to unfolds, the play seems like a comedy of manners by Congreve or Sheridan, in which an aggregation of unsympathetic characters are intent upon making fools of themselves for the audience's delectation. But we quickly become aware that all the characters will likely come to a bad end.

The curious-impertinent tale is actually a novelette "preserved in the amber of the great Spanish romance"[5] and set smack in the midst of Cardenio's lamentations and turf-hopping. Anselmo [Anselmus], a Florentine gentleman, asks his best friend Lotario [Votarius] to test the fidelity of Anselmo's beautiful, young wife, Camila [wife of Votarius]. Anselmo complains that he will have no rest until he is certain of her total devotion. After protesting, Lotario makes a mock test and is rebuked by Anselmo. Lotario's real test, during Anselmo's absence from town, results in the seduction of Camila. The tested and tester become lovers. Later, when Anselmo becomes suspicious, Lotario and Camila stage a "show" to allay his suspicions. As Anselmo watches from behind a curtain, Camila pretends to resist Lotario's advances. Meanwhile, Camila's maid, Leonella, who has discovered her mistress's secret love and threatens to betray her, has herself taken a furtive lover, Bellarius, whose shadowy visits to Leonella lead Anselmo to the conclusion that his wife has a lover. Eventually, the intrigues culminate in Anselmo's discovery that Camila and Lotario are lovers. As usual, Cervantes, after building up to a horrifying climax where fury and conflict and revenge are called for, lets the whole plot fizzle out. Lotario flies with Camila to a monastery. Leonella runs away. Anselmo writes a farewell note and then dies of remorse at his own folly for setting up the seduction of his wife. Lotario goes off to war and is slain in some far-off battle. Camila takes monastic vows and obligingly rounds off the tale by dying shortly afterwards. By ending the story with a whimper instead of a bang, Cervantes has left to Shakespeare and Fletcher the task of injecting vitality and power into the finale.

Without changing the cast, the two dramatists infuse the subplot of *Cardenio* or *The Second Maiden's Tragedy* with ominous forebodings from the very start, then allow a ruthless and preordained fate to lead the characters, all five of them, to their violent deaths. After a complicated interchange amongst the players that grows ever more menacing, the unnamed wife (Camila in *Don Quixote)* of Anselmus (Anselmo in *Don Quixote*) stabs Votarius (Lotario in *Don Quixote)* with a poisoned sword. Anselmus then kills Leonella (the maid), who has treacherously informed on her mistress, with the same poisoned weapon. Anselmus and Leonella's lover Bellarius fight a duel with swords and the wife of Anselmus deliberately runs between the clashing blades and is killed. Anselmus and Bellarius continue their combat and both are mortally wounded. In four minutes on the stage, the entire cast of the subplot is slain, four of them by the viper-like poisoned blade that pricks and slays. Taking them as a group, they were a sordid, unpleasant lot of simpletons and sluts whose lives prove nothing and whose deaths evoke no laments. It is, in fact, in the main plot of *Cardenio* that the great power and beauty of this extraordinary play is revealed.

The fragile skein that ties the subplot and the main plot of *Cardenio* strongly suggests that the two sections of the play were separately written, then spliced together by the insignificant fact (for the plot) that Govianus, the deposed king and hero of the main plot, and Anselmus, the buffoon and cuckold in the subplot, are brothers.[6] Linking the characters by kinship doesn't pull the fusion off. The main plot and the subplot remain as Cervantes created them, separate and unrelated.

In studying *Cardenio*, I have paid special attention to Fletcher's technique and style in an effort to distinguish it from Shakespeare's. Not an easy task. Right from the start, however, I detected stylistic differences between the main plot and the subplot. I was quickly drawn to the conclusion that the main plot was by Shakespeare and the subplot by Fletcher. In O.L. Hatcher's *John Fletcher: a Study in Dramatic Method* (1905) appears a lengthy, cogent analysis of Fletcher's approach to the art of dramatic writing, brilliantly summarized by Lawrence B. Wallis. Basing her study upon fifteen Fletcher plays written without collaboration, Miss Hatcher has hit upon most of the theatrical effects and techniques that are conspicuous in the subplot of *Cardenio,* or *The Second Maiden's Tragedy:*

> In both plotting and characterization Fletcher's dependence on stage conventions was marked. Since he lacked depth, subtlety and strong creative faculty, he could not highly individualize the type, whether in character or situation.

But his choice of conventions was discriminating, and he wove them into the structure of his plays with rare agility.

Among his conventions of plot, disguise (especially of girls as boys) was the one most overworked; yet the gay mix-ups and mischief of his comic plots owed much to it. The most unconvincing one, except in some farcical instances, was his unmotivated use of "conversion," in order to give rise to new situations or speed the dénouement. Retribution, or the deed returning upon the doer, was happily used for comic purposes, as were the abundant asides, unnatural, unsubtle, yet helpful in keeping spectators abreast of the briskly moving turns of action. But these "commonplaces of the theatre" were often inappropriate and vexing when used in tragicomedy or tragedy.

Conventional types of character were the natural outgrowth of such plotting, since behavior patterns were determined by the action. The figures, frequently resembling one another from play to play, echoed the exaggerations and absurdities of the situations in which they were placed. Diverse stories did, however, give some differentiation to individuals of the same type. They were, in general, conscienceless creatures.

The main characters were, for practical reasons, of the upper classes; they thus lent themselves readily to spectacle, and had leisure for adventure and merry intrigue. But a sympathetic interest in the lower classes was reflected in a host of minor figures. Fletcher's major types were the clever maid-in-love, the merry scapegrace, the sentimental hero or "mooning youth," and the brave soldier; minor ones included the chaste maid or matron, the clever servant, the wrathful gentleman, the merry old man, the evil king or duke, and the scheming favorite. If these figures, seldom much individualized and never original, had small human interest compared with Shakespeare's, Fletcher nonetheless selected perennial favorites almost unerringly.

From her study of our playwright's stagecraft, Miss Hatcher concluded that he had a nearly infallible "stage manager's instinct." He expended much energy upon stirring his audience to a sense of bustling activity. His characters came and went constantly; the stage group kept shifting in "kaleidoscopic fashion." Anyone bound for anywhere crossed the stage, but paused to tell his errand. Changes in scene, normally not involving much distance, were numerous. Characters frequently had just returned from their travels, or were about to set out on them, and there was much talk of journeys; trips were sometimes prepared for with much bustling about, and then countermanded. Moreover, Fletcher could visualize to the full the possibilities of the inner and upper stages, of the doors, windows, balconies and other structural features of his playhouse. Hence he could, with rare flexibility, bring two or more groups to interact on each other, whether in eavesdropping scenes, serenades, battlefields, masques or play-within-a-play. All this made for an "air of commotion" well suited to comedy, if unrestful in more serious plays.

In his technique, Fletcher observed the unities of time and place adequately; the first by creating the impression of an almost continuous time-sequence, and the second by making careful transitions between his frequent, but short-distance, changes of place. He flagrantly violated unity of action, however—a grievous fault in his serious plays. Since he sought to combine in one drama as many groups as he could, he did not focus on "some powerful personal center."

> So, as Coleridge had suggested, he gave his plays no "inner coherence" or "strongly vitalized relations." Two or more plots might be joined so loosely as to be virtually independent; linking devices were usually the flimsy ones of kinship or service. Such plotting, however, always provided abundant activity, and sometimes furnished a contrasting tone, or intensified the mood. But only in the comedies was the absence of "general centralization" relatively harmless or even, at times, almost advantageous.
>
> As for other matters of technique, Fletcher quickly sketched-in the essential "exposition" in the opening conversation of a play, and thereafter allowed his loquacious characters to talk everything into crystal clearness. Preferring the fillip of surprise to adequate motivation, he left many major turns of the action unprepared, a "fault" which "ran riot" in the tragicomedies and comedies. His dénouements were always spectacular if dubiously dramatic, with every possible closing-scene convention packed into them, and every effect heightened indiscriminately. To create conflict, except of the more tangible kinds, was beyond his powers; his "whole moral endowment was against the portrayal of the tragic life," with its deeper, spiritual issues. Hence tragic heroes. . .lacked any inner struggle, and villains were base and bestial without adequate motivation.[7]

The pitfalls for any critic who attempts to identify the writers in any collaboration are obvious. In the case of Shakespeare and Fletcher, the tendency, of course, is to assign the good writing to Shakespeare and the not-so-good writing to Fletcher.[8] Even this method may prove difficult. Professor Schoenbaum notes: "Collaborations. . .and revisions are less likely to manifest stylistic individuality than the unrevised work of a single author. The partners may adjust their styles to one another; the reviser may imitate his predecessor. In *Eastward Ho,* Jonson, Marston and Chapman—three of the age's most individualistic writers—pooled their talents to produce a play with remarkable consistency of texture. . ."[9]

In discussing the authorship of *The Second Maiden's Tragedy,* Professor Anne Lancashire writes: "Collaborate authorship is no longer considered a real possibility; the play is stylistically, thematically and linguistically of a piece."[10] The acceptance of this simple, categorical assertion paves the way for the attribution of the play to the most popular candidate—Thomas Middleton. *But I cannot agree that in theme, style, and language the plot and subplot indicate a common authorship.*

Concerning the collaboration of Shakespeare and Fletcher, Richard Garnett and Edmund Gosse pointed out the possible explanation for Professor Lancashire's opinion: "Nothing else in English is so like Shakespeare as a successful scene from a romantic comedy of Fletcher. Superficially, the language, the verse, the mental attitude often seem absolutely identical, and it is a singular tribute to the genius of the younger poet that he can endure the parallel for a moment."[11] Certainly, the difference between the writing of Shakespeare and Fletcher can be tantalizingly subtle. A most astute critic, E.K. Chambers, commented on Shakespeare's romance plays in *Shakespeare: A Survey* (pp. 287–88): ". . .the general scope of the later tragicomedies of Shakespeare and that of the early tragicomedies of Beaumont and Fletcher is much the same. They have many devices of construction and many types of character in common. Wickedness triumphs for a time, but never in the end. Truth and charity pass through the furnace and come out unscathed. . . ." Arthur H. Bullen, a distinguished critic of half a century ago, pinpointed the characteristics of Fletcher's writing:

> Fletcher excelled as a master of brilliant dialogue and sprightly repartee. In the management of his plots and the development of his characters he was careless and inconsistent. But in his comedies the unceasing liveliness and bustle atone for structural defects; and in tragedy his copious command of splendid declamation reconciles us to the absence of rarer qualities. Fletcher's metrical characteristics are strongly marked. He sought by various devices to give greater freedom to the movement of blank verse. Thus he introduces redundant syllables in all parts of the line, and he is particularly fond of ending the line with an emphatic extra monosyllable, a practice in which he stands alone. . .Fletcher's verse, however, becomes monotonous, owing to his habit of pausing at the end of the line; and for tragic purposes it is wanting in solidity. His metrical peculiarities are of importance in helping us to distinguish his work from the work of his coadjutors.[12]

And now, having described all these booby traps for the unwary scholar who presumes to separate the styles and techniques of Shakespeare and Fletcher, I shall stick my neck out and hazard the supposition that Fletcher wrote the subplot, or most of the subplot. There are, however, parts of the subplot that I believe may be the work of Shakespeare and parts of the main plot that I think may be the work of Fletcher. My original intention was simply to assign the main plot to Shakespeare and the subplot to Fletcher and thus elude the difficult problem of naming the scenes on which the two dramatists may have collaborated. But since I have so frequently committed myself on controversial subjects, and in fairness to the reader, I presume that a further attribution of scenes based upon style, characterization, versification and originality of language is in order: Shakespeare: Ii, III, IVii and Vii; Shakespeare and Fletcher, Iii, IIi and IIiii; Fletcher, IIii, IVi and Vi.

Scholars have often observed that Fletcher, as well as Beaumont, liked a ready-made plot, with ready-made characters. A.S.W. Rosenbach pointed out that "Beaumont and Fletcher stayed close to the source, even in minor details and the language used by the characters."[13] If my attribution is correct, this is precisely what Fletcher may have done with the curious-impertinent tale. To illustrate how Fletcher exploited his sources, here are two comparative passages:

Cardenio	*Don Quixote*
What profit can return to you by knowing That which you do already,	Tell me, Anselmo, if heaven or thy fortunes had made Thee Lord and lawfull possesor

with more toil?
That a man needs, in having
a rich diamond
Put it between a hammer
and an anvil,
And not believing the true
worth and value,
Break it in pieces to find
out the goodness
And in the finding, lose it?
(I, ii, 300-06)

of a most precious Diamante, of whose goodnesse and qualitie all the Lapid-arists that had viewed the same would rest satisfied, and that all of them would joyntly and uniformely affirme that it arrived in quality, goodnes, and finesse to all that, to which the Nature of such a stone might extend it selfe, and that thou thy selfe didst beleeve the same, without witting anything to the con-trary: would it be just that thou shouldest take an humour to set that Diamant betweene an Anvile and a hammer; and to trie there by force of blowes whether it be so hard and fine as they say? And farther, when thou didst put thy designe in execution, put the case that the stone made resistance to thy foolish triall, yet wouldest thou adde thereby no new valour or esteeme to it? and if it did breake, as it might befall, were not then all lost?[14]

Cardenio

What labour is't for a woman
to keep constant. . .
That's never tried or
tempted?. . .
O, what a lazy virtue
Is chastity in a woman if
no sin
Should lay temptation to't
(I, ii, 279-80, 286-88)

Don Quixote

For what thanks is it. . .for a woman to be good, if no bodie say or teach her ill? What wonder that she be retired and timerous, if no occasion be ministred to her of dissolution. . . . [15]

There are numerous other passages that are similar in the two works that you can locate with ease; or, if you prefer, you will find many of them listed in Professor Lancashire's edition of *The Second Maiden's Tragedy.*[16]

Scholars have frequently essayed the primrose path to determine the authorship of anonymous or obviously misattributed plays by counting feminine endings, caesural pauses, images, oxymorons, line run-ons, verse irregularities, frequency of word usage, neologisms (often found in Shakespeare's work), contractions, and abbreviations. The advantage of this easy method, which is often of some value, is that the critic is not required to possess any literary taste. Even if he has zinc ears, all he need do is feed his computer to find the answer to the question, "Did Shakespeare write this play (or scene or passage)?"

The tough method with attributions to Shakespeare is to learn enough about drama to determine whether a play is tightly knit, redolent with power, and reveals the admirable craft (Shaw notwithstanding) of most of the other plays of the Master. And is the blank verse forceful and at times startling and beautiful?

One of the most effective of the easy methods, in my opinion, is that of Professor Hoy who, in a series of seven installments, issued a study entitled, "The Shares of Fletcher and His Collaborators in the Beaumont and Fletcher Canon."[17] As Fletcher wrote many plays on his own as well as with different collaborators, this is an important and engrossing subject. Hoy's method, however, is somewhat flawed because he had no access to any manuscript of Fletcher or any of his collaborators.

Following the method of Professor Hoy and occasionally drawing on a few of his conclusions, I have prepared a chart showing the frequency of certain word abbreviations or contractions in *The Maid's Tragedy* (Beaumont and Fletcher), *Henry VIII* (Shakespeare and Fletcher), *Cardenio* (Shakespeare and Fletcher) and *The Two Noble Kinsmen* (attributed to Shakespeare and Fletcher). All four plays date from approximately 1610 to 1613, so that the usage of contractual phrases should not be much affected by the time span, as would be the case if one compared the contractions in *Titus Andronicus* with those in *The Tempest.*

The startling variations in the appearance of word contractions in the four plays is very suggestive. Professor Hoy tells us that in Fletcher's unaided work the following (also favorites of Middleton) are constant in every scene: *o'th'*, *i'th'*, *ye,* and *'em.* While Professor Hoy is aware of the possibility of scribal intervention in the text, he does not deal with what can legitimately occur when Beaumont prepares the promptbook of a Beaumont and Fletcher play, or Shakespeare prepares the promptbook of a Shakespeare and Fletcher play, or Fletcher prepares the promptbook of a Shakespeare and Fletcher play. Clearly, the book, which likely would require minor changes and adjustments even during the copying, could not be entrusted to a clerk whose only talent was his legible chirography.

	Maid's Tragedy	*Henry VIII*	*Cardenio*	*Two Noble Kinsmen*
o'th'	——	23	——	31
i'th'	1	16	2	22
ha'	15	——	12	——
th'	——	44	3	26
ye	2	66	3	27
do't	5	——	10	1
'em	9	57	35	55
in's	——	5	——	2
see't	1	——	2	——
for't	1	——	11	6
on't	——	6	19	6
y'are	7	10	8	——
is't	4	5	6	4
in't	3	4	12	9
was't	1	——	1	1
t'ot	4	8	6	1

Frequency of Abbreviations and Contractions in *The Maid's Tragedy* (Beaumont and Fletcher), *Henry VIII* (Shakespeare and Fletcher), *Cardenio* or *The Second Maiden's Tragedy* (Shakespeare and Fletcher) and *The Two Noble Kinsmen* (Shakespeare and Fletcher).

After an examination of this chart, and, knowing as we do that the manuscript of *Cardenio* or *The Second Maiden's Tragedy* is in Shakespeare's handwriting, I think we can reasonably hypothecate that the printer's copy of *The Maid's Tragedy* by Beaumont and Fletcher was also the promptbook, very likely in Beaumont's hand; and both *Henry VIII* and *The Two Noble Kinsmen* were in Fletcher's hand. I believe we are justified in the further hypothecation that Beaumont and Shakespeare, in copying the portion of each play that was in Fletcher's hand, changed Fletcher's *ye*'s into *you*'s, his *i'th*'s into *in the*'s, and his *o'th*'s into *of the*'s, and his *th*'s into *the*'s. Beaumont was evidently not partial to '*em*'s and changed many of them into *them*'s. Such minor changes in the text of a collaborator were evidently the prerogative of the co-author saddled with the onerous task of preparing the book.

I have looked over the manuscript of *Cardenio* with great cunning and cannot find even so much as a pen scratch of Shakespeare's collaborator, John Fletcher. (A manuscript poem signed by Fletcher is illustrated in this chapter, together with a detailed identifying analysis.)

Late in his career, Shakespeare developed a partiality for the verb *bless (blessed, blessing).*[18] In his final five plays, the word *bless* and its derivatives occur ninety times, including eighteen times in *The Two Noble Kinsmen.* There are twelve usages in *Cardenio,* nine of them in the main plot.

That Shakespeare was a man of stringent morality and deep religious conviction is seldom questioned by scholars. In my previous work on Shakespeare, I mentioned that so rigorous was the dramatist's sense of morality that he had apparently cut out of his will (by deletion) a bequest to an old friend who had just been accused of being "unreasonably slack" with Stratford township funds.[19] One may, I think, surmise that Shakespeare, without being prudish, was not partial to oaths and rarely used them gratuitously or for metrical reasons in his dramas. It occurred to me to tabulate the Elizabethan oaths (very different from our curses today!) in the portion of *Cardenio* that I assigned to Shakespeare (the main plot) and the portion I assigned to Fletcher (the subplot). As the main plot comprises 1137 lines compared with 974 lines for the subplot, one might expect, if the expletives were evenly apportioned between the two plots, there would be about twenty percent more oaths in the main plot than in the subplot. Ignoring the censor's deletions, here is what the tabulation revealed: The writer of the main plot employed in all, twenty-three oaths in his lines, and the writer of the subplot incorporated forty-eight oaths, more than double the number in the main plot. Shakespeare's Elizabethan oaths, with frequency of usage, were *push* (two), *marry* (three), *life* (four), *troth* (three), *by my troth* (one), *O heav'n* (two), *faith* (six), *mass* (one) and *by th' mass* (one). Sir George Buc, the censor, or some other authorized official, had deleted *by th' mass* and ten usages of *life* (including those in the subplot) as being inappropriate language for public performance.[20] Alexander Schmidt records in all other plays of Shakespeare only one usage of *i'faith,* two usages of *push,* but numerous usages of *faith* and *by my faith.* The subplot contains seven usages of *i'faith.* Other oaths found in the subplot but not in the main plot or any other works of Shakespeare's are *cuds me, pist, byrlady* and *uds life.*

The magical word-usage of Shakespeare is perceptible throughout the five acts of *Cardenio.* His skill in devising apt neologisms by employing stale, ordinary words in a fresh sense is, as always, awesome. He often mints new adjectives by adding the prefix *un-*, or enlivens his lines with piquant compound words. In checking *Schmidt's Concordance,*[21] I found that some of the unusual words occur in other works of Shakespeare. Not found in other works: *perjurious* (line 1914), *catchpole* (line 1822), *long-nosed* (line 1397), *arch-subtlety* (line 914), *suspectful* (line 227), *virgin-victory* (line 1241), *risse* (for rose up, line 115), *city-pie* (line 1695) and *unlimitable* (line 263).

Words used elsewhere in Shakespeare's writings are: *dissemble, glorious, strumpet, everlasting, unhallowed, glister, disquiet, pavement, impudence, unpleasing* (five usages), *gross* (meaning easily perceptible), *shady* (meaning dark), *ingrateful* (ten usages), *durance* (ten usages).

Some words in *Cardenio* occur only once or twice in other writings of Shakespeare: *prisonment* (*Cardenio*, line 213; *King John,* III, iv, 161); *strange dish* (for conspiracy),

(*Cardenio*, line 361; *Winter's Tale*, III, ii, 73); *unfashionable* (meaning unpresentable), (*Cardenio*, line 832-34; *Richard III*, I, i, 22); *unpossible* (*Cardenio,* line 2116; *Richard II,* II, 2, 126); *twinkling* (*Cardenio,* line 1193; *Merchant of Venice,* II, ii, 177); *fleshly* (*Cardenio,* line 1446; *King John,* IV, ii, 245); *uncapable* (*Cardenio,* line 1455; *Merchant of Venice*, IV, i, 5 and *Othello,* IV, ii, 235); *chatter* (of teeth), (*Cardenio,* line 1655; *Lear,* IV, vi, 103); *roughness* (*Cardenio,* line 1807; *Lear,* II, ii, 103); *film* (meaning thin cover), (*Cardenio,* line 2089; *Hamlet,* III, iv, 147); *ungoverned* (*Cardenio,* line 1245; *Two Gentlemen of Verona*, IV, i, 45); *sneap* (meaning snub), (*Cardenio*, line 1126; *Henry IV, Part II,* II, i, 133);

Here are a few of the many phrases that are echoed elsewhere in Shakespeare's work:

Cardenio	Other Works of Shakespeare
When your discretion sucked (line 85)	when Hector's grandsire sucked (*Troilus & Cressida,* I, iii, 292)
steal a death (line 1181)	die the death (*Cymbeline,* IV, ii, 96)
robs the mind (line 882)	robs my tongue (*Richard II,* I, ii, 173)
beshrew your heart (line 521)	beshrew your heart (*Henry IV, Pt. II,* II, iii, 45)
unfashionable for pleasure (line 832)	lamely and unfashionable (*Richard III*, I, i, 22)
tossed between two tales (line 1834)	tossed between desire and dread (*Lucrece,* 171)
take acquaintance of my blood (lines 1939-40)	take a new acquaintance of thy mind (*Sonnet* 77, line 12)

It is, of course, quite possible that John Fletcher contributed some of the foregoing words and phrases to *Cardenio.* Whatever his contribution, his language was certainly reviewed and approved by Shakespeare at the time he wrote this manuscript of the play.

The blank verse in the subplot appears to me far more flexible, erratic, and undisciplined than in the main plot. Here are two random examples of the iambic pentameter from the subplot. The lines do not scan and are much too gauche to be from Shakespeare's pen:

> How earnestly y'are against us, as if we had robbed
> you (IV, i, 1351)
> To give you encouragement and advance your virtues
> (IV, i, 1359)

In attributing the subplot to Fletcher and the main plot to Shakespeare, I have kept in mind that the tone of the subplot is modern and in Fletcher's breezy style, whereas the main plot is old-fashioned, tightly knit and rigorously moral. The main plot characters are Shakespearean in the tradition of Hamlet and Macbeth. On the other hand, the subplot is daring and sophisticated, perhaps better adapted to the taste of the Court of James I.

John Fletcher. From an old print based upon a painting in the National Portrait Gallery, London.

Ther's not any Bruller of our tymes
inventing more; more misbegott wth ryme
Then I am at this Instant: But tys so
that I must write, yett hange mee Iff I knowe
of what; or to what End; for that maine sinne
of my fforgettfullnes (best of your kinde)
I knowe you have forgotten; for I am sure,
you are too good to lett your anger dure,
and so that subiects lost. Save then I strive
extreamely to commende you; Some doe thrive
by those same glorys; But they knowe what neede
such commendations; (as I knowe there neede
I take from; by additions:) Lett mee then
write something (Maddame) lyke those honest men
that have no busines; Something that affordes
some savor to the wrighter. Knights, and Lords
spring by your draughts, I will not treate of you
yt are too tearly: nor whether ytt bee true
wee shall have warre wth Spaine (I would wee might:)
nor what shall daunce ith Maske; nor what shall write
those brave things done: nor summe vp the expence;
nor whether ytt bee paid for ten yeare hence:
All these I overpasse; and come att Length
Out of myne owne dexteritie, and strength
to wish my selfe at Ashby: There I am sure
I should have Brawne, and Brakett, wch indure
Longer then twentie Tryumphs, and good Swan,
able to choake th'ambition of a churchman,
and Pyes cum privilegio, wthout sinne
forbydding all to make 'em, but Ralph Goodwin:
And you o Ladie I should see agen,
ther's all my maine end. you that every man,
and every tonge breaths well of, you that styll
lyke Eue before the fall must bee vnyll.
and though you have the power to doe amis
ye have the apple still to knowe what tys,
you I should see I saye, That of my all
service, and prayers, are originall.

Roome for a little prose, lyke a Dwarfe; There were certaine Bookes Maddame that Sr Thomas Beamont mentioned, and (as hee told mee;) for your Ladiship, wch shall bee very shortly sent downe, and some others to attend them. I am sure you will doe my service to my Lord; so I commytt you to your closett. maddame

All at your noble service
John ffletcher

Handwritten document signed by John Fletcher.

Although the signature on these verses addressed to the Countess of Huntington has, as you will perceive, a different visual appearance from the text of the document, a careful examination reveals that the text and signature are in the same writing. To the best of my knowledge, no other exemplar of John Fletcher's handwriting is known to exist.

To establish for yourself the common origin for the verses and signature, please observe first that the writing of the name has the identical stroke pattern, with approximately the same intensity, as the body of the document, and was apparently written in the same ink with the same quill. Further, the slant of the penmanship in the body of the document is the same as the slant in the signature.

Before you examine the individual letters of the signature, notice that the word *maddame* (two lines above the *John* of the signature) has the same visual appearance as the signature. The word *maddame* is written in a bastard combination of the modern round hand and the Elizabethan italic. Other proper names or foreign terms in the text are in italics, and the rest of the writing is in the secretary hand. Since nearly every educated person in the Elizabethan era could write in the secretary hand, italic, modern round hand, and court hand, as is evidenced by the surviving authorial manuscripts of the time, it is not unusual to find a writer using three or four different scripts in the same document. In the word *maddame* above Fletcher's signature, only the *d*'s are different from the same word (first word in line two of the five-line note just above the signature). The writing in this *maddame,* in turn, matches the italic printing in the text of the words *cum privelegio, Spaine, Ashby, Swan, Ralph Goodwin* and *Beamont.*

Now, examine the signature, *John Fletcher,* and compare it with the handwriting in the epistle. The *o* in *John* (there is no capital *J* in the epistle) matches perfectly the *o* in *too* (third word in line eighteen), a delicate circle attached to the letter that precedes it, but not to the letter that follows it. The *h* in *John* is the same *h* that appears in the name *Ashby* (center of line twenty-four from the top of the page). The *n* in *John* is much like the *n* in *then* (second word in line twenty-seven).

In the surname *Fletcher*, compare the second *f* in the word *affordes* (last word in line fifteen) with the capital *F*. the letter is identically formed. However, in the *F* in his signature, Fletcher put an extra crossbar through the letter, instead of using the double *ff,* to indicate that the letter was capitalized. The *l* in *Fletcher* may be found throughout the text, but a good example is in the word *apple* (fourth word in line eight from the bottom of the page). The Greek *e,* which occurs twice in *Fletcher,* is a little uncommon in Elizabethan handwriting. An identical Greek *e* may be observed in the word *Spaine* (seventh word in line nineteen from the top of the page). The *t* in *Fletcher* is a stubby, little stroke such as you will perceive in the word *Beamont* (fifth word in the fourth line above the signature). The *ch* in Fletcher's name is written in a sloppy, swift movement in the modern round hand and there are no characters in the verses that exactly match them. Fletcher concludes his signature with a bizarre *r* that appears to be a unique letter born from his imagination.

John Fletcher's Handwriting

too Ashby then affordes apple

Spaine Beamont

ohn flet

The matching letters, *ohn flet*, removed from the seven words in the epistle and placed for comparison below Fletcher's signature are powerful evidence that the entire epistle is in the dramatist's hand.

CHAPTER V

CARDENIO AND *THE MAID'S TRAGEDY*

The Maid's Tragedy (1610-11), a successful and famous play by Beaumont and Fletcher with probable retouching by Shakespeare, is a primary source for *Cardenio* or *The Second Maiden's Tragedy* (1611).

This categorical assertion, I must admit, as so often the case in this study, is at odds with the prevailing academic opinion. Professor Anne Lancashire has expressed the view held by most scholars. "The odd title of *S.M.T.* [*The Second Maiden's Tragedy*] originated with the censor, Sir George Buc. . . . It has generally been assumed that Buc so identified the play because it reminded him of Beaumont and Fletcher's *Maid's Tragedy,* which must therefore have passed through his hands not long before. The title could be related, however, to the non-extant *Proud Maid's Tragedy* acted at court by the Lady Elizabeth's Men on 25 February 1611/12, for as A.W. Ward has pointed out, *S.M.T.* has little in common with *The Maid's Tragedy* apart from the fact that both plays deal with a lustful tyrant. Both plays do, however, also depict tyrannicide. . . Buc's inappropriate and clumsy title has stuck to S.M.T. . . ."[1] My opinion, however, is that the main plots and style of *The Maid's Tragedy* and *Cardenio or The Second Maiden's Tragedy* are closely linked in many ways:

1. In both plays, the lust of a tyrannical monarch forces the woman he loves to commit suicide.

2. In both plays, the king's beloved murders him. In one, with a dagger; in the other, the ghost of the dead woman induces her real lover to poison the king.

3. The evil king in both plays makes the same proposal to each woman: Have a mock marriage to another and be my mistress and no one will suspect our affair. Evadne, in *The Maid's Tragedy,* accepts the proposal. The Lady in *Cardenio* rejects it.

4. In both plays, the lust of the king draws other members of his court into the intrigue. In *The Maid's Tragedy*, three innocent persons die; in *Cardenio,* two. However, the subplot of *Cardenio* supplies the Senecan touch, with five corpses on the stage at one time.

5. In both plays, the characters seem powered by destiny, with little control over their fate.

There are, of course, many incidents in each plot that would make the plays appear different and exciting, even to the sophisticated audiences of the time. In *The Maid's Tragedy*, Amintor, whose true love is Aspatia, marries the king's secret mistress Evadne (at the monarch's behest) as a coverup for the king's affair. Evadne has sworn to remain true to the king even after her marriage to Amintor. In the horrors that follow the mock wedding, Evadne stabs the king to death, then slays herself. Aspatia, who loves Amintor and had expected to wed him, is driven almost mad with grief when he marries Evadne. Dressed as a man, she provokes a duel with Amintor, who reluctantly kills her. After he discovers that he has slain Aspatia, Amintor commits suicide.

In *Cardenio,* the lustful king, a usurper, demands that The Lady become his queen or mistress and offers her a mock marriage with another man. She declines and the desperate king sends soldiers to capture her. She stabs herself and dies. The Tyrant's love is unabated and he transfers his passion for the living woman to her corpse. He exhumes the body of The Lady so he can adore her beauty even in death. In his necrophilic zeal, The Tyrant has The Lady beautifully embalmed by Govianus, the deposed king and lover of The Lady, who has disguised himself as a mortician. Govianus poisons the body of the dead Lady, whose ghost had appeared to exhort him to stop The Tyrant from abusing her body. The Tyrant dies after he kisses the poisoned corpse, and Govianus is restored to his throne. Truth has triumphed and the realm is at peace.

Despite the new plot twists, there is a consanguinity of style and organization in the two plays that hints at a common authorship. It seems likely that Shakespeare, as the senior dramatist of the Globe, still working at least part-time in the writing and production of new plays, overhauled and touched up *The Maid's Tragedy*.[2] Here are two speeches by Aspatia (truly a Shakespearean heroine!) that in my opinion outsoar the poetic reach of either Beaumont or Fletcher:

Come, let's be sad, my girls:
That down-cast of thine eyes, Olympias,
Shows a fine sorrow.—Mark, Antiphila;
Just such another was the nymph Oeone's,
When Paris brought home Helen.—Now, a tear
And then thou art a piece expressing fully
The Carthage-queen, when from a cold sea-rock,
Full with her sorrow, she tied fast her eyes
To the fair Trojan ships; and, having lost them,
Just as thine eyes do, down stole a tear. . .
(II, ii, 371)

Another speech that seems to carry the celestial ring of Shakespeare's verse is also delivered by Aspatia as she comments on some embroidery by Antiphilia:

These colors are not dull and pale enough
To show a soul so full of misery
As this sad lady's was. Do it by me,
Do it again by me, the lost Aspatia;
And you shall find all true by the wild island.
Suppose I stand upon the sea-beach now,
Mine arms thus, and mine hair blown with the wind,
Wild as that desert; and let all about me
Tell that I am forsaken. Do my face
(If thou hadst ever feeling of a sorrow)
Thus, thus, Antiphila: strive to make me look
Like Sorrow's monument; and the trees about me,
Let them be dry and leafless; let the rocks
Groan with continual surges; and behind me,
Make all a desolation. See, see, wenches,
A miserable life of this poor picture!
(II, ii, 372)

While I agree that parallels can be at times invidious, they are certainly no more invidious than identifying authorship by vocabulary, word or image clusters, and such things as the incidence of words like *hath* versus *has* and *'em* versus *them*. I shall therefore proceed with a few of the parallels between *The Maid's Tragedy* and *Cardenio* or *The Second Maiden's Tragedy.*

In both plays, the main plot is built upon the illicit sexual desires of a monarch and thus could prove offensive to King James, himself notorious for "his own royal and most gracious lust" (*Cardenio,* III, 1268). According to Anne Lancashire, "James was given to sudden favoritisms of handsome young men, upon whom he lavished gifts and titles; and sexual promiscuity at his court was widespread. Of particular note in 1611 was the promiscuity of the king's then favorite, Robert Carr, Viscount Rochester, whose influence over James was enormous."[3] Any mention of regicide had to be expressed with great delicacy. To avoid cuts in dialogue, dramatists for the King's Men usually incorporated a warning against any sort of violence against the king. In *The Maid's Tragedy* there were several such warnings, since the king in that play was a legitimate monarch, whereas in *Cardenio* the monarch was a usurper, and his murder was more acceptable in royal eyes. However, when Govianus contemplates the murder of The Tyrant, he is hesitant. Passages in *The Maid's Tragedy* and *Cardenio* indicate that the king was viewed as a godlike figure:

Cardenio	*The Maid's Tragedy*
A religious trembling shakes me by the hand	. . . there is Divinity about you, that

And bids me put by such unhallowed business,
But revenge calls for't, and it must go forward.
(V, ii, 2108-10)

strikes dead
My rising passions: as you are my king,
I fall before you, and present my sword
To cut mine own flesh, if it be your will. . .
(III, i, p. 382)

In both plays, there is a disconsolate lover who walks in the woods. In *The Maid's Tragedy,* Aspatia longs for her former lover Amintor, who has rejected her to wed the king's mistress. In *Cardenio,* Anselmus is so worried about his wife's possible infidelity that he cannot sleep at night. His wife describes his conduct:

Cardenio

He walks at midnight in thick shady [dark] woods
Where scarce the moon is starlight. I have watched him
In silver nights when all the earth was dressed
Up like a virgin in white innocent beams;
Stood in my window, cold and thinly clad
T'observe him through the bounty of the moon. . .
And when the morning dew began to fall,
Then was my time to weep.
(I, ii, 348-356)

The Maid's Tragedy

. . . this lady
Walks discontented, with her watery eyes
Bent on the earth. The unfrequented woods
Are her delight; where, when she sees a bank
Stuck full of flowers, she with a sigh will tell
Her servants what a pretty place it were
To bury lovers in; and make her maids
Pluck 'em, and strow her over like a corse.
She carries with her an infectious grief,
That strikes all her beholders. . .
(I, i, p. 344)

In both plays, the murderer of the king teases him before or while killing him. In *The Maid's Tragedy,* Evadne, who has tied the sleeping king to his bed, taunts him before she stabs him to death. In *Cardenio*, the hero and deposed king, having poisoned the body of The Lady, lays it before The Tyrant:

Cardenio

Tyrant: Hast done so soon?
Govianus: That's as your
grace gives approbation.
Tyrant: O, she lives again!
She'll presently speak to
me. Keep her up.
I'll have her swoon no more;
there's treachery [magic]
in't.
Does she not feel warm to
thee?
Govianus: Very little, sir.
Tyrant: The heat wants cher-
ishing, then. Our arms
and lips
Shall labour life into her.
Wake, sweet mistress!
'Tis I that call thee at the
door of life.
Kisses the body Ha!
I talk so long to death,
I'm sick myself.
Methinks an evil scent still
follows me.
Govianus: Maybe 'tis noth-
ing but the colour, sir,
That I laid on.
Tyrant: Is that so strong?
Govianus: Yes, faith, sir,
'Twas the best poison I
could get for money.
Throws off his disguise
Tyrant: Govianus!
Govianus: O thou sacri-
legious villain. . .
(V, ii, 2128-42)

The Maid's Tragedy

Evadne: O, you sleep soundly,
sir!
King: My dear Evadne,
I have been dreaming of thee:
come to bed.
Evadne: I am come at length, sir;
but how welcome?
King: What pretty new device is
this, Evadne?
What, do you tie me to you? By
my love,
This is a quaint one. Come, my
dear, and kiss me;
I'll be thy Mars; to bed, my
queen of love;
Let us be caught together, that
the gods may see
And envy our embraces.
Evadne: Stay, sir,
stay!
You are too hot, and I have
brought you physic
To temper your high veins.
King: Prithee, to bed, then:
let me take it warm;
There thou shalt know the state
of my body better.
Evadne: I know you have a sur-
feited foul body;
And you must bleed.
Draws a dagger,
King: Bleed!
Evadne: Ay, you shall bleed.
Lie still, and, if the devil,
Your lust, will give you leave,
repent. This steel
Comes to redeem the honour that
you stole. . .
(V, i, pp. 418-19)

In each play, the king's murderer confronts the monarch with his evil lust and predicts his damnation. Evadne's remarks are delivered as she raises the dagger to stab the king; and Govianus makes his speech just as he casts off his disguise:

Cardenio

Thou thief of rest, robber of
monuments!
Cannot the body after funeral
Sleep in the grave, for
thee? Must it be raised
Only to please the wickedness of thine eye?
Do all things end with
death, and not thy lust?
Hast thou devised a new way
to damnation,
More dreadful than the soul
of any sin
Did ever pass yet between
earth and hell?
(V, ii, 2143-2150)

The Maid's Tragedy

If thy hot soul had substance
with thy blood,
I would kill that too; which,
being past my steel,
My tongue shall reach. Thou
art a shameless villain;
A thing out of the overcharge
of nature,
Sent, like a thick cloud, to
disperse a plague
Upon weak catching [trusting]
women; such a tyrant,
That for his lust would sell
away his subjects,
Ay, all his heaven hereafter!
(V, i, pp. 419-20)

In both plays, the hero, tortured by his conflicting emotions as was Hamlet when he spoke the "To be or not to be" soliloquy, contemplates suicide, but rejects the idea of death, of which he has no fear, until he has completed one final earthly task:

Cardenio

Govianus: I'll make myself
Over to death too, and we'll
walk together
Like loving spirits: I
prithee let's do so.
—She's snatched away by fate
and I talk sickly;
I must dispatch this business
upon earth
Before I take that journey
(IV, iv, 1790-95)

The Maid's Tragedy

Amintor: There's something yet,
which I am loathe to leave;
There's man enough in me to meet
the fears
That death can bring; and yet
would it were done!
I can find nothing in the whole
discourse
Of death, I durst not meet the
boldest way;
Yet still, betwixt the reason
and the act,

> The wrong I to Aspatia did
> stands up. . .
> I will not leave this act un-
> satisfied
> If all that's left in me can
> answer it.
> (V, iii, p. 431)

In both plays, the songs are very similar and are written in similar meter (often used in songs of that era), mostly trochaic trimeter, but with some iambic tetrameter and trochaic dimeter. Compare a song from each drama:

From *Cardenio:*

Ĭf év/ĕr pí/tў wére/wĕll pláced (iambic tetrameter)

Ŏn trúe/dĕsért/ănd vír/tŭŏus hón/ŏur (iambic tetrameter)

Ít cŏuld/né'er bĕ/béttĕr/gracéd (trochaic trimeter)

Fréelў/thén, bĕ/stów't ŭp/ón hĕr. (trochaic tetrameter)

Névĕr/ládў/éarned hĕr/fáme (trochaic trimeter)

Ĭn vír/tŭe's wár/wĭth gréat/ĕr strífe (iambic tetrameter)

Tó prĕ/sérve hĕr/cónstănt/náme (trochaic trimeter)

Shĕ gáve/ŭp béau/tў, yóuth/ănd lífe. (iambic tetrameter)
(IV, iv, 1716-24)

From *The Maid's Tragedy:*

Láy ă/gárlănd/ón mў/héarse (trochaic trimeter)

Óf thĕ/dísmăl/yéw; (trochaic dimeter)

Máidĕns,/wíllŏw-/bránchĕs/béar (trochaic trimeter)

Sáy Ĭ/díed/trúe. (trochaic dimeter)

My love/was false/but I/was firm (iambic tetrameter)

From my/hour of/birth: (trochaic dimeter)

Upon/my bur/ied bod/y lie (iambic tetrameter)

Lightly/gentle/earth! (trochaic dimeter)

(II, i, p. 360)

For those not familiar with the conventions of Elizabethan verse, let me point out that occasional metrical deviations are permitted. The most common variant is the substitution of a spondee for an iamb or trochee; but occasionally, as in line two of the first stanza of the *Cardenio* poem, one finds an errant anapest. To avoid confusion I have not marked the deviant feet but have merely identified the meter intended by the poet.

In both plays, the visible power of inanimate objects in the presence of death is commented upon. In *Cardenio,* the tyrant king, about to turn body snatcher, perceives tears on the marble monument of the dead Lady. In *The Maid's Tragedy*, Amintor, the hero, comments on the power of death as he contemplates the body of Evadne, who has stabbed herself with the same dagger with which she slew the king:

Cardenio

Tyrant: How pity strikes
e'en through insensible
things. . .
(IV, iii, 1576)

The Maid's Tragedy

Amintor: There is some hidden
power in these dead things. . .
(V, iii, p. 430)

In both plays, there is a similar view of feminine honor, valued above all else in the world. In *Cardenio,* Govianus speaks of the dead *Lady* who killed herself rather than become the king's mistress. In *The Maid's Tragedy*, Evadne, who had sold her body to the king, is very aware of her tainted honor, and it is this taint she seeks to eradicate by her murder of the king. Both women are ready to die in defense of their honor.

Cardenio

Govianus: Eternal maid of
honour whose chaste body
Lies here like virtue's
close and hidden seed,
To spring forth glorious to

The Maid's Tragedy

Evadne: I was a world of honour,
virtue,
Till your cursed court and you
(hell bless you for't)
With your temptations on temp-

eternity
At the everlasting harvest. . .
(IV, iv, 1740-43)

tations
Made me give up mine honour;
for which, King,
I am come to kill thee.
(V, i, pp. 419-20)

In both plays, the guilt or innocence of an individual is read in the blush:

Cardenio

Votarius: His very name
shoots like a fever
through me,
Now hot, now cold. Which
cheek shall I turn toward
him
For fear he should read
guiltiness in my looks.
(II, ii, 794-96)

The Maid's Tragedy

King: I have thrown out words
That would have fetched warm
blood upon the cheeks
Of guilty men, and
he is never moved;
He knows no such thing.
(III, ii, p. 408)

In both plays there is an eloquent remark on the punishment of death for uttering an inacceptable statement:

Cardenio

Memphonius: Now by my
faith
His tongue has helped his
neck to a sweet bargain!
(IV, ii, 1502)

The Maid's Tragedy

Amintor:. . . make thy tongue
Undo this wicked oath, or on thy
flesh
I'll print a thousand words to
let out life!
(II, i, p. 367)

In both plays occurs the symbol of a house for the body, a sort of container for the soul. In *Cardenio,* The Lady, about to die by her lover's hand or her own, is reconciled. In *The Maid's Tragedy,* Amintor contemplates suicide without fear:

Cardenio

Lady: I am like one
Removing from her house. . .
(III, iii, 1198-99)

The Maid's Tragedy

Amintor: My soul grows
weary of her house. . .
(III, i, p. 430)

In both plays there are similar phrases:

Cardenio:	*The Maid's Tragedy*
Votarius: I praised the garden But little thought a *bed of snakes* lay hid in't. (I, ii, 480-81)	*Evadne:* I sooner will find out the *beds of snakes*. . . Than sleep one night with thee. . . (II, i, p. 365)

The dramatic scene in which The Tyrant kisses the poisoned body of the dead Lady is evocative of an earlier scene by Shakespeare in *Romeo and Juliet*. Juliet speaks:

> What's here? a cup, closed in my true love's hand?
> Poison, I see, hath been his timeless end:
> O churl! drunk all, and left no friendly drop
> To help me after? I will kiss thy lips;
> Haply some poison yet doth hang on them
> To make me die with a restorative. . .
> (V, iii, 161-66)

In addition to drawing on *The Maid's Tragedy,* Shakespeare and Fletcher may also have taken a few hints from Tourneur's *The Revenger's Tragedy,* a drama often attributed to Middleton. A very similar scene is the propping of the murdered duke's body by Vindice and his brother Hippolito against a wall so that it appears to be alive (*The Revenger's Tragedy,* IV, ii, 200-17), just as in *Cardenio,* Govianus leans Sophonirus's body against a door so that it will appear as if he were slain by the soldiers who break into the room (III, iii, 1243-48). Also, in *The Revenger's Tragedy,* Vindice poisons the skull of his mistress and the duke, who had raped her, kisses the skull and dies (III, v, 140-55), a scene that strongly parallels the murder of The Tyrant in *Cardenio.*

CHAPTER VI

CARDENIO AND THEOBALD'S *DOUBLE FALSEHOOD*

In the entire history of the British theater there is no more tantalizing mystery than what Dr. John Watson might call, "The Case of the Three Shakespeare Manuscripts." Lewis Theobald, an eighteenth-century editor and playwright, claimed that he owned three clerical copies of *Cardenio.* He refused to let anybody look at them, but to prove his contention, he wrote a drama called *Double Falsehood;* or, *The Distrest Lovers,* which he said was based upon his manuscript copies of *Cardenio,* a play originally written by Shakespeare. Strangely, the three manuscripts disappeared without a single soul ever seeing them. However, Theobald's play, *Double Falsehood,* survives. Thus the question before us now is, should the play by Theobald be renamed *Triple Falsehood* to commemorate three manuscripts that never existed; or should we admit that Theobald did have three manuscripts of *Cardenio* and used them to create his own version?

The storm center of this literary dilemma, Lewis Theobald (1688-1744), received only a modest private education which, by his linguistic talents, he parlayed into a brilliant scholarly background. He studied law, but quickly threw it over to become a Grub Street hack. In a "Preface" to his tragedy, *The Persian Princess,* Theobald claimed that the play was written and acted when he was only nineteen. Six years later, Theobald was eking out a living by translating Greek classics into racy English prose. He wrote and published uninspired verses and issued a series of controversial essays in three tiny volumes.

Aside from his poverty, the first major problem in Theobald's life came when he was accused of literary theft. John Churton Collins describes this celebrated incident which was to have a profound effect on Theobald's credibility:

> In 1715 appeared his tragedy, "The Perfidious Brother," which became the subject of a scandal reflecting very seriously on Theobald's honesty. It seems that Henry Meystayer, a watchmaker in the city, had submitted to Theobald the rough material of this play, requesting him to adapt it for the stage. The needful alterations involved the complete recasting and rewriting of the piece, costing Theobald, according to his own account, four months' labour. As he had "created it anew," he thought he was entitled to bring it out as his own work and take

> the credit of it; and this he did. But as soon as the play was produced Meystayer claimed it as his own, and in the following year published what he asserted was his own version, with an ironical dedication to the alleged plagiarist. A comparison of the two shows that they are identical in plot and very often in expression. But as Meystayer's version succeeded Theobald's, it is of course impossible to settle the relative honesty or dishonesty of the one man or of the other. The fact that Theobald did not carry out his threat of publishing Meystayer's original manuscript is not a presumption in his favour.[1]

After this literary *faux pas,* Theobald, ignoring whispers that he was a plagiarist, continued to grind out catchpennies. He produced an adaptation of Shakespeare's *Richard II* that brought him a hundred pounds enclosed in an Egyptian pebble snuffbox from Lord Orrery, but little else. Theobald became enmeshed in a critical battle with John Dennis (1657-1734), a pugnacious critic and dramatist, and made an implacable enemy of him. Then, in 1725, the publication of Alexander Pope's edition of Shakespeare gave him a chance to take on the Spider of Twickenham. It was the opportunity of a lifetime to destroy himself and Theobald seized upon it. He slashed, cut, and stabbed into shreds Pope's edition of Shakespeare. Almost everything he said about Pope was true, but truth was never any defense against the biting wit of the brilliant satirist who knew precisely how to demolish his enemies. Pope made Theobald the hero of his *Dunciad,* a poem still relishable for its clever assaults on Theobald's "pedantry, dulness, poverty and ingratitude."[2]

In 1733, Theobald published his seven-volume edition of Shakespeare's works, an excellent set still esteemed by scholars. For the balance of his life, however, he continued to lay down a constant barrage of hack works, mainly plays. He died without a groat to his name at 10 A.M. on September 18, 1744, leaving behind one grieving friend, Mr. Stede of Covent Garden Theatre, and two hundred and ninety-five rare old English plays in quarto editions.

The controversial play for which Theobald will always be remembered, *Double Falsehood,* premiered at the Drury Lane Theatre on December 13, 1727. It was a great hit. Theobald had revamped Cervantes's Cardenio tale, infused it with vitality, cut short the interminable meanderings of Cardenio, and, for the finale, produced a love-and-kisses dénouement that left his audience happy. The acting must have been outstanding, as there were two members of the Booth family in key roles. Barton Booth, who missed the first five performances because of illness, took the part of Julio, the hero (based upon the character of Cardenio), and Mrs. Booth was Violante (based on Dorotea, the seduced lady in Cervantes's story). The play had a run of ten performances, most unusual in that era of frequent one-night stands.

There is an "Epilogue" at the end of the play, "Written by a Friend and Spoken by Mrs. Oldfield" that ridicules the Elizabethan idea of honor, and perhaps explains why Theobald decided that *Cardenio* should be a comedy rather than a tragedy. Here are a few heroic couplets from this epilogue. which, had Pope not been a fierce enemy of Theobald, I might suspect were from his acerbic quill:

Well, Heaven defend us from these ancient Plays,
These Moral Bards of Good Queen Bess's Days!
They write from Virtue's Laws, and think no further;
But draw a Rape as dreadful as a Murther.
You modern Wits, more deeply vers'd in Nature,
Can tip the wink, to tell us, you know better;
As who should say—"'Tis no such killing Matter—
"We've heard old Stories told, and yet ne'er wonder'd,
"Of many a Prude, that has endur'd a Hundred:"
"And Violante grieves, or we're mistaken,"
"Not, because ravisht; but because—forsaken,—"
Had this been written to the modern Stage,
Her manners had been copy'd from the Age.
Then, tho' she had been once a little wrong,
She still had had the Grace to've held her Tongue;
And after all, with downcast Looks, been led
Like any Virgin to the Bridal Bed.[3]

Apparently, from the enthusiastic reception accorded the play, many persons believed that it was based upon the original *Cardenio,* then attributed to Shakespeare, rather than Shakespeare and Fletcher. Nobody at that time had seen the record of the play's performances at Whitehall in 1613; and apparently nobody knew that on September 9, 1653, Moseley had registered the play as "The History of Cardenio by Mr. Fletcher. & Shakespeare." Thus there seemed to be some truth in Theobald's claims. However, so vehement were the enemies of Theobald that Pope joined in the attack with the claim that Theobald had written the drama himself. A "young gentleman of Cambridge" composed a vicious jingle that was printed in *The Grub-Street Journal*, No. 98, November 18, 1731:

See Theobald leaves the lawyer's gainful train
To wrack with poetry his tortured brain;
Fired or not fired, to write resolves with rage,
And constant pores o'er Shakespeare's sacred page;
—Then staring cries, I something will be thought,
I'll write—then—boldly swear 'twas Shakespeare
wrote.
Strange! he in poetry no forgery fears,
That knows so well in law he'd lose his ears.[4]

The initial dispute over the authenticity of *Double Falsehood* eventually simmered down, but Professor S. Schoenbaum has alluded to it as one of those "puzzles which would in time arouse acrimonious debate. . . ."[5]

In his "Preface of the Editor" (1727), Theobald defended himself against the charge that he was lying when he claimed to own three manuscripts of *Cardenio,* a play believed to have been lost for over one hundred years. Here is the paragraph that launched a thousand quips:

> The Success, which this Play has met with from the Town in the Representation, (to say nothing of the Reception it found from those Great Judges, to whom I have had the Honour of communicating it in Manuscript;) has almost made the Purpose of a Preface unnecessary: And therefore what I have to say, is design'd rather to wipe out a flying Objection or two, than to labour at proving it the Production of *Shakespeare*. It has been alleg'd as incredible, that such a Curiosity should be stifled and lost to the World for above a Century. To This my Answer is short; that tho' it never till now made its Appearance on the Stage, yet one of the Manuscript Copies, which I have, is of above Sixty Years Standing, in the Handwriting of Mr. *Downes,* the famous Old Prompter; and, as I am credibly inform'd, was early in the Possession of the celebrated Mr. *Betterton,* and by Him design'd to have been usher'd into the World. What Accident prevented This Purpose of his, I do not pretend to know: Or thro' what hands it had successively pass'd before that Period of Time. There is a Tradition (which I have from the Noble Person, who supply'd me with One of my Copies) that it was given by our Author, as a Present of Value, to a Natural Daughter of his, for whose Sake he wrote it, in the Time of his Retirement from the Stage. Two other Copies I have, (one of which I was glad to purchase at a very good Rate,) which may not, perhaps, be quite so Old as the Former; but One of Them is much more perfect, and has fewer Flaws and Interruptions in the Sense.[6]

Even after two hundred and fifty years almost nobody writes about Shakespeare without a comment or two upon Theobald's claim. Some look upon Theobald as an outrageous liar; others contend he was almost certainly telling the truth. Kenneth Muir is a temperate critic:

> Theobald's account (in his *Preface*) is not above suspicion. He is vague on matters where one would like him to be precise. He does not tell us how he obtained possession of the Downes manuscript, nor the name of the Noble Person who supplied him with one of the manuscripts, nor does he make clear whether there were three or four manuscripts in all, nor does he give us the names of the "Great Judges" to whom he showed one manuscript. The tradition of Shakespeare's natural daughter reads like an invention, since the poet's plays were not his own property. It is odd that all the manuscripts should have disappeared, and, unless we assume that Theobald changed his mind about the authorship, it is strange that he did not include the play in his editions of Shakespeare.[7]

Ten pages later, Muir picks up his complaint and adds: "But one can understand the desire to relieve Shakespeare of all responsibility for a play which, in its present form, can add nothing to his reputation."[8]

For the affirmative side, I'd like to call E.H.C. Oliphant to the witness stand. After a lengthy discussion of *Double Falsehood*, with particular attention to the large number of feminine endings in the play that, he is convinced, proclaim the authorship of John Fletcher, Oliphant concludes that there is strong evidence that Theobald's drama was based upon one or more manuscript copies of *Cardenio:*

> I desire to point out that any one who refuses to regard the play as originally Elizabethan and looks on it as a shameless forgery by Theobald is driven to consider that, though he knew nothing of any supposition of a collaboration of Shakespeare and Fletcher in a drama on the subject, he yet about midway through the play abruptly changed his style and adopted what is at least a remarkably good imitation of the Fletcherian manner. Had he suspected such collaboration, he might possibly have done so; but in the circumstances the demand made upon us for an acceptance of the theory of mere coincidence is altogether too much. The weakness of Sir Sidney Lee's supposition that "Theobald doubtless took advantage of a tradition that Shakspere and Fletcher had combined to dramatize the Cervantes theme" is that there is no proof of such a tradition—that, in fact, there is the strongest reason for saying that Theobald had never heard the slightest hint of it. The play must therefore be regarded as based on an Elizabethan drama, and as containing passages that were contained in the original, and the early author of the latter portion of it must on internal evidence be set down as Fletcher. If we admit so much, we have made a big stride toward admitting the presence of Shakespeare—a circumstance that may cause many to deny Fletcher's participation. That both are present I have no doubt. Let me say, to avert misunderstanding, that I am not ascribing *Double Falsehood* partly to Shakespeare merely on the strength of a few odd lines bearing some resemblance to his style. I base my view on the strong case made for Fletcher by the combined external and internal evidence, and by the fact that the external evidence and the probabilities unite to make Shakespeare Fletcher's collaborator; wherefore, as certain passages bear the imprint of his style and manner of thought, I feel justified in regarding them as his.[9]

There is one passage in *Double Falsehood* acclaimed by Shakespearean enthusiasts, some of whom go overboard in extolling it. Robert Payne declares: "The play reads lamely but has magnificent lines which almost certainly derive from Shakespeare."[10] Whereupon he quotes:

> Strike up, my Masters;
> But touch the strings with a religious softness,
> Teach sound to languish through the night's dull ear,
> Till melancholy start from her lazy couch
> And carelessness grow convert to attention.
> (I, iii, p. 43)

I am willing to concede that the word *religious*, in the sense used may have come from *Cardenio:*

> A religious trembling shakes me by the hand
> And bids me put by such unhallowed business.
> (V, ii, 2107-08)

But there are lines that seem to me obscure or inaccurate in Theobald's passage, which, by the way, he insisted was his own creation.

There are better lines in Theobald's play:

> Poisoned with studied Language, and bequeathed
> To desperation. I am now become
> The Tomb of my own Honour; a dark Mansion,
> For Death alone to dwell in. . .
>
> (II, ii, p. 47)

By making *Double Falsehood* a fast-moving, modernized comedy, Theobald gave it audience appeal. He ignored the rather flip, obvious plot of the Curious Imperative in the Cardenio tale, and took the same story Shakespeare and Fletcher had transformed into a romance tragicomedy. However, he used only the material that would lend itself to comic situations, such as the ludicrous adventures of Cardenio in the mountains. Theobald started his action by adapting from Shakespeare and Fletcher the very obligatory scenes that Cervantes had left out of the Cardenio tale. Right off there were confrontations, a whole series of them, a seduction, and a wedding that never came off and almost ended in swordplay.

Theobald was not a great writer, but he knew how to instill life into a drama. He relieved the tedium of Cardenio, the human gazelle, by bringing together the characters of the play in a series of scenes that maintained the conflict. The bottom line is that he turned out a successful play without making it into a tragedy.

Possibly some earlier dramatist, other than Shakespeare and Fletcher, had already adapted *Cardenio* or *The Second Maiden's Tragedy* for the changing taste of audiences, and Theobald had acquired three copies of this revision in various states of repair. Shakespeare's plays, long out of date, had been fair game for renovators for more than half a century before Theobald wrote *Double Falsehood.* Shakespeare's dramatic methods were antiquated even at the time John Dryden revamped *Antony and Cleopatra* in 1678. The revolt against the "out-of-date" and "vulgar" language of Shakespeare's plays had led Restoration dramatists to make changes so drastic that almost nothing except the author's name was left unaltered. Whole scenes and acts were deleted. Passages of soaring poetry were transformed into blank verse as flat as the oak-planked stage on which they were declaimed. Samuel Pepys had found the original version of *Twelfth Night* "but a silly play" and *A Midsummer Night's Dream* "the most insipid play that ever I saw in my life."[11] But Pepys merely echoed the taste of his era, an age that regarded itself as far above the low comedy and bloody tragedy for which Shakespeare was then notorious. Professor Louis Marder wrote: "In theatres where the candles frequently hurt the eyes of the spectator. . . the audience sat on wooden benches and. . . if they went to *Romeo and Juliet* they had a choice of seeing it as a tragedy one day or as a comedy, with the lovers preserved alive, the next."[12]

Sir William Davenant, who claimed to be an illegitimate son of Shakespeare and who tried to compensate for his lack of a nose (eroded away by a syphilitic affliction) by dandifying his name to D'Avenant, was one of the chief reformers of Shakespeare's plays. He produced a *Macbeth* "drest in all its finery, as new Cloath's, new Scenes, Machines, as Flyings for the Witches; with all the Singing and Dancing in it—it being all Excellently Perform'd, being in the nature of an Opera. . . "[13] F.E. Halliday described a few of Davenant's assaults on Shakespeare's great play:

> Davenant is at his excruciating worst in the tremendous third scene of the last act. In the original play, when the terrified servant comes to report the advance of Malcolm and his forces, the half-demented Macbeth turns on him with:
>
> "The devil damn thee black, thou cream-faced loon!
> Where got'st thou that goose look?"
>
> This is polished into,
>
> "Now, friend, what means thy change of countenance?" . . . And why, oh why did Davenant change the line "The way to dusty death. Out, out brief candle!" into "To their eternal homes: out, out that candle!"
>
> . . . If Davenant's version were an original play it would pass as a remarkable Restoration tragedy, the silliness redeemed by flashes of magnificent poetry, and it is only when compared with what Shakespeare wrote that it is so deplorable. The greater part is no more than a pedestrian paraphrase in limp blank verse, and, by attempting to elevate, Davenant succeeds merely in depressing the poetry to his own level. He left nothing to his audience's imagination, and, worst of all, perhaps, is his maddening trick of flattening Shakespeare's imagery into literal statement: "Their daggers unmannerly breech'd with gore—being yet unwiped;" "Screw your courage to the sticking-place"—"Bring but your courage to the fatal place;" the list could be almost indefinitely extended.[14]

Just as drastic were the "improvements" on Shakespeare made by the noted actor Thomas Betterton in his adaption of *A Midsummer Night's Dream,* which he renamed *The Fairy Queen*. Professor Louis Marder calls it "perhaps the most fantastic if not the most elaborate version of that play ever staged. . . a dance of six monkeys, a Grand Dance of twenty-four Chinese, and swans that turned into fairies. . . "[15]

As Theobald stated that one of his three copies of *Cardenio* had belonged to the great actor, Thomas Betterton (c. 1635-1710), and was above sixty years old (hence probably written in the early 1660s), it is very possible that Theobald owned an original revision by Betterton, who might have transformed the tragedy of Shakespeare and Fletcher into a ribald comedy for the delectation of the merry monarch, Charles II. If so, all of Theobald's copies may have been slightly variant transcripts of Betterton's version.

Even the most sophisticated playgoer of Theobald's time might have been shocked by the Shakespeare and Fletcher drama that featured a sexual assault on the corpse of a beautiful woman. Thus Theobald, or a predecessor in the revision of *Cardenio,* produced a timely comedy, retaining only the obligatory scenes, the exciting confrontations that were an important feature of *Cardenio. Since not a single one of these scenes occurred in Cervantes's tale, it would certainly be an unbelievable coincidence if Theobald or any other dramatist had conceived the start of the play in precisely the same manner as Shakespeare and Fletcher without reference to their manuscript or a modified version of it.*

Except for the addition of the confrontation scenes, Theobald's action follows pretty closely the story in *Don Quixote*. All of Theobald's characters from the Cardenio tale get new names: Don Fernando, the villain, becomes Henriquez; Cardenio becomes Julio; Luscinda, beloved of Cardenio, becomes Leonora; Don Bernard is Leonora's father, the panderer; and Dorotea is Violante.

One might expect that Theobald would occasionally make use of the precise language of Shakespeare and Fletcher, but possibly the original *Cardenio* had been so extensively overhauled by Betterton or some other adapter of the Restoration that the text of Shakespeare and Fletcher was totally obliterated. A comparison between identical scenes and situations in the two plays is most interesting.

In *Cardenio,* when The Lady is paraded before The Tyrant, just before the contemplated wedding arranged by The Lady's pandering father, The Tyrant is shocked by her gloomy appearance. In *Double Falsehood,* the villain Henriquez suffers an identical shock when Leonora, bargained away to Henriquez by her pandering father, appears with a dark, foreboding face at the wedding ceremony:

Cardenio

Tyrant: Black! Whence risse that
cloud? Can such a thing
be seen
In honour's glorious day,
the sky so clear?
Why mourns the kingdom's
mistress? Does she come
To meet advancement in a
funeral garment?
Back! She forgot herself.
'Twas too much joy
That bred this error, and
we heartily pardon't.
Go, bring me her hither
like an illustrious
bride
With her best beams
about her; let

Double Falsehood

Henriquez: Why, Leonora, wilt
Thou with this Gloom
Darken my Triumph; suff'ring
Discontent,
And wan Displeasure, to subdue
that Cheek
Where love shold sit inthron'd?
Behold your slave!
Nay, frown not; for each Hour of
growing Time
Shall task me to thy Service. . .
(III, ii, pp. 58-59)

her jewels
Be worth ten cities;
that beseems our
mistress,
And not a widow's case a
suit to weep in.
(I, i, 115-24)

In *Cardenio*, The Lady tells The Tyrant of her contempt for all the pomp and show he is offering her. In *Double Falsehood,* the villain, Henriquez, abandons his "royal" attitude to win Violante, who is not impressed by his wealth:

Cardenio

Lady: Fortunes are but the
outsides of true worth.
It is the mind that sets
his master forth.
(I, i, 179-80)

Double Falsehood

Henriquez: The Dignities we
wear, are Gifts of Pride;
And laugh'd at by the Wise,
as mere Outside.
(I, iii, p. 45)

In *Cardenio*, the pandering Helvetius, who has literally sold his daughter to The Tyrant, berates her for refusing to wed the king she despises. In *Double Falsehood,* the pandering Don Bernard, who has bargained away his daughter to the nobleman Henriquez, a seducer and liar, roundly castigates his daughter for not accepting Henriquez's proposal of marriage:

Cardenio

Helvetius: Base-spirited girl,
That can'st not think above
disgrace and beggary,
When glory is set for thee
and thy seed,
Advancement for thy father,
beside joy
Able to make a latter spring
in me
In this my fourscore summer,
and renew me
With a reversion yet of heat

Double Falsehood

Don Bernard: Come, Leonora,
You are not now to learn, this
noble Lord
(Whom but to name, restores my
failing Age.)
Has with a Lover's Eye beheld
your Beauty;
Thro' which his Heart speaks
More than Language can;
It offers Joy and Happiness to
You,
And Honour to our House.

and youth!
Thy very seed will curse thee
in thy age
When they shall hear the
story of thy weakness:
How in thy youth thy fortunes
tendered thee
A kingdom for thy servant,
which thou left'st
Basely to serve thyself. . . .
(II, i, 605-11, 624-28)

Imagine then
The Birth and Qualities of him
that loves you;
Which, when you know, you can-
not rate too dear.
(II, iii, p. 49)

In *Cardenio*, The Lady, under immense pressure from her pandering father Helvetius to marry The Tyrant, answers him eloquently. In *Double Falsehood,* Leonora also has an eloquent reply to her pandering father:

Cardenio

Lady: I owe to you a reverence,
A debt which both begins and
ends with life,
Never till then discharged;
'tis so long-lasting
Yet could you be more precious than a father,
Which, next a husband, is the
richest treasure
Mortality can show us, you
should pardon me
(And yet confess too that you
found me kind)
To hear your words, though I
withstood your mind.
(II, i, 637-641)

Double Falsehood

Leonora: My Father, on my
knees
I do beseech you
To pause one Moment on your
Daughter's Ruin.
I vow, my Heart ev'n bleeds,
that I must thank you
For your past Tenderness; and
yet distrust
That which is yet behind.
Consider, Sir,
Whoe'er's th' Occasion of
another's Fault,
Cannot himself be innocent. O,
give not
The censuring World Occasion
reproach
Your harsh Commands; or to my
Charge lay That
Which most I fear, the Fault
of Disobedience.
(I, iii, p.49)

In *Cardenio,* the pandering father, Helvetius, having been scolded in a memorable rebuke by Govianus, recants and offers an apology. In *Double Falsehood,* the father, Don Bernard, also recants and apologizes for all the trouble he has caused by pandering his daughter:

Cardenio

Helvetius: Blessing reward
thee! Such a wound as
mine
Did need a pitiless surgeon.
Smart on, soul;
Thou'lt feel the less here-
after. Sir, I thank you.
I ever saw my life in a false
glass
Until this friendly hour.
With what fair faces
My sins would look on me!—
But now the truth shows
'em,
How loathsome and how mon-
strous are their forms!
(II, i, 735-42)

Double Falsehood

Don Bernard: This comes of
forcing Women where they hate:
It was my own Sin; and I am rewarded.
Now I am like an aged Oak,
alone.
Left for all Tempests.—I would
cry, but cannot;
I'm dry'd to Death almost
with these Vexations.
Lord! What a heavy Load I
have within me.
(III, iii, p. 64)

In *Cardenio,* Votarius, who has seduced his best friend's wife, fears that his blushes will betray him. In *Double Falsehood,* Violante has been seduced by Henriquez and is fearful that a blush may reveal her secret:

Cardenio

Votarius: His very name
shoots like a fever through
me,
Now hot, now cold. Which
cheek shall I turn toward
him,
For fear he should read
guiltiness in my looks?
(II, ii, 794-96)

Double Falsehood

Violante: Whom shall I look
upon without a Blush?
There's not a Maid, whose Eye
with Virgin Gaze
Pierces not to my Guilt. . .
(II, ii, p. 46)

In *Cardenio*, the hero, Govianus, having poisoned the tyrant king, replies contemptuously to the threats of the still menacing monarch. In *Double Falsehood,* the hero, Julio, boldly answers the threats of the highborn Henriquez, who is about to marry Julio's beloved, Leonora:

Cardenio

Govianus: I smile at thee.
Draw all the death that ever mankind suffered
Unto one head, to help thine own invention,
And make my end as rare as this thy sin,
And full as fearful to the eyes of women!
My spirit shall fly singing to his lodging
In midst of that rough weather. Doom me, Tyrant.
Had I feared death, I'd never appeared noble
To seal this act upon me, which e'en honours me.
(V, ii, 2156-64)

Double Falsehood

Julio: You have wrong'd me;
Wrong'd me so basely, in so dear a Point,
As stains the Cheek of Honour with a Blush;
Cancells the Bonds of Service; bids Allegiance
Throw to the Wind all high Respects of Birth,
Title, and Eminence; and, in their Stead,
Fills up the panting Heart with just Defiance. . .
Forego this bad Intent; or with your Sword
Answer me like a Man. . .
(III, ii, p. 60)

Although the sources for *Double Falsehood*, with the exception of its notable source, *Cardenio,* do not fall within the purview of this book, it is interesting that Theobald also utilized the same sources as Shakespeare and Fletcher: *Don Quixote,* Shakespeare's earlier plays, and *The Maid's Tragedy.*

The use of *Don Quixote* in *Double Falsehood* is obvious, and Theobald frequently dogs the adventures of Cardenio. As for Shakespeare's plays, Theobald, as an editor of Shakespeare, could hardly avoid the influence of his favorite dramatist.[16] For instance, compare Shakespeare's speech of Desdemona to her father in *Othello* with Theobald's speech of Leonora to her father Don Bernard when he asks that she renounce her lover, Julio:

Othello

Desdemona: My noble father,
I do perceive here a divided duty;

Double Falsehood

Leonora: I've heard my Mother say a thousand Times,
Her Father would have forced

To you I am bound for life
and education;
My life and education both do
learn me
How to respect you; you are
the lord of duty;
I am hitherto your daughter;
but here's my husband,
And so much duty as my
mother show'd
To you, preferring you before
her father,
So much I challenge that I
may profess
Due to the Moor my lord.
(I, iii, 180-89)

her Virgin Choice;
But when the Conflict was
'twixt Love and Duty,
Which should be first
obey'd, my Mother quickly
Paid up her Vows to Love, and
married You.
You thought this well, and she
was praised for This;
For this her Name was honour'd. . .
My case is now the same;
You are the Father, which You
then condemn'd;
I, what my Mother was. . .
(II, iii, p. 51)

The imitations of Shakespeare—I shan't call them plagiarisms because they were likely unconscious cribs—in *Double Falsehood* are, as Kenneth Muir indicated, very abundant.[17] Less obvious are the influences of *The Maid's Tragedy*,[18] of which I shall point out only one. In *The Maid's Tragedy*, the speech on men's fickleness is delivered by Aspatia, to whom are accorded nearly all the great speeches in the play. In this speech one may observe the beautiful image clusters and remarkable word power of Shakespeare. In *Double Falsehood,* Violante, who has been betrayed by Henriquez, philosophizes upon the fickleness of men:

The Maid's Tragedy

Aspatia: Then, my good girls,
be more than women, wise;
At least be more than I was;
and be sure
You credit any thing the
light gives life to
Before a man. Rather believe
the sea
Weeps for the ruined merchant,
when he roars;
Rather, the wind courts but
the pregnant sails
When the strong cordage

Double Falsehood

Violante: You Maidens, that
shall live
To hear my mournful Tale, when
I am Ashes,
Be wise; and to an Oath no
more give Credit,
To Tears, to Vows, (false
Both!) or any Thing
A man shall promise, than to
Clouds, that now
Bear such a pleasing Shape,
and now are nothing.
For they will cozen, (if They

cracks; rather, the sun
Comes but to kiss the fruit
in wealthy autumn,
When all falls blasted. If
you needs must love,
(Forced by ill fate,) Take
to your maiden-bosoms
Two dead-cold aspics [asps],
and of them make lovers. . .
(II, ii, pp. 370-71)

may be cozen'd.)
The very Gods they worship,—
Valour, Justice,
Discretion, Honesty, and all
they covet,
To make them seeming Saints,
are but the Wiles
By which these *Syrens* lure us
to Destruction.
(IV, ii, p. 76)

And now, concluding as I do, that Theobald owned three copies of a revised, greatly altered *Cardenio,* all doubtless attributed to Shakespeare, what happened to those copies? The answer may be very simple. Theobald may have realized from the defective plots and limping poetry that his *Cardenios* were little more than travesties on the original, which by his own admission he never possessed. Therefore, rather than risk obloquy as an inept Shakespearean scholar by publishing his copies, and perhaps at the same time impugning Shakespeare's reputation, he may have silently consigned them to the flames and, then, just as silently omitted them from his seven-volume edition of Shakespeare.

CHAPTER VII

OTHER CANDIDATES FOR AUTHORSHIP OF *CARDENIO*

The number seven is symbolic, provocative, mysterious. Consider the seven ages of man, the seven wonders of the ancient world, the seven cities that claim Homer, and now, the seven candidates for authorship of *Cardenio* or *The Second Maiden's Tragedy* —Massinger, Tourneur, Chapman, Middleton, Ford, Fletcher, and Shakespeare.

In 1955, Professor S. Schoenbaum tabulated twelve critics who had recorded their opinions on the authorship of this controversial drama.[1] I've added another thirteen to bring the list up-to-date, and I've followed Professor Schoenbaum's convenient format, beginning with Ludwig Tieck who in 1829 speculated that Massinger was the author.

1829	Tieck	Massinger
1830	Beddoes	Tourneur
1874	Bullen	Tourneur
1875	Swinburne	Chapman or Middleton
1875	Shepherd	Chapman
1891	Fleay	Author, *Revenger's Tragedy*
1892	Hopkinson	Chapman
1894	Boyle	Massinger or Tourneur
1902	Rosenbach	Tourneur
1911	Oliphant	Middleton
1919	Sykes	Tourneur
1929	Nicoll	Tourneur
1945	Everitt	Middleton and Shakespeare
1954	Stenger	Middleton
1955	Schoenbaum	Middleton
1960	Oras	Middleton
1966	Brodwin	Chapman, Middleton, or Ford
1970	Lieblein	Middleton
1976	Levin	Middleton
1978	Lancashire	Middleton
1978	MacDonald	Middleton

1993	Hamilton	Shakespeare and Fletcher
1993	Briggs	Middleton
1993	Taylor	Middleton
1993	Wiggins	Middleton

In the sixteen decades that have elapsed since Tieck put forth his claim for Massinger, only two critics, both of them lamely, have supported his view. In 1912, Watson Nicholson casually noted that "*The Second Maiden's Tragedy* is probably the work of Philip Massinger."[2] Leonora Brodwin dismisses Massinger's candidacy with a deft put-down: "My major objections to Massinger's authorship are that he is neither as great a poet nor as complex a thinker as the author of the anonymous play."[3]

George Chapman has faded badly as a contender since the death of his main sponsor, Algernon Charles Swinburne. Swinburne was a superb writer and could roll out a sentence like a Persian carpet, but his critical faculties were often blighted by bias. My own view is that Swinburne was influenced by Keats's immense enthusiasm for Chapman. Leonora Brodwin arrived at her opinion that Chapman was the author by a process of elimination. Middleton, she noted, was preoccupied with "sexual transgression," and this disqualified him, since The Lady and The Tyrant "were anything but sexually obsessed."[4] However, with an ambivalence that is delightful, Ms. Brodwin does not rule out Middleton or even, as a final possibility, John Ford.

An oft-touted candidate for *The Second Maiden's Tragedy* authorship is Cyril Tourneur, also believed by many scholars to be the author of *The Revenger's Tragedy* and *The Atheist's Tragedy.* H. Dugdale Sykes, one of the foremost proponents for Tourneur's candidacy, is very positive, one might almost say dogmatic, in his views.[5] Even before he presents his evidence, Sykes fires his conclusions at us in strong terms: "It is inconceivable that either Chapman or Shakespeare can have had a hand in this play. . . There is no doubt whatever in my mind that all three plays [*The Atheist's Tragedy, The Revenger's Tragedy* and *The Second Maiden's Tragedy]* are the work of one hand, and that the hand of Cyril Tourneur."[6] Sykes points out that "the colloquial contractions of the smaller parts of speech—and especially *'t* for *it* were especially common in both plays [*Revenger's Tragedy* and *Atheist's Tragedy*]. On examining *The Second Maiden's Tragedy* I found these contractions even more numerous. . . "[7] Sykes mentions *do't, for't, in't, by't, bestow't* and others similar. He allows, however, that Middleton also uses similar abbreviations in great abundance. Sykes neglects to record the fact that in *The Revenger's Tragedy* there appear sixteen usages of *o'th'* but none at all in *The Second Maiden's Tragedy.* Also, in *The Revenger's Tragedy* occur fourteen usages of *i'th'*, as opposed to only two in *The Second Maiden's Tragedy.*

In *The Second Maiden's Tragedy,* Sykes finds a proliferation of vice and corruption, with an ingenuity for devising horrible situations, just as one sees in Tourneur's two plays. The only admission Sykes makes that might weaken his case is that the author of *The Atheist's Tragedy* shows great partiality for nouns ending in *ion* and the author of *The Second Maiden's Tragedy* does not. Sykes concludes his presentation by pointing out that "there are. . . sufficient traces in *The Second Maiden's Tragedy* of the language and sentiments of *The Atheist's Tragedy* [published 1611] and *The Revenger's Tragedy* [published 1607] to exclude any doubt as to their common authorship."[8] Perhaps the strongest part of Sykes's argument is that similar scenes (the poisoned skull in *The Revenger's Tragedy* and the poisoned body in *The Second Maiden's Tragedy)* suggest a common author, but this view is predicated upon the presumption that an author plagiarizes himself, not another author.

Despite all his legerdemain with contractions, there is a big flaw in Sykes's theory. *The Revenger's Tragedy* and *Cardenio* or *The Second Maiden's Tragedy* are written in vastly different styles and embody a vastly different philosophy of life. The remarkable mystic, Cyril Tourneur, if it be he who wrote *The Revenger's Tragedy*, belongs in the pantheon of a small but élite group of poets who sought the bone beneath the flesh, the reality under the visible. Tourneur's poetry is often emitted in lyrical spasms, gorged with words used in a strange sense, totally unlike the writing in *The Second Maiden's Tragedy*. Sometimes the deeper current of Tourneur's symbolism is submerged in the crashing surf of his metaphors. He is the Ezra Pound of the Elizabethan era. Like Arthur Rimbaud, a later symbolist, Tourneur carries on a poetic dalliance with colors: "scarlet hid in lawn," "silver years," "black serpent," "yellow labors," "painted red with wine," "skin of gold," "green-color'd maids," "white father," "heaven turn black," "golden spurs," "red with shame," "my sins are green," and so on.

T.S. Eliot, certainly a soul mate of Tourneur's, unwittingly described the author of *The Revenger's Tragedy* when he wrote of John Donne:

> He knew the anguish of the marrow
> The ague of the skeleton
> No contact possible to flesh
> Allayed the fever of the bone.

Tourneur would have understood, I think, Eliot's skulls that "leaned backward with a lipless grin" and "the dice of drowned men's bones" that Hart Crane wrote about when he stood at Melville's grave.

If anything further is required to show that the same dramatist who wrote *The Revenger's Tragedy* did not write *Cardenio* or *The Second Maiden's Tragedy,* here are the keynote lines with which Tourneur begins his mystical masterpiece:

> O, that marrowless age
> Should stuff the hollow bones with damn'd desires,
> And 'stead of heat kindle infernal fires
> Within the spendthrift veins of a dry duke,
> A parch'd and juiceless luxur [lecher].
> (I, i, 5-8)

The preoccupation with bright colors and white bones in *The Revenger's Tragedy* builds to a climax when the seducer dies after kissing the poisoned skull of the woman he betrayed.

Many leading scholars have endorsed Thomas Middleton's candidacy for authorship of *The Second Maiden's Tragedy.* Here are twenty reasons why I believe this drama was not written by Middleton:

1. The manuscript of *The Second Maiden's Tragedy,* subsequently converted into a promptbook, is not in Middleton's hand. It is in the same hand as Shakespeare's will. (See Chapter II, Part I, for the charts comparing the handwriting in the will with the handwriting in *The Second Maiden's Tragedy.*)

2. In October 1611, when *The Second Maiden's Tragedy* was reviewed and named by the censor, Middleton is thought to have been affiliated with Philip Henslowe's acting company, the Admiral's Men, chief rivals of the King's Men. In any event, it seems unlikely that the King's Men, producers of *The Second Maiden's Tragedy,* would have employed an outside writer when they already had in their company three expert dramatists—Shakespeare, Fletcher, and Beaumont.

3. There are no manuscript corrections or notations of any kind by Middleton in the promptbook of *The Second Maiden's Tragedy,* even though it was customary for authors then, as now, to participate in the production and rehearsal of dramas.

4. To explain the numerous corrections and alterations made in the manuscript promptbook of *The Second Maiden's Tragedy,* nearly every one of which is in the same hand that wrote the entire manuscript, the proponents of Middleton's claim have invented a scrivener. This imaginary scrivener, say they, transcribed Middleton's original manuscript either literally, with all errors, or so ineptly that he was obliged to pin accidental omissions on the margins of pages and disfigure his text with interlinear additions. Further, unlike others of his exacting profession, he was unable to copy the play without frequent spelling mistakes, such as extra syllables and omitted portions of words. He was also delinquent in punctuation.

5. A few adherents of the Middleton authorship theory contend that the manuscript of *The Second Maiden's Tragedy* is in the hand of a noverint, or apprentice lawyer, who worked for Shakespeare's solicitor, Francis Collins. They further allege that Collins's noverint, or scrivener, wrote Shakespeare's will, and this would explain why the handwriting in *The Second Maiden's Tragedy* is identical with the handwriting in Shakespeare's will. But it requires a mighty elasticity of imagination to transport an incompetent legal clerk to London just to mangle a poetic drama.

6. The plain fact is that *The Second Maiden's Tragedy* is not a clerical copy. It does not look like a clerical copy. It has none of the characteristics of a clerical copy. In fact, it is in every respect an original, authorial manuscript. During the course of nearly sixty years as a handwriting expert, I have examined and identified thousands of original manuscripts and clerical copies from the period of Henry VII to Elizabeth II. The difference between a clerical copy and an authorial manuscript is that the clerical copy is expected

to be, and nearly always is, meticulously transcribed, beautifully penned, and accurate in every detail; whereas the author's original draft is apt to be laced with errors in spelling, punctuation, and even omitted words, since the author is primarily concerned with setting his thoughts down quickly and is often heedless of the manner in which he indites them.

7. Further evidence against the theory that the manuscript of *The Second Maiden's Tragedy* is a clerical copy lies in the fact that it was the draft submitted to the censor. If this manuscript were a clerical copy, as Middleton proponents claim, the question at once arises as to why Middleton's original draft was not submitted. From Middleton's surviving handwriting in his play, *A Game at Chesse,* we know that his script was neat and legible. Hence, a clerical copy of his original manuscript would certainly not be required for the censor or the promptbook.

8. Some Middleton supporters have averred that since Shakespeare was rich and famous in 1611, it would be ridiculous to presume that he would stoop to the menial task of transcribing a play. The fallacy in this argument is that this is not a transcribed play but the original draft in the hand of its co-author. It reveals how Shakespeare worked with a collaborator. Apparently he integrated Fletcher's manuscript of the subplot with the main plot, correcting, altering, deleting, adding and improving Fletcher's text as he composed his own portion of the play.

9. A few scholars who support Middleton's claim argue that their candidate *has to be* the author of *The Second Maiden's Tragedy* because the manuscript is all in the same handwriting, whereas if the play were written by Shakespeare and Fletcher, it would be in two different hands. However, a manuscript in two separate sections would never do as a promptbook! The leaves would need to be the same size, consecutively paginated, legible and consistent. The characters would have to be properly identified throughout, the action unified, and all inconsistencies eradicated. The entire play would have to be skillfully melded with the main plot and subplot fused for unity of action. This could be accomplished only with a linkage of the two manuscripts by a single author. The confusion engendered by an attempt to use two separately written manuscripts, however, would certainly create a most interesting comedy of errors.

10. Some of the Middleton proponents insist that *The Second Maiden's Tragedy* is by Middleton merely because (they contend) it is not the lost *Cardenio,* based upon the tale of Cardenio in *Don Quixote*. While they admit that the subplot is clearly taken from the Cardenio tale, despite the fact that the ending is entirely different, they insist that the main plot is not. This view is palpably incorrect for the main plot of *The Second Maiden's Tragedy* utilizes the same characters, and begins in almost the same way, as Cervantes's tale of Cardenio. That the plot unfolds and ends very differently, as is the case with Fletcher's subplot, is a tribute to Shakespeare's genius. Most Elizabethan scholars who have studied Shakespeare's literary techniques would admit that while he has been accused of being a plot bandit, his wondrous imagination was often ignited by nothing more than a mere hint from an arcane book or obscure tract. To contend that the

main plot in *The Second Maiden's Tragedy* was not influenced by the Cardenio tale because Shakespeare used only a portion of it and developed it differently is specious. It also argues an ignorance of Shakespeare's creative methods. Some of the plot and scene ideas that inspired him were so completely metamorphosed by the great dramatist that they are virtually unrecognizable, and it has become a favorite scholarly pastime to track them down.

In a clear, authoritative exposition of how Shakespeare used his sources, Watt, Holzknecht and Ross point out:

> First, it must be remembered that excepting where the source was itself a drama, and this was relatively seldom, the original was written to be read, whereas Shakespeare's product was composed for the stage—it was, in other words, made dramatic. Thus what was originally narrative, historical, lyrical, or expository became not only dialogue but dialogue involving passion, suspense, climax, and other elements presented not in cold type but in the vivid mimicry of life. It cannot be said that Shakespeare's respect for his sources very often checked his expression of his sense for the dramatic. He did not hesitate, therefore, to combine details from plots originally unrelated or to change episodes by re-emphasizing them or altering them completely. Furthermore, he often changed the proportions of the original story, he expanded scenes from the barest of hints, he reversed a conclusion, he even added episodes from another story or from his own fertile brain. He sometimes introduced realism to contrast with romance or a bit of clowning to dull the bitter edge of grief. The mood of the material he often changed, sentimentality becoming sentiment, the cynical becoming the wholesome, the immoral, the moral. For the original geographical setting, moreover, he had no respect if it stood in the way of his higher purposes. With his characters he was just as free; he frequently retained both name and characteristics of a figure in his original or, on the contrary, he changed both. Where his sense of dramatic economy dictated, he dropped a character out entirely, or he added one or more not in the original. These and a dozen more liberties with his sources will be found in any extended comparisons of the plays and their originals.[9]

In the case of *Cardenio* or *The Second Maiden's Tragedy,* Shakespeare appropriated what he wanted from Cervantes and then invented the rest of his plot. He took the middle-class characters from the Cardenio tale and transformed them into kings and dukes. He jettisoned the prolix lamentations and goatlike antics of Cardenio and changed him from a mealmush weakling into a man of tempered steel. Finally, and most importantly, he then pitched out the rest of the meandering plot of the tale, which would never have worked on the stage, and replaced it with an exciting story of love and lunacy.

As for the assertion of Middleton claimants that *The Second Maiden's Tragedy* cannot be the lost *Cardenio* because it does not literally follow Cervantes's boring plot, it seems incredible that any reputable scholar would have the naïveté to contend that a great playwright like Shakespeare would try to dramatize this soporific tale and then compound his theatrical misdemeanor by adding a gauche "happy ending," as did Cervantes.

11. Scholars unanimously concur that the lost play, *Cardenio,* is based upon the tale of Cardenio in Cervantes's *Don Quixote,* not published in English until 1612. This brings up an interesting question. Does it not seem incredible that Shakespeare and Fletcher wrote their play *Cardenio* at approximately the same time that Middleton allegedly wrote the untitled play known as *The Second Maiden's Tragedy* (1611), *with both plays based upon the identical tale from Cervantes and produced by the identical players' company, the King's Men?* Would Shakespeare or Fletcher or any stockholders have for a moment sanctioned the writing and production of two romance plays on the same source, with one of them by an outside dramatist usually employed by their leading rival? Reflect, too, on the anomaly that the drama by the far more famous authors, Shakespeare and Fletcher, is supposedly lost, while the lesser-known, untitled play attributed to Middleton is treasured in the British Museum Library.

12. The eighteenth-century dramatist, poet, and noted editor of Shakespeare's plays, Lewis Theobald, wrote a drama called *Double Falsehood* (1727), which he claimed was based upon three mid-seventeenth-century transcripts of Shakespeare's *Cardenio* he had obtained from several sources. (Theobald was unaware of Fletcher's co-authorship.) Theobald never showed these versions of *Cardenio* to anyone, and the manuscripts subsequently disappeared, probably because Theobald regarded them as butchered adaptations of Shakespeare's original *Cardenio* by Restoration hacks. Theobald incorporated into *Double Falsehood* a series of four very important obligatory speeches (or confrontations), not one of which appears in the Cardenio tale by Cervantes, but all four of which occur in the identical manner and in the identical situations in *The Second Maiden's Tragedy.* These obligatory speeches (quoted and discussed in detail in Chapter VI), together with other striking similarities between *The Second Maiden's Tragedy* and *Double Falsehood,* need to be explained away by Middleton adherents before they can even begin to address the question of their candidate's authorship of *The Second Maiden's Tragedy.*

13. Middleton is regarded by literary historians as a woman hater. His women are frequently bed-hopping doxies or fist-shaking viragos. His men are mostly unconscionable seducers, or money-grubbers who would filch a farthing from a blind man's cup. Middleton did not believe in "true love." He equated love with sex, as Professor David L. Frost so aptly pointed out in the "Introduction" to this book. It thus seems improbable that Middleton could have created The Lady in *The Second Maiden's Tragedy,* an idealistic woman who spurned wealth and power and, pure of heart and body, laid down her life on the alter of chastity. Nor could Middleton have created The Tyrant, a colorful ruler so smitten with heroine worship for The Lady that, by his own admission, he usurped the throne solely for the purpose of winning her affections. So wildly enamored was The Tyrant with The Lady that he descended into the depths of evil for her, and ultimately, driven insane by unrequited love, sacrificed his kingdom and his

life just to possess her corpse. Bear in mind that as king, The Tyrant could have had any beautiful woman he desired, or any score of beautiful women; but he loved only one woman. He was at heart a visionary and a poet, an incurable romantic, as his moving speech at her casket reveals. In my opinion, both The Lady and The Tyrant are characters of Shakespearean stature, molded by the Stratford dramatist and far beyond the comprehension or creative powers of Middleton.

14. In *The Second Maiden's Tragedy,* there is a perceptible dichotomy in characterization, plot development, and poetic technique between the traditional main plot and the racy subplot. The iambs are adroitly marshalled into pentameter in the main plot, with only occasional deviations from the stately measures of its blank verse; but in the subplot the iambs often frolic with trochees and dactyls. Indeed, the versification in the subplot is so "footloose and fancy-free" that some catalectic feet go far beyond Fletcher's characteristic feminine endings and transform his lines into erratic heptameters or ill-disguised prose. In my opinion, two writers authored *The Second Maiden's Tragedy.* Further in evidence of this belief is that the linkage between the main plot and the subplot is adventive and frivolous, depending upon nothing more than a few allusions to kinship. There is hardly any interaction between the characters in the two plots, as almost certainly would be the case if the entire play had been written by a single author as skilled and experienced as Middleton.

15. Middleton's characters seldom uttered the type of epigrammatic remarks and poetic phrases for which Shakespeare is famous. It is significant that *The Second Maiden's Tragedy* is virtually a cornucopia of superb poetry and brilliant "sayings" that evoke the masterful touch of the Stratford dramatist. Consider that Middleton merits only a total of eighteen memorable sayings or phrases in John Bartlett's *Familiar Quotations,*[10] but of Shakespeare there are well over a thousand.[11] It is obvious, I think, that should Middleton's authorship of *The Second Maiden's Tragedy* be accepted unanimously by scholars, his position in literature would be enhanced and his contribution to Bartlett would be doubled or tripled.

16. There are many striking similarities in plot, scenes, dramatic technique, word and phrase usage, and moral tone between *The Second Maiden's Tragedy* and *The Maid's Tragedy,* both produced a year or two apart by the King's Men. These similarities, discussed in detail in Chapter V, strongly suggest a common authorship for the two plays. We know that Fletcher was the co-author of *The Maid's Tragedy*. It is also very probable that Shakespeare, as the leading dramatist of the King's Men, would have looked over *The Maid's Tragedy* and likely touched up parts of it, as he is believed to have done with many other plays. Certainly, the censor, Sir George Buc, detected the striking similarity between *The Maid's Tragedy,* which he apparently had censored a year or two earlier, and the untitled play submitted to him. He thus gave the no-name play the designation, "this second Maiden's tragedy." If, as many scholars insist, Middleton did in fact write *The Second Maiden's Tragedy,* so clearly derivative from *The Maid's Tragedy*, it would not be amiss to charge him with a bit of not-very-deceptive plagiarism.

17. The tale of Cardenio in *Don Quixote* had not been published in English or French in 1611 when *The Second Maiden's Tragedy* was written. Since both the main plot and subplot were partially based on the Cardenio story, we must confront the question of how the author, or authors, acquired their knowledge of Cervantes's tale. It is, of course, possible that whoever wrote *The Second Maiden's Tragedy* had access to the proofs or a manuscript copy of Thomas Shelton's translation. We do not know whether Shakespeare or Middleton could read Spanish, but we do know that Fletcher used Spanish sources frequently and that he likely was fluent in the language. As the co-author of *Cardenio,* he could have sight translated all or portions of the Cervantes tale for his friend and collaborator William Shakespeare.

18. As an illustration of the flimsy, almost frivolous base on which many Middleton adherents build their case for his authorship, let me cite the arguments that Dr. David L. Lake, senior lecturer in English at the University of Queensland, advanced in his *Canon of Thomas Middleton's Plays.*[12] Lake's purpose in writing his book was to "solve by statistics the many problems of disputed authorship that surround the work of Thomas Middleton."[13] Dr. Lake begins by citing Schoenbaum's observation in *Middleton's Tragedies* (p. 196) that "the not very common oath *cuds me* is used in *Second Maiden* and Middleton."[14] Lake continues:

> I have found that neither *cuds me* nor any other oath including the form *cuds* occurs in the unassisted work of any other known author between 1600 and 1627, whereas there are 13 instances of *cuds* in Middleton's undoubted assisted plays. . . including 10 of *cuds me*. . . This oath is much more distinctive than even the exclamation *push* for which Middleton is so famous. There are three instances of *push* [two by Shakespeare; one by Fletcher] in *Second Maiden,* whereas no author in 1620-1627 other than Middleton has more than one *push* per play. Another highly significant marker is the contraction *I've,* of which there are eight instances in *Second Maiden* [three by Shakespeare; five by Fletcher]; such a frequency of *I've* is not equalled, apart from Middleton, by any seventeenth century dramatist before Davenant. . . With the co-occurrence of these three unique indications—of *cuds*, 3 *push*, 8 *I've*—the author of *Second Maiden* is clearly identified as Middleton.[15]

Dr. Lake discusses briefly some other computer evidence for Middleton's authorship, all of it far more tenuous and far less convincing than the paragraph I have quoted above. He concludes: "I think Middleton's authorship is beyond reasonable doubt."[16] To Dr. Lake's remarks, I might add that the oath *cuds me* occurs in Fletcher's subplot of *The Second Maiden's Tragedy* and, according to Alexander Schmidt[17] was never used by Shakespeare in any of his works.

19. A leading proponent of Middleton's candidacy, Professor Richard H. Barker, notes that "The oath *in faith* (or *faith* or *by my faith*). . . appears twenty-five times in the play [*The Second Maiden's Tragedy].*"[18] In its variations, writes Barker, the expletive *faith* occurs fifty-seven times in Middleton's *A Chaste Maide in Cheapside* [c. 1613],

with twenty-eight usages of *i'faith*.[19] Fletcher uses the expletive *i'faith* seven times in *The Second Maiden's Tragedy*, but there is not a single usage of *i'faith* in Shakespeare's main plot, which comprises more than half the play.

For those scholars who reject literary quality as a valid method of determining authorship and rely upon computerized evidence, Professor Barker has thus eliminated Middleton as the author of *The Second Maiden's Tragedy* and, at the same time, established Shakespeare as the playwright. In fact, Barker's computer evidence for Shakespeare's authorship (as opposed to Middleton's) is placed beyond cavil, for Alexander Schmidt[20] records only one usage of *i'faith* in the entire body of Shakespeare's plays and poems.

20. The supporters of Middleton's authorship point to the hero's name (Govianus) in the manuscript of *The Second Maiden's Tragedy* as evidence that this drama cannot be Shakespeare's lost play about Cardenio. True, Shakespeare had originally selected the name Govianus for his hero, a character based upon Cervantes's character Cardenio. However, several months later, the incredible, electrifying success of Cervantes's great novel apparently induced Shakespeare to capitalize on the fantastic fame of Don Quixote's friend Cardenio. A shrewd judge of public taste, the poet often seized upon currently popular characters and plots for his dramas, and since there were no international copyright laws in Shakespeare's day, he was at liberty, if he so chose, to borrow the name Cardenio, or any other names or plot hints, from *Don Quixote*. Doubtless, as was the custom at that time, the title *Cardenio* was written on the cover or wrapper of the play, which, if lost, as covers often were, left only the censor's makeshift title, *The Second Maiden's Tragedy,* at the end of the manuscript. As previously explained in the Introduction, just a single individual (the book-keeper or stage prompter) would be apt to consult Shakespeare's original manuscript, then the promptbook, and it would have been ridiculous for Shakespeare and Fletcher to invest several days in changing the names of the characters when the stage prompter could orally introduce the name changes should it ever be necessary during rehearsals or performances.

The first elaborate case for Middleton's authorship of *The Second Maiden's Tragedy* was made in 1945 by Professor Richard H. Barker who, after a cavalier dismissal of Shakespeare and Chapman as possible candidates, presents a detailed analysis of why he finds Middleton, rather than Tourneur, to be the author:[21]

Irony. It is typical of Middleton's plays, Barker states, that his characters insist upon "undoing themselves." He cites as evidence the subplot [Cervantes's curious-impertinent tale] in which Anselmus tests the fidelity of his wife and thus forces her into infidelity. The fallacy in Barker's argument is that most tragic characters undo themselves. Do not Macbeth and Hamlet undo themselves, for example, the first by ambition and the second by indecision?

Style. Barker quotes Swinburne, who finds the style of *The Second Maiden's Tragedy* very similar to that of the later Middleton. Barker writes: " 'When Glorie is set for thee and thy seed,' 'Pursued almost to my eternal hazard'—lines like these are unmistakably

Middleton's. . . "[22] These lines, in my opinion, are a little ambiguous and pretentious and barely elude triteness. They could certainly have been written by Middleton or by almost any other Jacobean or Elizabethan dramatist.

Diction. Barker writes: "The author of the play shares with Middleton a fondness for certain abstract words that are rich in associations—words like *joy, blessing, comfort, grace, glory, peace,* and *sin.*"[23] No reference to a concordance is necessary for the student of Shakespeare to recognize these words so often used by the Stratford dramatist.

Versification. Barker introduces at this point a chart of feminine endings to show how often Middleton uses them compared with Tourneur.[24] However, his chart is powerful evidence that John Fletcher, very partial to feminine endings, was the co-author of *The Second Maiden's Tragedy.*

Parallels. This is the least convincing of Barker's evidence that Middleton wrote *The Second Maiden's Tragedy.* Barker uses no fewer than nine plays of Middleton from which to draw parallels with *The Second Maiden's Tragedy.*[25] Most of the comparison plays were written years after the Shakespeare-Fletcher play, and thus any parallels could be inadvertent plagiarisms and hence possess little if any value. Further, from nine plays of nearly any prolific dramatist one could certainly abstract some similarities to any Elizabethan or Jacobean play you care to name by the same author or any other author.

In 1955, Professor S. Schoenbaum, a world-renowned expert on Shakespeare and Middleton, continued Barker's work, amplifying it and expanding the thesis that Middleton was the author of *The Second Maiden's Tragedy.*[26] In a review of Schoenbaum's book,[27] A.J. Bryant, Jr. wrote:

> The first part [of two] is a chronological survey of Middleton's development as a writer of tragedy in five plays (*The Revenger's Tragedy, The Second Maiden's Tragedy, Hengist, King of Kent, Women Beward Women,* and *The Changeling)* of which only the last three are generally accepted as containing Middleton's work. The second part is a textual study, presenting the evidence—diction, metrical tests, parallel passages etc.—on which the author's determination of the Middleton canon has been based. . . . To begin with, Schoenbaum's addition of some new sets of parallel passages to the pile of evidence amassed by previous scholars leaves us still with only a presumptive case. . . . Another kind of evidence that Schoenbaum sets great store by is the presence of an "ironic method". . . but this turns out to be the weakest evidence of all. The ironic reversals of plot which he cites to prove Middleton's authorship might just as easily have been used to prove that Marston wrote these plays (listed earlier in this paragraph), and the "ironic twists" in metaphor serve merely to illustrate something that was the common property of all Jacobean dramatists of consequence, including Shakespeare.[28]

During the investigative work on his distinguished study, *Middleton's Tragedies,*[29] Professor Schoenbaum unknowingly turned up all the data necessary to prove that *The Second Maiden's Tragedy* is not by Middleton, but is actually the lost play *Cardenio.* One by one, he uncovered the vital facts.

Professor Schoenbaum was aware, of course, that the lost play was twice performed by the King's Men at Court in 1612-13, was written by Shakespeare and Fletcher, and was based upon the tale of Cardenio in Cervantes's *Don Quixote*. These known facts, common knowledge among scholars for more than a century, formed a granite base on which to build a solid case for the acceptance of *The Second Maiden's Tragedy* as the original draft of *Cardenio*.

Since neither Schoenbaum, nor anybody else, could identify the handwriting in which the manuscript was written, and it appeared to be a neat script, Professor Schoenbaum accepted the prevailing dictum (1910) of Sir Walter Greg that it was a clerical copy. However, Greg was not a handwriting expert and should never have made a declaration *ex cathedra* on the subject. His ill-founded assertion later proved very damaging to the world of scholarship, as it was accepted without question by numerous students of drama. In fact, Greg's promulgation was the only unsubstantiated evidence Schoenbaum cited in evaluating *The Second Maiden's Tragedy*, but it may have been the very evidence that prevented him from discovering *Cardenio*.

In his analysis of the anonymous play, Schoenbaum quite properly ignored the eighteenth-century comments on the manuscript's cover by prior owners, one of whom had attributed the play to Shakespeare. Schoenbaum was aware that such attributions, not infrequent on manuscript poems in commonplace books of the seventeenth and eighteenth centuries, warrant only a cursory examination and are usually nothing more than booby traps for novice scholars.

In reviewing the statement by the censor, Sir George Buc, at the end of the manuscript play, Schoenbaum observed that the drama had not been titled by the author or authors. Some of the characters, including the protagonist, were still nameless; other characters may have had only tentative names. Buc gave the unnamed play a working title that was to stick: "Second Maiden's Tragedy." He completed his censorship task on October 31, 1611, a date that fits closely with the two known performances of *Cardenio* at Court in 1612-13. These sundry facts raised the nascent possibility that this play from the repertoire of the King's Men might be the lost *Cardenio*. However, nobody had ever suggested or even suspected that *The Second Maiden's Tragedy* could be *Cardenio,* including Professor Schoenbaum, who shared the prevailing dogma that it was an indifferent play, not worthy of Shakespeare—sans beauty, sans character motivation, sans believable plot, sans practically everything except fustian and melodrama.

Middleton scholars were unanimous that the play was written by a single author. Schoenbaum studied it carefully and observed that it "lacks unity of action. . . the two stories [main plot and subplot] being joined together in a clumsy and arbitrary fashion."[30] Since Middleton was a skilled dramatist and not likely to have written a disjointed play, this important discovery should have alerted Schoenbaum to the possibility that *The Second Maiden's Tragedy* was authored by two collaborators and then pieced together by the co-author charged with melding the two plots. Schoenbaum was aware, of course, that the King's Men boasted two of the greatest authorship teams of the century, perhaps of all time—Beaumont and Fletcher, and Shakespeare and Fletcher, the latter duo having collaborated also on *Henry VIII* and *The Two Noble Kinsmen*. However, so focused was Professor Schoenbaum on the premise that *The Second Maiden's Tragedy* was the work of a single author and in the hand of a professional scrivener that he totally discounted the idea of a collaboration.

Schoenbaum continued his examination: "In the year 1611 or not long before, Middleton read in *Don Quixote*, a *novella* which embodied that ironic view of life to which he was profoundly attracted."[31]* Here, at last, was a really important clue, for Schoenbaum must now have realized that, like the lost play of *Cardenio*, the untitled play known as *The Second Maiden's Tragedy* was at least partially based upon Cervantes's tale of Cardenio. Had Schoenbaum reconnoitered further and perused the Cardenio story in *Don Quixote*, he would have discovered, I am convinced, what no other scholar had detected—that the main plot, as well as the subplot, was inspired by the Cardenio *novella*. It is possible he might then have realized that *The Second Maiden's Tragedy* was actually *Cardenio*.

Still under the impression that he was investigating a play by Middleton, Schoenbaum turned his attention to a comparison between *The Maid's Tragedy* by Beaumont and Fletcher and *The Second Maiden's Tragedy*. He noted the views of earlier critics, then wrote: "When Sir George Buc gave *The Second Maiden's Tragedy* its title, he was thinking, no doubt, of Beaumont and Fletcher's *The Maid's Tragedy*. This designation is regarded by Greg as 'not very appropriate.' [Professor A. W.] Ward goes further: 'Except that the subject is again the guilty passion of a tyrant,' he writes, 'the play bears no resemblance to Beaumont and Fletcher's [Maid's] tragedy.' "[32] To his credit, Schoenbaum ignored this gross inaccuracy by Ward, who evidently had not read *The Maid's Tragedy* or else was woefully lacking in perception. (See Chapter V in this book.) Schoenbaum commented: ". . . if *The Second Maiden's Tragedy* cannot be classified as a sequel to *The Maid's Tragedy*, its main plot does show the very considerable influence of Fletcherian melodrama. It is an important influence and one which is evident in all of Middleton's later [1620s] tragedies and tragicomedies."[33]

Even though Schoenbaum had detected a marked difference in treatment and literary style between the main plot and the subplot, he remained oblivious of the double authorship. He found the characters in the main plot unbelievable [typical of Shakespeare's romance plays] and the subplot far more effective. Of the main plot, Schoenbaum wrote: "It has the sensationalism and unconvincing motivation, the spectacular effects of good and evil [all typical of Shakespeare's romance plays] that one expects from Fletcher. It capitalizes on a striking contrast between lust and chastity." [34] Even Fletcher's pervasive literary presence did not propel Schoenbaum to the inevasible conclusion that this was the lost drama of which Fletcher was the co-author. Nor did Schoenbaum perceive that

*I have been unable to substantiate Schoenbaum's statement that Middleton read the tale of Cardenio prior to its publication in English (1612) or that he knew Spanish well enough to read it in the original.

the anonymous play contained all the other customary ingredients of Shakespeare's romance plays.

To conclude the case for *Cardenio,* it only remained for Schoenbaum to establish that *The Second Maiden's Tragedy* was, as other critics had pointed out, very different from all previous plays written by Middleton. Schoenbaum effectively did this when he stated: ". . . in the remarkable lesser action of *The Second Maiden's Tragedy,* Middleton reveals for the first time an interest in mental processes and emotional disturbances. . . ."[35]

I have presented here, not necessarily in the order of discovery, much of the evidence that Professor Schoenbaum adduced for Middleton's authorship of *The Second Maiden's Tragedy,* but which instead virtually established the anonymous drama as Shakespeare and Fletcher's lost play.

There was still to come from Professor Schoenbaum, eleven years later, a dramatic reversal of opinion. With a scholarly stance that left open the door for further changes of position, he conceded that there was another factor to be considered in the manuscript of *The Second Maiden's Tragedy,* which "although scribal, has corrections that (in Greg's words) 'imply a knowledge of the author's own preference or intention.' Most investigators concerned with the play's parentage have overlooked the possible evidential significance of these revisions. While not ignoring them in my discussion of Middleton's claim to *The Second Maiden's Tragedy,* I have (I now feel) attached insufficient weight to their presence. The hand responsible for these corrections does not belong to Middleton."[36]

With his admission that at least part of the manuscript play could be in the author's hand, Schoenbaum concluded his persuasive evidence that *Cardenio* and *The Second Maiden's Tragedy* are one and the same play and thus unwittingly established himself as my stellar witness in the case of William Shakespeare and John Fletcher *versus* Thomas Middleton.

NOTES

Notes to Introduction

1. Napoleon was once asked why he had so often risked his life in battle. Was it for patriotism, power, fame, or wealth? "For none of these," replied the emperor. "It was so I could possess all the beautiful women I fell in love with." The motive of The Tyrant in *Cardenio* is certainly a logical and powerful one.

2. This phrase is Elizabethan underworld argot and means "whores and thieving sluts who would lift up their petticoats for a farthing."

3. David L. Frost, *Selected Plays of Thomas Middleton* (Cambridge: University Press, 1978), ix.

4. *Ibid.*, xi.

5. Harold L. Stenger, Jr., *The Second Maiden's Tragedy* (Ph.D. thesis, University of Pennsylvania, 1954), 9.

Chapter I

1. John Heminges and Henry Condell, ed., *First Folio of Shakespeare,* Norton facsimile (New York: 1968), 7.

2. While we have no direct evidence that Shakespeare owned printed quartos of any of his plays, since they were not regarded as literary works, it is very possible that he possessed at least a few of the quartos; thus, should a new production of one of his plays be called for, he could overhaul the text in the privacy of his study.

3. *First Folio of Shakespeare*, 7.

4. There is a detailed technical description of the manuscript in Anne Lancashire's edition of *The Second Maiden's Tragedy* (Manchester: 1978), 4-7, as well as in W.W. Greg's Malone Society Reprint (London: 1910), v-xi.

5. I have used the phrase "claim to the title" rather than the word "copyright," because the rights of literary ownership were not so explicit and inflexible in the seventeenth century as they are today. In his excellent handbook, *Shakespeare: An Illustrated Dictionary,* Stanley Wells explains the complicated function of the *Stationers' Register* (p. 167): "In Shakespeare's time, printing and publication were the monopoly of the

Stationers' Company. Members who wished to publish a book were required to enter the title in a register, and to pay a fee, which gave them a copyright in it. Not all bothered to do so, but the register is a valuable source of information."

6. Sir George Buc or Buck (d. 1623) was a historian, poet, and master of the revels. Among Buc's writings is *The History of the Life and Reign of Richard the Third* (published in 1646). Buc was knighted by King James I on June 21, 1603, the day before James's coronation. On the same day Buc was granted the mastership of the revels which gave him the authority to censor and license works for publication or plays for performance. By 1620, according to an official communication of the period, "Old Sir George Buck, master of the revels, has gone mad." He officially retired in 1622. Arthur Henry Bullen, "Sir George Buc," *Dictionary of National Biography*, III, 170-72.

7. *The Second Maiden's Tragedy* (Ph.D. thesis, University of Pennsylvania, 1954), 19-31.

8. *Ibid.*, 29.

9. *Ibid.*, 30-31.

10. Robert Payne, *By Me, William Shakespeare* (New York: 1980), 149.

11. D.H. Lambert, *Cartae Shakespeareanae. Shakespeare Documents* (London: 1904), 54.

12. The spelling of the play's name, clearly penned in the secretary hand, has been variously transcribed by scholars. In his article on John Fletcher (*Dictionary of National Biography*, VII, 303-311) Arthur Henry Bullen alludes to "the lost play 'Cadema' or 'Cardano' acted in 1613."

13. Samuel A. Tannenbaum, *Shakespere Forgeries in the Revels Accounts* (New York: 1928), 65, 66.

14. Charles William Sutton, "Humphrey Moseley," *Dictionary of National Biography*, XIII, 1074.

15. When the theaters were closed down by the Puritans in 1647, Moseley may have bought the manuscript promptbooks from the King's Men. Many years earlier, the promptbooks of all plays that had been published were likely relegated to final service in fireplaces, kitchens, and outhouses.

The list of Moseley's registered plays includes four by Middleton, ten by Massinger, and two (Greg records three, including the doubtful Hen: Y^{e} 2d) attributed in full or in part to Shakespeare (W.W. Greg, *Collected Papers* (1966), "The Bakings of Betsy," 59-61).

16. *Dramatic Documents from the Elizabethan Playhouses,* Commentary Volume (1931), 195.

17. *The Second Maiden's Tragedy* has occasionally been labeled as a play that got misnamed. F.G. Fleay, an expert on Elizabethan drama, incorrectly identified it as *Love's Pilgrimage* (1647), a drama probably by Fletcher, based upon one of Cervantes's *Novelas Exemplares*. J. Ludwig Tieck thought it was the lost Massinger play, *The Tyrant,* entered in the *Stationers' Register* in 1660 and listed by Warburton among the plays acci-

dentally destroyed by his cook. The German translation, published by Tieck, is named after the protagonist in the play, *Der Tyrann*, and bears the same subtitle that may have been given to the drama by The King's Men: *die zweite Jungfrauen-Tragoedie*.

18. Some scholars contend that Shakespeare planned a sequel to *Henry IV, Part I* because in the "Epilogue" he wrote: "If you be not too much cloy'd with fat meat, our humble author will continue the story, with Sir John [Falstaff] in it, and make you merry with fair Katherine of France, where, for anything I know, Falstaff shall die of a sweat. . ." In my opinion, Shakespeare was far too clever to write a sequel until he was assured of success with the initial effort, nor could he have anticipated the immense popularity of Falstaff. Thus the "Epilogue" was doubtless added to the play after it became a hit and after Shakespeare was already at work on, or had written, the promised continuation.

19. Greg, *Collected Papers*, 61.

20. Frederick G. Netherclift, *Handbook of Autographs* (London, 1857), 28.

21. Greg. *Collected Papers* 51-53.

22. *Ibid.*, 53.

23. Anne Lancashire, *The Second Maiden's Tragedy* (Manchester: 1978), 3.

Chapter II

1. Joseph Quincy Adams, whose *Life of William Shakespeare* (Boston & New York: 1923) was for many years the standard one-volume biography of the dramatist, writes (pp. 460-61): "On the twenty-fifth [of March, 1616] the poet was so ill that he sent for his lawyer, Francis Collins, to make important changes in his will. This document. . .had been drawn up by Collins, a solicitor then residing in Warwick, but formerly of Stratford, where he was held in high esteem. Devised while the poet was, according to legal parlance at least, 'in perfect health,' and neatly written on three sheets of paper fastened together, it had, I think, been duly published on its completion. At the end the poet signed in a clear bold hand 'By me, William Shakespear,' and Collins added 'Witness to the publishing hereof, Fra: Collyns.' " Virtually all the foregoing remarks are ancient fictions, repeated so often that some scholars have come to believe them. Further, had Professor Adams taken a closer look at a copy of Shakespeare's manuscript will, he would have perceived that it was not "neatly written" and Shakespeare's signature was not "in a clear bold hand," but in a tremulous, infirm script.

2. Charles Hamilton, *In Search of Shakespeare: A Reconnaissance into the Poet's Life and Handwriting* (New York: 1985), 116.

3. *Shakespeare's Lives* (New York: 1970), 608.

4. *In Search of Shakespeare,* 66-83.

5. *Ibid., passim.*

6. London: 1910, vi. Sir Walter Wilson Greg (1873-1959) was one of the most illustrious British scholars of the 20th century. Educated at Harrow and Oxford, he was accorded many honors in the field of English literary history. Greg was president of the

Malone Society, devoted to the study of Shakespeare, and the author of a distinguished work on facsimiles.

7. *Ibid.*, vi.
8. *The Second Maiden's Tragedy*. Manchester, 1978, 6.
9. Harold L. Stenger, Jr., 5-6.
10. *Ibid.*, 15.
11. *Ibid.*, 16.
12. Pierce Butler, *Materials for the Life of Shakespeare* (Chapel Hill, N.C.: 1930), 176.
13. For a detailed discussion of the Langleat *Titus* page, see Hamilton, *In Search of Shakespeare*, 148-57.
14. Oxford Press, 1987, 20-22.
15. *Ibid.*, 20.

Chapter III

1. This is conjecture. But the odds against Shakespeare and Cervantes having met, other than in their writings, are astronomical.
2. Shakespeare: old style calendar; Cervantes: new style.
3. London and New York, 1933.
4. *Bibliographica,* Vol. I, Westport, CT, 1895, 474-98.
5. *Ibid.*, 487.
6. The title of this celebrated tale is translated in various ways: Samuel Putnam's translation: "Story of the One Who was Too Curious for His Own Good"; Walter Starkie's translation: "The Tale of Ill-Advised Curiosity"; Peter Motteux's translation: "The Novel of the Curious Impertinent."
7. Thomas Shelton, *Don Quixote* (Tudor Edition, 1896), Book III, 264-65.
8. *Ibid.*, 268.
9. *Ibid.*, 268-69.
10. *Ibid.*, 270-72.
11. A. Edward Newton, *The Greatest Book in the World* (Boston: 1925), 194.
12. Bantam Books (New York: 1988), 159.

Chapter IV

1. The plays of Shakespeare's era usually consisted of five acts with no designated scenes. However, there were pauses for entrances, exits, and music that may have filled the function of scenes.
2. "Beaumont and Fletcher," *Encyclopedia Britannica,* 14th ed., III, 275.
3. *Brief Lives*, "Francis Beaumont," (London: Folio Society, 1975), 47.

4. *Letters Written by Eminent Persons*, II, Pt. 1, 352.

5. A.S.W. Rosenbach, "The Curious-Impertinent in English dramatic literature before Shelton's translation of Don Quixote," *Modern Language Notes* (17, 1902), 360-62.

6. Possible evidence that the main plot and subplot were written by two different persons is that the writer of the main plot did not at first take the names of his characters from the Cardenio tale in *Don Quixote,* whereas the subplot author for the most part appropriated the names from the Cervantes story.

7. *Fletcher, Beaumont & Co.*, 1947, 112-15.

8. S. Schoenbaum, *Internal Evidence and Elizabethan Dramatic Authorship* (Evanston: 1966), 35, discusses James Spedding's effort to determine the respective shares of Shakespeare and Fletcher in *Henry VIII* on the basis of literary quality: "On the basis of such a perusal, [Spedding] assigns to Shakespeare the scenes in which he finds vigor, reality, impassioned language, and figurative richness; those scenes which are, in a word, *excellent.* To Fletcher he gives the episodes that are conventional, diffuse, languid—in short, inferior."

9. *Ibid.*, 168.

10. *Second Maiden's Tragedy* (Manchester: 1978), 17.

11. *English Literature: An Illustrated Record* (London & New York: 1903), II, 322.

12. "John Fletcher," *Dictionary of National Biography*, VII, 305-06.

13. "The Curious-Impertinent," 362.

14. *Don Quixote*, Tudor edition, Shelton's trans., 1896 Lib. IV, Chapt. VI, 70.

15. *Ibid.*, 65.

16. Lancashire, 298-301.

17. *Studies in Bibliography,* VIII (1956), IX (1957), XI (1958), XII (1959), XIII (1960), XIV (1961), XV (1962).

18. Theodore Spencer, *Selected Essays* (New Brunswick: 1966), 287.

19. *In Search of Shakespeare* (New York: 1985), 86-87.

20. In connection with deleting expletives, Watson Nicholson points out in his article, "The Second Maiden's Tragedy," *Modern Language Notes,* xxvii, 2 (Feb. 1912), 36, that James I was strictly averse to profanity on the stage and "it should be remembered that *The Second Maiden's Tragedy* was written in the year of the King James Bible, and, besides, the most blasphemous of the Stuarts was likewise the most pious."

If the deletions of some of these oaths appears highhanded to you, since none of them is considered an expletive today, let me quote the Act of 1606, known as the Profanity Act, that guided George Buc: ". . . any person or persons [who] in any stage play, interlude, show, maygame, or pageant, justingly or profanely speak or use the holy name of God or Jesus Christ, or of the Holy Ghost or of the Trinity [should] forfeit for every such offense by him or them committed ten pounds."

21. *Shakespeare Lexicon,* 3rd ed. (New York: 1968).

Chapter V

1. Ann Lancashire, 15.

2. Dunn, E.C. *Eight Famous Elizabethan Plays (The Maid's Tragedy),* (New York: Modern Library, 1950), 340-434.

3. Ann Lancashire, 15.

Chapter VI

1. "Lewis Theobald," *Dictionary of National Biography*, XX, 599.

2. *Ibid.*, 600.

3. Walter Graham, ed. *Double Falsehood,* Western Reserve Studies 1:6 (Western Reserve University, Cleveland, Ohio, 1920), 33.

4. *Ibid.*, 10.

5. *Shakespeare's Lives* (Oxford & New York: 1970), 61.

6. *Double Falsehood,* 29.

7. *Shakespeare as Collaborator* (London: 1960), 150-51.

8. *Ibid.*, 60.

9. *Plays of Beaumont and Fletcher* (New Haven: 1927), 150-51.

10. *By me, William Shakespeare* (New York: 1980), 334.

11. F.E. Halliday, *The Cult of Shakespeare* (New York: 1957).

12. *His Exits and His Entrances: The Story of Shakespeare's Reputation* (Philadelphia & New York: 1963), 49.

13. *Ibid.,* 49-50.

14. Halliday, 22-23.

15. *His Exits and His Entrances,* 50.

16. In *Shakespeare as Collaborator* (pp. 154-58), Kenneth Muir cites a number of passages in *Double Falsehood* that add up to "wholesale echoes of Shakespeare's previous work."

17. *Ibid.*, 154-58

18. Theobald edited an edition of Beaumont and Fletcher's plays (published 1750) that was left incomplete at his death, but he had entirely finished the editing and notes for *The Maid's Tragedy.*

Chapter VII

1. *Middleton's Tragedies: A Critical Study* (New York: 1955), 185.

2. "The Second Maid's Tragedy," *Modern Language Notes*, xxvii (No. 2, 1912), 34.

3. "Authorship of The Second Maiden's Tragedy. A Reconsideration of the Manuscript Attribution to Chapman," *Studies in Philology*, 63 (1966), 74.

4. *Ibid.*, 73.

5. "Cyril Tourneur: The Revenger's Tragedy: The Second Maiden's Tragedy," *Notes & Queries,* 137 (Sept., 1919), 225-29.

6. *Ibid.*, 226.

7. *Ibid.*, 227.

8. *Ibid.*, 228.

9. *Outlines of Shakespeare's Plays* (New York: Barnes & Noble, Inc., 1934), 16.

10. (Boston, 1980, 15th ed.), 261.

11. *Ibid.*, 184-250.

12. Cambridge Univesity Press, London & N.Y.: 1975, 187-88.

13. *Ibid.*, on dust jacket.

14. *Ibid.*, 187.

15. *Ibid., 187-88.*

16. *Ibid.*, 190.

17. *Shakespeare Lexicon.*

18. "The Authorship of *The Second Maiden's Tragedy* and *The Revenger's Tragedy," Shakespeare Association Bulletin*, XX (1945), 56.

19. *Ibid.*,

20. *Op. cit.*, 50-62.

21. *Op. cit.*, 51-62

22. *Ibid.*, 55.

23. *Ibid.*, 56.

24. *Ibid.*

25. *Ibid.*

26. *Op. cit.*, 16-68.

27. "Four Critics of Drama, Academic and Otherwise," *Sewanee Review* (Fall, 1956), 508-09.

28. *Ibid.*

29. First Edition, 1945.

30. *Ibid.*, 37.

31. *Ibid.*, 38.

32. *Ibid.*, 52.

33. *Ibid.*, 37.

34. *Ibid.*

35. *Ibid.*

36. *Internal Evidence and Elizabethan Dramatic Authorship* (Evanston, 1966), 173.

SOME WORDS OF THANKS

For the help and encouragement of the following, I am enormously grateful: the staff of the New York Public Library, who graciously helped to ferret out elusive old lore that was vital to this book; The Shakespeare Birthplace Trust in Stratford-upon-Avon, a long-time friend to all bardolaters; the Huntington Library, an old haunt of mine when I was a graduate student at U.C.L.A. in the late 1930s, and who generously provided a photocopy of a manuscript epistle by John Fletcher that enabled me to identify his script; the British Museum Library, possessor of the original manuscript of *Cardenio* or *The Second Maiden's Tragedy*. The courtesy and cooperation of the British Museum Library is legendary among scholars. Another great font of knowledge to whom I owe much is the Bodleian Library at Oxford. The public Record Office in London also put me in its debt. I am further indebted to the Grolier Club for the use of documents in their library.

I have never before expressed in print my gratitude to three former members of the U.C.L.A. faculty who helped me to develop an inquisitive mind and instilled in me a fierce skepticism—Professors Franklin P. Rolfe, Alfred E. Longueil, and Louis B. Wright. Professor Wright, then also head of the manuscript division of The Huntington Library in San Moreno, subsequently became director of the great Folger Shakespeare Library in Washington, D.C. I wish now to thank these three distinguished scholars for the assistance and encouragement they gave me more than half a century ago.

Especially helpful to me was Professor John Baker of Centralia, Washington, who generously took the time to read the first draft of this book and annotated nearly every page with valuable, creative comments and suggestions, many of which I accepted with gratitude. I wish also to acknowledge the significant criticisms of Professor Susan Olsen. Finally, I should like to thank my assistant Dianne Barbaro, who aided me in many special ways. As always, I wish to thank my wife Diane, who tolerated my fits of inspiration and helped me enormously when inspiration failed.

BIBLIOGRAPHY

Adams, Joseph Quincy. *A Life of William Shakespeare*. Boston: 1923.

Altick, Richard D. *The Scholar Adventurers*. New York: 1950.

Anders, H.R.D. *Shakespeare's Books. A Dissertation on Shakespeare's Reading and the Immediate Sources of His Works*. Berlin: 1904.

Andrews, John F. (ed.) *William Shakespeare: His World, His Work, His Influence*. 3 vols. New York: 1985.

Arber, Edward (ed.) *A Transcript of the Registers of the Company of Stationers of London: 1554-1640*. 5 vols. 1875-94.

Astle, Thomas. *The Origin and Progress of Handwriting*. 1784.

Aubrey, John. *Brief Lives*. London: 1975.

Autographic Mirror. 4 vols. London & New York: 1864.

Barker, Richard H. "The Authorship of *The Second Maiden's Tragedy* and *The Revenger's Tragedy*." *Shakespeare Association Bulletin*, XX, 1945, 51-62.

Baynes, T.S. *Shakespeare's Studies*. n.p. 1893.

Bentley, Gerald E. *Shakespeare: A Biographical Handbook*. New Haven: 1961.

______. "Shakespeare and the Blackfriars Theatre." *Shakespeare Survey*, 1, 1948.

Bertram, Paul. *Shakespeare and The Two Noble Kinsmen*. New Brunswick: 1965.

Bradbrook, M.C. *The Living Monument: Shakespeare and the Theatre of His Time*. Cambridge: 1976.

Bradley, Jesse Franklin, and Joseph Q. Adams. *The Jonson Allusion Book*. New Haven: 1922.

Brodwin, L. "Authorship of *The Second Maiden's Tragedy*. A Reconsideration of the Manuscript Attribution to Chapman." *Studies in Philology*, 63, 1966.

Brooke, C.F. Tucker. *The Shakespeare Apocrypha*. Oxford: 1967.

______. *Shakespeare of Stratford: A Handbook for Students*. New Haven: 1926.

Brown, Ivor, and George Fearon. *Amazing Monument: a Short History of the Shakespeare Industry*. Port Washington, New York: 1939.

Bryant, A.J., Jr. "Four Critics of Drama, Academic and Otherwise." *Sewanee Review*, Fall, 1956, 508-20.

Bullen, Arthur Henry. "Sir George Buc." *Dictionary of National Biography*, III, 170-72.

______. "John Fletcher." *Dictionary of National Biography*, VII, 303-11.

Burgoyne, Frank J. *Collotype Facsimile and Type Transcript of an Elizabethan Manuscript. . .(Northumberland Manuscript)*. London & New York: 1904.

Cadwallader, John. "Theobald's Alleged Shakespeare Manuscript." *Modern Language Notes*, 55, 1940, 108-09.

Campbell, Oscar J., and Edward G. Quinn. *Reader's Encyclopedia of Shakespeare*. New York: 1966.

A Catalogue of the Shakespeare Exhibition Held in the Bodleian Library. Oxford: 1916.

Chambers, E.K. *William Shakespeare: A Study of Facts and Problems*. 2 vols. Oxford: 1930.

Chambers, R.W. "The Expression of Ideas. . .in the 147 Lines. . .of Sir Thomas More." *Modern Language Review*, July, 1931.

Chambrun, Clara de. "The Book Shakespeare Used—a Discovery." *Scribner's Magazine*, July, 1936.

______. *Shakespeare: a Portrait Restored*. London: 1957.

______. *Shakespeare Rediscovered*. New York: 1938.

Combe, John. *Last Will and Testament* (orig. ms.). Public Record Office. London: Prob. II, 126.

Collins, John Churton. "Lewis Theobald." *Dictionary of National Biography*, XX, 599.

Courtney, W.P. "John Warburton (1682-1759)." *Dictionary of National Biography*, XX, 755.

Croft, P.J. *Autograph Poetry in the English Language*. Vol. 1. 1973.

Dawson, Giles E., and Laetitia Kennedy-Skipton. *Elizabethan Handwriting, 1500-1650. A Manual*. New York: 1966.

Des Moineaux, Edwin J. *Manuscript Said to Be Handwriting of William Shakespeare Identified as the Penmanship of Another Person*. Los Angeles: 1924.

Eccles, Mark. *Shakespeare in Warwickshire*. Madison: 1961.

Edmund Ironside. (orig. ms.) British Museum Library. Egerton: 1994.

Elton, Charles Isaac. *William Shakespeare: His Family and Friends*. London: 1904.

Erdman, David V., and Ephim G. Fogel. *Evidence for Authorship: Essays on Problems of Attribution*. Ithaca: 1966.

Everitt, E.B. *The Young Shakespeare*. Copenhagen: 1954.

Fido, Martin. *Shakespeare*. Maplewood, New Jersey: 1978.

Flower, Desmond, and A.N.L. Munby. *English Political Autographs*. London: 1958.

Fox, Levi. *The Shakespeare Handbook: The Essential Companion to Shakespeare's Works, Life and Times*. Boston: 1987.

Frazier, Harriet C. *A Babble of Ancestral Voices: Shakespeare, Cervantes and Theobald*. The Hague: 1974.

French, Marilyn. *Shakespeare's Division of Experience*. N.Y.: 1982.

Furnivall, F.W. "Shakespere's Signatures." *Journal of the Society of Archivists and Autograph Collectors*, no. 1, June, 1895.

Garnett, Richard, and Edmond Gosse. *English Literature: An Illustrated Record*. 4 vols. London & New York: 1903.

Gordon, Cyrus H. *Forgotten Scripts*. New York: 1982.

Graham, Walter (ed.) *Double Falsehood. Western Reserve Studies*, 1:6. Cleveland, Ohio: 1920.

Granville-Barker, H. and G.B. Harrison. *A Companion to Shakespeare Studies*. New York: 1934.

Green, A. Wagfall. "Shakespeare's Will." *Georgetown Law Journal*, xx, March, 1932.

Greenwood, George. *Shakespere's Handwriting*. New York: 1920.

______. *The Shakespere Signatures and "Sir Thomas More."* London: 1924.

Greg, Walter W. *The Book of Sir Thomas More*. Oxford: 1911.

______. *Collected Papers*. 1966.

______. *Dramatic Documents from the Elizabethan Playhouses. Commentary Volume*. 1931.

______. *The Editorial Problem in Shakespeare: a Survey of the Foundations of the Text*. Oxford, 1942.

______. *English Literary Autographs, 1550-1650*. 3 vols. London: 1932.

______. *The Second Maiden's Tragedy*. London: 1910.

______. *The Shakespeare First Folio* (reprint). London: 1969.

Halliday, F.E. *The Cult of Shakespeare*. London: 1957.

______. *The Poetry of Shakespeare's Plays*. London: 1954.

Hamilton, Charles. *The Book of Autographs*. New York: 1978.

______. *Collecting Autographs & Manuscripts*. Norman, Oklahoma: 1961.

______. *Great Forgers and Famous Fakes*. New York: 1980.

______. *In Search of Shakespeare: A Reconnaissance into the Poet's Life and Handwriting*. New York: 1985.

______. *Scribblers & Scoundrels*. New York: 1968.

Halliwell-Phillipps, James O. *An Historical Account of New Place, Stratford-upon-Avon*. London: 1864.

______. *The Life of Shakespeare*. London: 1848.

______. *Outlines of the Life of Shakespeare*. 2 vols. London: 1887.

Hanley, Hugh A. "Shakespeare's Family in Stratford Records." *The Times Literary Supplement,* May 21, 1964.

Harbage, Alfred. "Elizabethan—Restoration Palimpsest." *Modern Language Review,* 35, 1960, 287-319.

Harrott, Thomas M. *William Shakespeare: A Handbook*. New York: 1934.

Hector, L.C. *The Handwriting of English Documents*. London: 1958.

Hotson, J. Leslie. *I, William Shakespeare*. 1938.

Hoy, Cyrus. "The Shares of Fletcher and His Collaborators in the Beaumont and Fletcher Canon." *Studies in Bibliography,* VIII (1956), IX (1957), XI (1958), XII (1959), XIII (1960), XIV (1961), XV (1962).

Ireland, William Henry. *Confessions*. London: 1805.

Jeaffreson, J.C. "A New View of Shakespeare's Will." *The Athenaeum,* nos. 2844, 2847, 2848, 2906.

Keen, Allan, and Roger Lubbock. *The Annotator. The Portrait of an Elizabethan Reader of Halle's Chronicle*. New York: 1954.
Knight, W. Nicholas. *Shakespeare's Hidden Life: Shakespeare at the Law, 1585-1595*. New York: 1973.

Lake, David J. *The Canon of Thomas Middleton's Plays*. London & New York: 1975.
Lambert, D.H. *Cartae Shakespeareanae. Shakespeare Documents*. London: 1904.
Lancashire, Anne. (ed.) *The Second Maiden's Tragedy*. Manchester: 1978.
Laroque, Francois. *The Age of Shakespeare*. N.Y.: 1993.
Lee, Sir Sidney. "An Elizabethan Bookseller." *Bibliographia,* Vol. 1. Westport, Connecticut: 1895.
______. *A Life of William Shakespeare*. New York: 1899.
Leech, Clifford. *The John Fletcher Plays*. Cambridge: 1962.
Lewis, Benjamin R. *The Shakespeare Documents*. 2 vols. Stanford: 1940.

McLaren, Moray. *By Me. . .A Report upon the Apparent Discovery of Some Working Notes of William Shakespeare in a Sixteenth Century Book*. London: 1949.
Madden, Frederic. *Observations on an Autograph of Shakespeare*. London: 1838.
Majault, Joseph. *Shakespeare*. Geneva, 1969.
Marder, Louis. *His Exits and His Entrances: The Story of Shakespeare's Reputation*. Philadelphia and New York: 1962.
Maxwell, Baldwin. *Studies in Beaumont, Fletcher, and Massinger.* New York: 1974.
Metz, G. Harold. *Four Plays Ascribed to Shakespeare*. New York and London: 1982.
Middleton, Thomas. *Selected Plays*. Cambridge: 1978.
______. *The Witch* (orig. ms.) Bodleian Library Ms., Malone 12.
______. *Works* (7 vols.). London: 1885.
Muir, Kenneth. *Shakespeare as Collaborator*. London: 1960.
______. *The Sources of Shakespeare's Plays*. London and New Haven: 1978.

Neilson, William A., and Askley H. Thorndike. *The Facts about Shakespeare*. New York: 1916.
Netherclift, Frederick G. *Handbook of Autographs*. London: 1857.
Newton, A. Edward. *The Greatest Book in the World*. Boston: 1925.
Nichols, John Gough. *Autographs of Royal, Noble, Learned, and Remarkable Personages*. 1829.
Nicoll, Allardyce. (ed.) *Shakespeare Survey 4*. Cambridge: 1951.
Nicholson, Watson. "The Second Maid's Tragedy." *Modern Language Notes,* No. 2, 1912, xxvii, 24.
Norman, Charles. *The Muses' Darling*. Drexel Hill, Pennsylvania: 1950.
______. *So Worthy a Friend: William Shakespeare*. New York: 1947.
Oliphant, E.H.C. (ed.) *Plays of Beaumont and Fletcher.* New Haven: 1927.
Oras, Ants. " 'Extra Monosyllables' in *Henry VIII* and the Problem of Authorship." *Journal of English and Germanic Philology,* 52, 1953, 198-213.
______. "Pause Patterns in Elizabethan and Jacobean Drama: An Experiment in Prosody."

University of Florida Monographs (Humanities), No. 3, Winter, 1960, 1-59.
Osborn, Albert S. *Questioned Documents*. 2nd ed. Albany: 1929.

Papp, Joseph, and Elizabeth Kirkland. *Shakespeare Alive!* New York: 1988.
Payne, Robert. *By me, William Shakespeare*. N.Y.: 1980.
Pearson, Hesketh. *A Life of Shakespeare*. New York: 1961.
Plimpton, George A. *The Education of Shakespeare*. London and New York: 1933.
Pollard, Alfred W. "The Manuscripts of Shakespeare's Plays." *Library* 7, Series 3. London: 1916.
______. *Shakespeare's Hand in the Booke of Sir Thomas More*. Cambridge: 1923.
Proudfoot, G.E. "*The Two Noble Kinsmen* and the Apocryphal Plays," in Stanley Wells's *Shakespeare: Select Bibliographical Studies*. London: 1973.

Quennell, Peter. *Shakespeare*. Cleveland: 1963.

Rawlins, Raymond. *Stein and Day Book of World Autographs*. New York: 1978.
Receipt for Purchase of The Second Maiden's Tragedy (orig. ms.) Grolier Club Library, New York.
Reese, M.M. *Shakespeare: His World and His Work*. London: 1953.
Rendall, Gerald H. *Shake-speare: Handwriting and Spelling*.
Revels Accounts. Bodleian Library, Rawl. A 239, fol. 47.
Rosenbach, A.S.W. *Books and Bidders*. Boston: 1927.
______. "The Curious-Impertinent in English dramatic literature before Shelton's translation of *Don Quixote*." *Modern Language Notes*, 17, 1902, 360-62.
Rowse, A.L. *Shakespeare the Elizabethan*. New York: 1977.
______. *William Shakespeare: A Biography*. New York: 1963.

Schmidt, Alexander. *Shakespeare Lexicon*. 3rd ed., New York: 1968.
Schoenbaum, S. *Internal Evidence and Elizabethan Dramatic Authorship: An Essay in Literary History and Method*. Evanston: 1966.
______. *Middleton's Tragedies: A Critical Study*. New York: 1955.
______. *Shakespeare: The Globe and the World*. New York: 1979.
______. *Shakespeare's Lives*. New York: 1970.
______. *William Shakespeare. A Documentary Life*. New York: 1975.
______. *William Shakespeare. Records and Images*. London: 1981.
The Second Maiden's Tragedy (orig. ms.) British Museum Library, Lans. 807, fol. 56A.
Shakespeare, William. *First Folio*. Norton Facsimile. New York: 1968.
______. *Last Will and Testament*. Public Record Office, London, Prob. II/126.
Shelton, Thomas (trans.) *Cervantes' Don Quixote*. 1896.
Spencer, Hazelton. *Art and Life of William Shakespeare*. New York: 1940.
Spencer, Theodore. *Selected Essays*. New Brunswick, New Jersey: 1966.
Stalker, Archibald. "Is Shakespeare's Will a Forgery?" *Quarterly Review* 274 (1940).
Staunton, H. *Memorials of Shakespeare Comprising the Poet's Will*. London, 1864.
Stenger, Harold L., Jr. *The Second Maiden's Tragedy*. (Unpublished Ph.D. thesis).

University of Pennsylvania, 1954.

Sutton, Charles William. "Humphrey Moseley." *Dictionary of National Biography*, XIII, 1074.

Swinburne, Algernon Charles. "Beaumont and Fletcher." *Encyclopaedia Britannica*, 14th ed., III, 275.

Sykes, H. Dugdale. "Cyril Tourneur: *The Revenger's Tragedy: The Second Maiden's Tragedy.*" *Notes & Queries*, 137, 225-29. September, 1919.

Tannenbaum, Samuel A. *The Booke of Sir Thomas Moore*. New York: 1927.

______. *The Handwriting of the Renaissance*. New York: 1930.

______. *A New Study of Shakespeare's Will*. Baltimore: 1926.

______. *Problems in Shakespeare's Handwriting*. New York: 1927.

______. "Reclaiming One of Shakespeare's Signatures." *Studies in Philology*, XXII, no. 3. July, 1925.

______. *Shakespeare and "Sir Thomas Moore*." New York: 1929.

______. *Shakespere Forgeries in the Revels Accounts*. New York: 1928.

______. *Shakespere's Unquestioned Autographs*. Baltimore: 1925.

Thompson, Edward M. *Shakespeare's Handwriting*. Oxford: 1916.

______. *Shakespeare's Hand in the Play of Sir Thomas More*. Cambridge: 1923.

Thurston, Herbert. "Shakespeare's Handwriting." *Month*, 123. London: 1914.

Tourneur, Cyril. *The Revenger's Tragedy* (Ed. Lawrence J. Ross). Lincoln, Ne:, 1966.

Ure, Peter. "Shakespeare and the Drama of His Time." *A New Companion to Shakespeare Studies*. (ed. Kenneth Muir and S. Schoenbaum). Cambridge: 1971.

Wallis, Lawrence B. *Fletcher, Beaumont & Co.; Entertainers to the Jacobean Gentry.* New York: 1947.

Warburton Catalogue, 1759. Grolier Club Library, New York.

Wells, Stanley. *Shakespeare: An Illustrated Dictionary.* (Revised ed.) Oxford: 1986.

______., and Gary Taylor. *William Shakespeare: A Textual Companion*. Oxford: 1987

Williams, Frayne. *Mr. Shakespeare of The Globe*. New York: 1941.

Wilson, J. Dover. *The Manuscript of Shakespeare's Hamlet and the Problems of Its Transmission*. (2 vols.) Cambridge: 1963.

Wright, Louis B. *The Folger Library. Two Decades of Growth: An Informal Account.* Charlottesville, Virginia: 1968.

Wright, Thomas. *Court Hand Restored.* New edition, 1891.

Yeatman, John Pym. *Is William Shakespeare's Will Holographic?* 1901.

Zesser, David M. *Guide to Shakespeare*. New York: 1976.

INDEX